FRONTIERS OF BELONGING

WORLDS IN CRISIS: REFUGEES, ASYLUM, AND FORCED MIGRATION
Elizabeth Cullen Dunn and Georgina Ramsay, editors

FRONTIERS OF BELONGING

THE EDUCATION OF UNACCOMPANIED REFUGEE YOUTH

ANNIKA LEMS

INDIANA UNIVERSITY PRESS

This book is a publication of

Indiana University Press
Office of Scholarly Publishing
Herman B Wells Library 350
1320 East 10th Street
Bloomington, Indiana 47405 USA

iupress.org

Manufactured in the United States of America

First printing 2022

Cataloging information is available from the Library of Congress.

ISBN 978-0-253-06178-2 (hardback)
ISBN 978-0-253-06179-9 (paperback)
ISBN 978-0-253-06180-5 (ebook)

CONTENTS

ACKNOWLEDGMENTS

THIS BOOK IS THE PRODUCT of many collaborations. It owes its ethnographic vitality to the sixteen young people from Eritrea, Guinea, and Ethiopia who generously allowed me to accompany them in their everyday pathways. Given the often desperate legal, social, and emotional struggles they were involved in, I do not take their readiness to let a researcher into their lives for granted. I share their hope that foregrounding the difficulties they encountered in the Swiss asylum and education landscape might contribute to improving the situation for future generations of refugee youth. I am also thankful to the social pedagogues, teachers, and legal guardians who often went at great lengths to accommodate my research interests. If my assessments of the Swiss education landscape in this book are often critical, this does not diminish the respect I have for the difficult social and emotional work pedagogues have to perform. At a time when refugees' access to public resources has become a highly politicized question, they often find themselves in impossible situations. While attempting to fulfill their educational mandates, they constantly have to avoid stumbling into sociopolitical minefields. Hopefully this book will offer a new and constructive perspective to pedagogues involved in the education of migrant youth, in Switzerland and beyond.

The ethnographic fieldwork this book is based on emerged as part of a larger research project entitled "Transnational Biographies of Education: Young Unaccompanied Asylum Seekers and their Navigation through Shifting Social Realities in Switzerland and Turkey." The project was led by Sabine Strasser from the University of Bern and Kathrin Oester from the University of Teacher Education (PH Bern) and funded by the Swiss National Science Foundation (Project Number 156476). On the basis of Kathrin's initial idea, we developed the project proposal together, and while I was responsible for the research in Switzerland, Eda

Elif Tibet conducted research in Turkey. The regular team meetings as well as the workshops and conferences we organized as part of the project offered a fantastic opportunity to discuss and think through my ethnographic observations. Many of the ideas I present in the book are a product of this spirit of collaboration. I thank Sabine and Kathrin for supporting me throughout the research phase and encouraging me to publish my findings as a book. The interdisciplinary special issue we coedited for the *Journal of Ethnic and Migration Studies* (Lems, Oester, and Strasser 2020; Lems 2020) formed an important point of departure for this undertaking.

Throughout the three and a half years I was based at the Institute of Social Anthropology at the University of Bern, I received invaluable support from my colleagues there. I am particularly thankful to Darcy Alexandra, Danae Leitenberg, Gerhild Perl, Julia Rehsmann, and Veronika Siegl, who accompanied my work in all its stages, from fieldwork to publication. I am also deeply indebted to my friend and long-term collaborator Jelena Tošić. Our joint efforts to look at im/mobility through an existential prism greatly influenced this book's conceptual angle. Some of these ideas were first published in a special issue that appeared in the journal *Soumen Anthropologi: Journal of the Finnish Anthropological Society* (Lems 2019; Lems and Tošić 2019). Furthermore, I want to thank Sebastien Bachelet, Milena Belloni, Heath Cabot, Elaine Chase, Heike Drotbohm, Paolo Gaibazzi, Laura Gilliam, Judith Hangartner, Edward Lowe, Hans Lucht, Francesca Meloni, Christine Moderbacher, Laura Otto, Henrik Vigh, Ulrika Wernesjö, Agnieszka Pasieka, Julia Pauli, Josefine Raasch, Georgina Ramsay, Madeleine Reeves, Samuli Schielke, and Michael Schnegg, who read and commented on drafts of the chapters I presented at various conferences, seminars, and publication workshops.

The book would not have been possible without the support of the Max Planck Institute for Social Anthropology in Halle. Since my move there in January 2019, it has been a fantastic academic home, and the vibrant international research community the institute accommodates has tremendously enriched my thinking and writing. A special thank you is owed to the members of my research group, Antje Berger, Danae Leitenberger, Christine Moderbacher, Vera Wolter, and Markus Wurzer. Our discussions about the everyday histories of exclusion permeating the German-speaking Alpine region were an important motivator for completing this book. Furthermore, I am indebted to the two anonymous reviewers whose thoughtful readings helped sharpen my arguments and writing. Given the many pressures academics are under in a neoliberal university landscape that does not reward such acts of solidarity, I do not take their readiness to invest so much time and energy in improving my work for granted. Finally, I want to thank

Elizabeth Cullen Dunn and Georgina Ramsay, the editors of the Worlds in Crisis book series, as well as Allison Chaplin and Sophia Hebert, the acquisition editors at Indiana University Press, for their generous advice and support. Georgina's encouragement a few years ago to think about my ethnographic data in terms of a book project formed the very beginning of this journey. I thank her for believing in me and my work and for incentivizing me to keep going.

Last but not least, this book would have never come into the world if it were not for the exceptional support of my husband, Paul Reade. He did not just patiently put up with my writing moods but often put aside his own work to read, edit, and comment on my chapters. By now he has read the book so many times that he must be truly thankful to get rid of it. I cannot thank him enough for his help and support.

FRONTIERS of BELONGING

INTRODUCTION

A POST-IT NOTE

In early August 2015 I made my first visit to an education institution in a small village on the outskirts of Zürich. I was there to meet Abel, Kibrum, and Aaron, three young men from Eritrea who had just moved in.[1] In the following weeks, five more boys were to join them and become part of a unique educational pilot project: over the next year, these eight teenagers from Eritrea, aged between fifteen and eighteen, who had come to Switzerland as unaccompanied minor asylum seekers, were to receive intensive German language classes as well as work experience in the different workshops that were located on the premises. After the orientation year, they were to start an apprenticeship in one of these trades. All up, they would live for three years in shared apartments, be supervised by a group of in-house social workers, and receive support from work pedagogues in the trades they were to learn.

This kind of project was unique in the canton of Zürich. Although the number of unaccompanied underage refugees lodging asylum applications in Switzerland had risen dramatically since 2014, most of them did not gain access to public (particularly secondary) schooling. While the UN Convention on the Rights of the Child—the core body of laws guiding the treatment and reception of refugee children in Switzerland—guarantees the right to free compulsory education for all children regardless of their nationality, the convention remains rather vague on access to education beyond the obligatory schooling age (UNCRC 1989, article 8). As the majority of the unaccompanied minor asylum seekers in Switzerland are between sixteen and seventeen years old and thus beyond the age for compulsory schooling, the migration and educational authorities are of two minds about their right to be included in the public education system. The pilot project where I was conducting fieldwork was an attempt by a privately funded institution to create pathways into the apprenticeship stream of education for a select group of unaccompanied minors past the obligatory schooling age.

That day at the beginning of August when I was introduced to Abel, Kibrum, and Aaron, I observed their joyous, almost ecstatic reactions to the institution. On inspecting the newly furnished apartments where they were going to live in groups of three, the workshops where they would work, the classroom where they would receive German lessons, and the sports grounds where they could play soccer in their free time, the boys were overwhelmed by the fortune of having been chosen to participate in this project. They walked across the premises singing and making little dance moves, pinching each other's hands in happiness.

One of the boys who struck me as particularly delighted that day was sixteen-year-old Abel. As we inspected the carpentry workshop, he told me that he had arrived in Switzerland one and a half years before and that he had spent most of that time in a home for unaccompanied minors not far from Zürich. Much later, when I got to know him better, he told me that he had left Eritrea on his own when he was twelve years old, after his father had been arrested by the Afewerki regime, leaving his mother impoverished and struggling to fend for him and his four younger siblings. On foot, he had crossed the border into Ethiopia, where he had spent two years in a refugee camp before attempting the dangerous journey through Sudan and Libya and across the Mediterranean—a time of extreme hardship, and a time that, as he once put it, still follows him "like a shadow."

Abel had received a temporary permit to stay in Switzerland on humanitarian grounds a few months before I first met him. The decision on the young men's asylum applications had major impacts on their educational possibilities. None of the participants in the education pilot had been granted full refugee status. Instead, they had received temporary humanitarian protection visas. This translated into fewer opportunities, blocking them in vital areas of their lives, such as the amount of social welfare they received, the impossibility of family reunification, the funds available for educational measures, access to the labor and apprenticeship market, the chance of receiving permanent residency, and the chance to move from shared refugee accommodation into private apartments. Because of Abel's temporary status, his legal guardian had not been able to find any other accommodation, and so he had had to remain in the cantonal shelter for unaccompanied refugee youth until he received the offer to join the educational pilot project. That afternoon as we worked in the carpentry workshop, Abel told me that he was happy that he had left the youth asylum seekers' home behind, that he would never go back there, "not even to visit my friends." When I asked why, he gave me an ironic glance. He said that he had been very unhappy there, especially because he had not been allowed to go to a "normal" school. I asked what that was, a "normal" school. Abel explained that a normal school was "a real school." Unlike the language class he had attended in the home for unaccompanied minors, it was a place where he would have been able to meet Swiss peers and learn subjects other than German. He said that the school in the refugee shelter was "good for nothing," that the teacher had kept repeating the same things, and that he had spent his days sleeping to kill the feeling of boredom—in brief, he had felt stuck and isolated there. "And what about this place?" I asked. This pilot project, Abel was convinced, would finally allow him to move ahead and "become integrated."

Fast-forward three weeks later: I was working with Abel, Aaron, and Kibrum in the carpentry workshop. Together with Daniel, the trainer, we were putting together bedside tables that were to be placed in the apartments of the unaccompanied minors who were set to arrive the following week. On returning to our task after the morning coffee break, I noticed that the boys were gathered around Abel, gesticulating and talking excitedly in Tigrinya. Abel, however, was not reacting. He was standing still, his arm resting on the workbench, staring into the distance. As I went nearer to see what was happening, I noticed that he had stuck a Post-it note to his chest. In crooked handwriting and broken German, he had written the following words: "I am not alive. Maybe dead. I am in heaven. Do I still live on this earth?"[2]

THE LOGIC OF INCLUSIVE EXCLUSION

Abel's Post-it message and his stoic, removed glance went right through me. What had happened? How had his perception of the educational institution shifted so dramatically from a place that would allow him to move forward in his life to the ultimate embodiment of a terminus? How could a project that was celebrated among many practitioners in the refugee sector as a best-practice example for integration be perceived so dramatically differently by the young people it was directed at, namely as a space of stagnation and exclusion?

To answer these questions, I need to dig deep. So deep indeed that I need to move beyond the immediate realms of the Post-it note and describe the complex and deeply ambiguous social and political processes that play into Abel's everyday life and shape his educational possibilities in Switzerland. I have to outline the core paradox that will preoccupy me throughout this book: the ambiguous interlocking of inclusionary language and exclusionary practice characterizing the responses to the unprecedented numbers of unaccompanied young asylum seekers arriving in Switzerland in the wake of the European refugee crisis—a dynamic Kathrin Oester and I have elsewhere described as *inclusive exclusion* (Oester and Lems 2019). By sketching the contours of this logic of inclusive exclusion, we will see how the treatment of unaccompanied minors as vulnerable victims in need of protection and integration, on the one hand, and as threats to the economic and cultural integrity of the Swiss "national order of things" (Malkki 1995), on the other, produces paradoxical dynamics whereby young people find themselves left outside while seemingly being allowed "in" (Lems 2020). I took my cue from Abel's dramatic note and the questions about the links among education, being, and nothingness it forced me to confront almost from the minute my research started, and this entire book can be read as an attempt to understand the political, social, and existential struggles that propelled him to write it.

In deploying inclusive exclusion as a conceptual metaphor, I can build on the work of scholars who have thought a great deal about the ambiguous entwinement of inclusion and exclusion in contemporary sociopolitical life (Kronauer 2010a; De Genova 2013). Since the 1980s, inclusion and exclusion have become key notions for capturing the ways late capitalist welfare societies deal with questions of poverty, inequality, and diversity. The concept of exclusion has long been used to describe marginalized groups' exclusion *from* society. However, Martin Kronauer (2010b, 44) makes an important point when he suggests that in welfare societies marked by global capitalist transformation processes, these dynamics have fundamentally changed. Today, *exclusion* needs to be used to analytically capture the dynamics whereby certain groups come to be excluded *in* society. Inclusion and exclusion thus form an important conceptual pair that need to be thought of together. Their ambiguous interplay reveals the simultaneity of inside and outside marking contemporary approaches to the societal participation of the marginalized (Kronauer 2010a, 25). Anthropologists of migration have pointed out the profound ways these dynamics have shaped the reception and treatment of migrants and refugees in Western societies (Fassin 2005; Cabot 2014; Ramsay 2017). The claim to accommodate cultural diversity and invest in mechanisms that enable refugees' societal participation are counterpoised by the intensification of legal, bureaucratic, and social hurdles that make this aim unachievable. In Switzerland, this can be seen in the state's growing investment in integration projects since the turn of the millennium, which went hand in hand with the increased distribution of short-term humanitarian permits that disqualify refugees from accessing these resources (Kamm et al. 2003).

To comprehend how the logic of inclusive exclusion plays out in young people's everyday lives, it is important to spell out the multiple societal, political, and educational processes underlying its formation. Because the emergence of the unaccompanied minor as a discursive figure plays a crucial role for understanding the ascriptions the young people this book focuses on have to deal with, I will first take some time to think through the divergent and oftentimes conflicting ideas

and expectations attached to this figure. Embedding the ambiguity of the unaccompanied minor in the ambivalence of wider public discourses on the integration of migrants and refugees in Switzerland will show that the logic of inclusive
exclusion inherent in policy responses needs to be read against the backdrop
of a much larger project of exclusion that is based on the increased distinction
between deserving and undeserving citizen subjects. The bridging schools for
refugee youth where I conducted research reveal the ambivalent shape this form
of exclusion takes on: while relying on inclusionary language and ideas, it repro-
duces distinct practices of segregation.

Following in the footsteps of scholars working at the intersection of migration,
anthropology, and education, this book starts from the premise that educational
spaces are not innocent sites of future-making but powerful social spaces where
the frontiers of belonging are continuously delineated, negotiated, policed, and
challenged. In conversation with the work of Ann Laura Stoler (2018), I see the
classroom as an example par excellence from where the formation, preservation,
and defense of "interior frontiers" can be observed. These frontiers are the everyday affective thresholds of belonging that create unspoken distinctions between
self and other, familiar and alien, desirables and undesirables. In describing these
vernacular delineations as interior frontiers, Stoler builds on Etienne Balibar's
reading of the work of nineteenth-century German philosopher Johann Gottlieb
Fichte. Fichte first coined the term *interior frontier* (*innere Grenze*) in his 1808
Reden an die deutsche Nation (Addresses to the German Nation). In response to
the Napoleonic occupation of Germany, Fichte (often described as the father of
German nationalism) gave a series of lectures in Berlin in the winter of 1808–9.
In these speeches he called on the German people to unify by taking up moral
arms rather than military ones (Fichte 1845, 377–95). In the face of the destruction and ruination Germany was facing, Fichte argued that the national space
should not be thought of as defined by external, politically defined borders but
by inner frontiers of belonging: "The first, primordial, and truly natural frontiers
of states are without a doubt their inner frontiers" (Fichte 1845, 459).[3] He used the
notion of the interior frontier as a unifying concept, as a moral barricade against
the erosion of the national self (Stoler 2018, 3). However, as Stoler points out, the
concept almost immediately revealed its dark underside, through "the raw and
visceral and passionately protected distinctions" it gave rise to (3). According to
Fichte, the interior frontier was determined by a shared language and culture,
which created invisible bonds and a sense of mutual understanding. He believed
that the people sharing these bonds naturally belonged together and formed a
harmonious whole. They could therefore not "absorb" (*in sich aufnehmen*) people
of different heritage without profoundly disturbing the balance of the national
community (Fichte 1845, 459; cf. Stoler 2018).

Etienne Balibar picked up on the dark potential of Fichte's concept in the 1990s to think through the silent and implicit yet persistent forms of racism—the ways contemporary societies come to exclude people marked as other, not on the basis of biology but on that of cultural difference. Balibar stresses that the conceptual metaphor of the interior frontier allows one to grasp the "classical aporias of interiority and exteriority" marking processes of racialized exclusion (Balibar 1994, 63). On the basis of this reading of Fichte's work, Stoler uses the notion of the interior frontier as an analytical means to grasp the ambiguous ways exclusion enters the domain of everyday relations, how it creates "deep tectonic shifts not readily visible with the conceptual tools at hand" (Stoler 2018, 2). The "affective delineations of difference" (2) interior frontiers are based on could easily be over-looked, as they often do not appear in the form of openly racist or exclusionary ex-pressions. The effectiveness of interior frontiers stems precisely from the fact that they are not delineated by barbed wires but by the small, seemingly unimportant barricades between self and other set up and defended in everyday interactions.

These processes of boundary drawing are particularly visible in the schooling of migrant and refugee youth, where the dividing line between claims to integra-tion and assimilative practices becomes increasingly blurred. I take Stoler's work as a point of departure to investigate the social nature of such interior frontiers—the ways they form not just discursively constructed ideas but also phenomeno-logical realities that insert themselves into the texture of the everyday. Over the course of this book, it will become apparent how educational practitioners work-ing with young unaccompanied refugees make use of a liberal vocabulary of hope-fulness and integration to justify a grammar of exclusion. Within these politically charged environments, young people like Abel—people whose journeys to Swit-zerland were often propelled by the hope of a sense of forward movement through education—find themselves stuck at the threshold of Swiss society, looking on at a world they are denied full entry into. Kept waiting at these thresholds, they continuously have to prove that they deserve the future prospects opened up to them through education, while simultaneously remaining stuck in segregated educational tracks where they are labeled as problem cases in need of special inter-vention and care. Yet, as Abel's Post-it note powerfully testifies, the young people do not passively succumb to the symbolic and structural violence emanating from interior frontiers. The everyday strategies they deploy in response to the environ-ment they find themselves thrown into—strategies that may sometimes appear in little, intangible gestures, while at other times erupting in loud and decisive actions—are therefore at the heart of the book. While the chapters that follow will pay full attention to the young people's lifeworlds, thoughts, and actions, this introductory chapter forms an attempt to give an insight into the shifting social and political landscapes that form the backdrop of these actions and reactions.

THE FIGURE OF THE UNACCOMPANIED MINOR

Abel's arrival in Switzerland and my research project were situated in the midst of a major transformative period—not just in terms of the rising numbers of unaccompanied minors seeking asylum in Switzerland but also in terms of a general shift in perception. Until shortly before the start of my fieldwork in June 2015, the broader public in Switzerland was not aware of unaccompanied minors seeking asylum. A quick Google media search with the keyword *unaccompanied minors* (*unbegleitete Minderjährige*) shows that until 2014 the word was mainly used in connection to children having to take international flights without their parents. From the summer of 2014, this changed dramatically. During these months the number of unaccompanied underage people lodging asylum applications in Switzerland doubled from 346 in 2013 to 795 in 2014. In 2015 this quadrupled to 2,736 (SEM 2016). These figures correspond with a Europe-wide trend that became most pronounced during the turbulent summer of displacements in 2015, when more than a million refugees lodged asylum applications in EU member states. Among them were a great number of children and teenagers traveling without adult guardians. While in 2013 12,725 unaccompanied minors applied for asylum in the European Union, in 2014 this figure rose to 23,150, peaking in 2015 with 95,206 applications (Eurostat, n.d.). Abel and the other young people this book focuses on thus arrived at a particular moment in time when the independent movements of underage people from war-torn countries in Africa and the Middle East—many of whom had spent years in refugee camps or protracted situations—gained momentum. When I started my research in 2015, the majority of the unaccompanied refugee youths seeking asylum in Switzerland were male (82.1%), between sixteen and seventeen years old (66%), and from Eritrea (1,191) or Afghanistan (909) (SEM 2016). The vast majority of them had reached Switzerland only after surviving perilous journeys across deserts, mountain ranges, and seas and escaping the imprisonment, kidnappings, and violence that characterizes many of the migrant journeys through transit countries such as Libya, Morocco, or Turkey—countries the European Union has de facto turned into its extended border zone (Strasser and Tibet 2020).

With the increased number of young refugees making their way to Switzerland on their own, the term *unaccompanied minor* has become inextricably linked to ideas of vulnerability. Whereas until the summer of 2014 the media and broader public in Switzerland tended not to differentiate between various categories of asylum-seeking youth, since then the clearly distinct figure of the unaccompanied child asylum seeker has entered the scene. It is a figure that is identified through certain attributes, such as innocence, trauma, lostness, or need for protection, and it is a figure that is imbued with specific rights (namely children's rights), particularly in terms of housing but also in terms of psychological well-being and education. While until 2014 there were only a handful of institutions targeted specifically at unaccompanied minors in Switzerland, there has been a strong push for child-specific housing, supervision, and education ever since. This shift led not just to the opening of many homes and school programs specialized in the reception and education of unaccompanied minors but also to strong efforts to harmonize these offers across the different cantons.[4]

Most Western states, including Switzerland, pride themselves on adhering to the UN Convention on the Rights of the Child and have recognized unaccompanied minor asylum seekers as a particularly vulnerable refugee category in need of special protection and care. As a result, young people arriving in Switzerland as underage asylum seekers receive preferential treatment in terms of housing, supervision, education, and the asylum procedure. The sense of vulnerability surrounding the figure of the unaccompanied minor could thus be seen to work as a protective shield against the threat of deportation, and it gives the young people access to special treatment. Yet the empirical case studies presented in this book will show that the moral conceptualization of childhood underlying these policies acts like a double-edged sword: while it sets out to protect the rights of children, it also leads to institutionalized expectations about what determines the "proper" refugee child. These expectations are based on specific Western ideas of childhood that frame it as a time of innocence and vulnerability and create a sharp division between childhood and adulthood. The growing number of age-dispute claims and age assessments concerning underage asylum seekers in the European Union prove how quickly the question of who is and is not regarded to be a "real" refugee child turns into a moral and political battleground (Crawley 2007; Kvittingen 2010). This can also be seen in Switzerland, where immigration authorities have been criticized for making excessive use of questionable age-assessment procedures as a means of racializing refugee youth (Oertli 2019). In 2016 the newspaper *Blick* published an investigative report about the practices of the Swiss immigration authorities, revealing the unusually high number of young asylum seekers classified as eighteen years old, especially among unaccompanied, young, male Afghans (Lenz 2016). The journalists suggested that migration officers rely on the weak method of bone analysis to turn underage men into adults. Being labeled as adults, they are no longer subject to the special protection of the UN Convention on the Rights of the Child and can be deported without much further bureaucratic ado if they receive a negative decision on their asylum applications.

Research from different parts of the world has shown that the increased arrival of young unaccompanied refugees has provoked paranoid reactions in policy-makers and the wider public that shift back and forth in labeling these youths as "at risk" and "*the* risk" (Nardone and Correa-Velez 2016; Heidbrink 2014; Bryan and Denov 2011) or as "vulnerable victims" and "impossible children" (Allerton 2018). The flip side of morally charged discourses on childhood, then, is the vilification of those who subvert these categories. Julia Hess and Dianna Shandy (2008, 767) compare the way the state deals with young refugees to a pendulum that keeps swinging back and forth between the urge to protect the most vulnerable members of society and the desire to treat them as risks in need of discipline, policing, or expulsion. In his groundbreaking work on the moral economy of immigration policies in Europe, Didier Fassin (2005) has described this movement as one between compassion and repression. Within an increasingly restrictive asylum landscape, acts of compassion toward refugees only appear as "privileged moments of collective redemption" directed at individual cases labeled humanitarian exceptions (375). These exceptional cases are deemed deserving of the (often temporary) protection of European states on the basis of humanitarian reasons, such as incurable illnesses, vulnerability, or psychopathology. Refugeehood is turned into a rare good that is only bestowed on the exceptional few, while the majority of asylum seekers are classed as "illegal," "bogus," or "economic" migrants (377).

The determination of refugee protection is shaped by international refugee law, but its interpretation and application are inextricably linked to political interests and priorities (Chimni 1998; Ludi 2014). These priorities constantly change, thereby also shifting who is regarded as deserving of refugee protection and who is not. Over the last decades, a distinct asylum hierarchy has taken shape in European refugee legislation. At the top of this hierarchy stands the figure of the political refugee who receives constitutional asylum for his or her fight against oppression—and, in Switzerland, a permit B. While this permit has to be renewed every five years, it holds the promise of being turned into a permanent residency after ten years of living in Switzerland. During the time of my research, only 19.2 percent of all asylum applicants were granted such a permit (SEM 2017a). Located lower in the asylum hierarchy is the figure of the transitional refugee who receives temporary protection. This humanitarian protection status, described as permit F (*Ausweis F*) in Switzerland, has to be renewed annually and gives less access to social welfare and education resources than a permit B. At the time of my research, 23.5 percent of all asylum applicants were granted such a permit. While this temporary permit is designed to create a status that is as precarious as possible to complicate future claims for permanent residence, it offers at least a minimum degree of stability and protection from deportation. At the bottom of the asylum hierarchy are the masses of asylum seekers who are classed as undocumented migrants and are subsequently deported or chased by the police. From the 31,299 people who applied for asylum in Switzerland in 2016, around 20,000 were rejected (SEM 2017a). In Europe's contemporary moral economy of asylum, the figure of the unaccompanied minor is treated as a refugee category worthy of special protection. Nevertheless, the chances of gaining refugee protection status are heavily dependent on the current asylum policy regarding the young people's countries of origin. While some youth receive permission to remain in Switzerland, others stand little chance of extending their stay beyond their eighteenth birthday, when the special protection status vanishes.

Over the last decade, intensified by the refugee crisis, European politics of asylum have been characterized by the formation of distinct scales of un/deservingness. Categorizations of un/deservingness are used to legitimize or contest access to resources such as refugee protection, social welfare, education, or citizenship. These categorizations are not based on rights but on individuals' moral characteristics. While by virtue of their perceived extreme vulnerability unaccompanied minors can be said to form the "perfect victims" (Ticktin 2016, 257) placed at the tops of these scales, the status of deservingness this affords them comes at a great cost. Expecting unaccompanied minors to display innocence to prove their deservingness does not just depoliticize their stories. It has the potential to provoke a backlash against those who do not act according to these morally charged expectations and are subsequently penalized, silenced, and excluded.

Similar dynamics can be observed in the reception and treatment of unaccompanied minors in Switzerland. Compared to the deep sense of suspicion that marks the reception of adult asylum seekers, the figure of the unaccompanied minor initially received a more positive public response in Switzerland. In the summer months of 2015, this figure even became *the* human face of the European "refugee crisis" in Switzerland. Media outlets produced countless stories about the traumatic journeys the young people had been through, provoking a wave of compassion. Throughout the summer of 2015, the home for unaccompanied minors in the countryside of Bern where I was conducting fieldwork was faced with a groundswell of sympathy by locals. While often extremely suspicious of adult (particularly Black, Muslim, and male) asylum seekers, locals were deeply moved by the media stories of the unaccompanied minors who had survived harrowing journeys on their own. The home got inundated with clothes donations and volunteering bids, to the point that it had to install a position dedicated solely to managing the help offers from the public. The education projects for unaccompanied refugee minors this book focuses on need to be read against the backdrop of these dynamics: it was during the peak of this compassion wave that attempts by refugee aid practitioners to install post–compulsory education programs for young unaccompanied asylum seekers managed to gain enough public and political support to get funded.

Yet just as the goodwill of the masses welcoming the Syrian refugees arriving in German and Austrian train stations in the summer months of 2015 quickly turned into a deep-seated racialized fear of being outnumbered in one's own country, so the narrative of the innocent unaccompanied refugee child morphed into one of the dangerous youth. As Miriam Ticktin (2016, 256) has pointed out, responses to refugees that are driven by a politics of humanitarian exception are built on an extremely unstable ground because they are not based in rights but in a "narrow emotional constellation" that is always in danger of collapsing like a house of cards. It is therefore hardly surprising that the scales of deservingness in Switzerland (as elsewhere in Europe) constantly shift back and forth, sometimes in favor of but also, in the wake of the rise of right-wing narratives fostering moral panics about immigration, increasingly against refugee youth.

How quickly ascriptions of deservingness can morph into undeservingness has become visible in the canton of Bern. Between May 2015 and November 2016, when I conducted fieldwork, Bern was often presented as a best-practice example for the German-speaking part of Switzerland, as it had taken its obligation under the UN Convention on the Rights of the Child to guarantee special protection to unaccompanied minors seriously and had invested in the establishment of child-appropriate accommodation and supervision infrastructure. Although the public generally approved of the establishment of several new homes to accommodate the more than five hundred unaccompanied refugee youth who had been allocated to the canton of Bern throughout the summer months of 2015, this sentiment radically swung around in May 2017, when the right-wing populist SVP party won a referendum aimed at stopping the funding of the "luxury" treatment of unaccompanied minors. Throughout the debates surrounding this event, the populist discourse cast doubt on the genuineness of the young people's claim of being "real" children or refugees, instead introducing a narrative of their parents as irresponsible and calculating villains, whose attempts at sending off their kids to live as parasites off the Swiss social system should not be rewarded. In the context of the UK debate, Stephanie Silverman (2016) has described this as the emergence of the "imposter child," an increasingly accepted narrative throughout Europe that accuses child asylum seekers of faking their age and identity to gain access to the welfare system. Similar debates can be found in the United States, where the normalization of terms such as *parachute children* or *anchor babies* points at the politicization of migrant youth (Heidbrink 2014, 6).

The example of Bern, where the right-wing success in the popular vote against the special treatment of unaccompanied minors legitimized debates about their deportability, shows just how powerful such debates are. Eritrean refugee youth—the group that contributed the most to the peak in unaccompanied minor asylum seekers in Switzerland in 2015—formed the main target of these public attacks. Although throughout the summer of displacements, when public sentiments had been in their favor, young Eritreans had received refugee or humanitarian protection across the board, right-wing populist interventions succeeded in turning this sentiment around by continuously casting doubt on Eritrea's classification as a dictatorship. Through highly dubious "fact finding missions" to Eritrea organized by SVP party members, it aimed to contradict reports by the UN (2016) and other international human rights bodies that had described the country as one of the cruelest contemporary totalitarian regimes. As a result of the mounting public pressure, the Swiss Federal Department of Justice and Police changed its recommendations for the handling of Eritrean asylum cases in 2017, leading to a wave of rejections. This backlash contributed to a sharp decrease in asylum applications from unaccompanied minors in Switzerland. In 2017 the overall number plummeted to 733, of which only 87 were lodged by youth from Eritrea (SEM 2017b). These developments show the volatile nature of the scales of un/deservingness: scarcely had the unaccompanied minor appeared in the public discursive arena as an exceptional humanitarian figure deserving of special protection and care, when it started to mingle with other, less deserving figures, such as the bogus economic migrant, the welfare scrounger, or the male migrant sexual predator. And no sooner was there a public outcry about a child refugee "crisis" than it disappeared into thin air again.

CRISIS TALK

It is important to note that the figure of the unaccompanied minor as an exceptional humanitarian category did not appear out of the blue. The emergence of this figure in Switzerland goes hand in hand with a strong international preoccupation with the plight of tens of thousands of unaccompanied minors from Latin America crossing into the United States in the summer of 2014, which quickly came to be labeled a "humanitarian crisis" (Ticktin 2016, 255). It also needs to be read against the backdrop of a growing number of newspaper articles, policy recommendations, and reports across the world that started to make children's autonomous roles in migratory movements more visible. The sudden peak in unaccompanied minors across the world thus takes place within this specific discursive context. While the phenomenon of independent child migration has existed for a long time, it was only recently that the legal system has started to see and react to it (Heidbrink 2014, 10). Importantly, the emergence of the unaccompanied minor as an exceptional humanitarian category cannot be separated from the dynamics of what I have elsewhere described as "crisis talk" in Europe (Lems 2020). The arrival of a large number of refugees in Europe throughout 2015 provoked a politics of crisis that went hand in hand with the narratives of economic and political crisis already permeating the public discursive scene.

Within these dynamics, refugee crisis talk quickly degenerated into a means of justifying harsh, extremely exclusionary responses.

In the brief time between the beginning and end of the summer of 2015, Europe rebordered—in both a physical and a metaphorical sense: in a concrete, physical sense in that it erected fences, reopened border checkpoints, and introduced hot-spot systems to crack down on the most frequently traveled refugee routes, and in a metaphorical sense in that it shifted the dominant narrative about the motives of the people on the move. European political leaders and policymakers used the smoke screen of the refugee crisis to justify a rigid distinction between undeserving "economic" migrants and deserving "real" refugees, arguing that many (if not most) of the people crossing the Mediterranean had taken advantage of the crisis situation to secure entry into the EU (Crawley and Skleparis 2018, 49). The ceaseless talk about the multiple economic, political, and identity crises confronting Europe allowed for the emergence of a dominant political and media discourse that suggested that even people who had been forced to leave their countries because of war and persecution were to be seen as migrants in search of economic opportunities rather than as refugees deserving of the protection of European states. The conception of un/deservingness this narrative follows is that refugeehood should only be bestowed on pure victims as a matter of last resort and that this should happen in the first safe country refugees enter. That these "safe" countries are often marked by poverty and political instability and do not offer refugees any future prospects beyond life in large-scale refugee camps does not matter. Because most asylum seekers in western and northern European states have to travel through such camps and countries before arriving at their destinations, they expose themselves as "bogus" refugees whose main goal is to gain access to wealthier states in Europe rather than to save their bare lives. In the realms of crisis talk, the pendulum of deservingness thus swings less often in favor of the displaced, leaving room only for the recognition of particular lives that should be valued and mourned, rather than life in general (Ticktin 2016, 256). As Bridget Anderson (2017, 7) poignantly puts it, the European refugee crisis did not only put into question the principles of freedom of movement and asylum. It challenged the very idea of Europe as "a space of liberal values, freedom, moral equality, and human rights" (7). The so-called refugee crisis should be understood as a "multidimensional crisis of solidarity between member states" of the European Union (7). Because many European states have experienced years of austerity and diminishing sovereignty, the sudden arrival of a large number of refugees provoked these problems to surface (8).

The sense of crisis surrounding the figure of the unaccompanied minor in Switzerland also needs to be read against the backdrop of a historically ingrained tradition of crisis talk in relation to migration. This becomes particularly visible in national debates about integration. At the turn of the millennium, there was widespread optimism among migration scholars in Switzerland that the newly introduced government focus on integration would overcome former immigration policies that had been driven by an excessive use of control, assimilation, and exclusion (Wicker 2003; Niederberger 2004). In recent years this hope has been tarnished. In this vein, Hans-Rudolf Wicker (2009, 26) warns of the deception in Swiss policymakers' increased language of integration. He argues that current migration policies show an astonishing continuity with former exclusionary approaches to migration. One key component is a deep-seated fear of *Überfremdung*, a word that only exists in the German language and is particularly prevalent in the Swiss context. While it is frequently translated into English as "foreign infiltration," the more appropriate translation would be "over-foreignization." In Switzerland, the fear of *Überfremdung* has a long history and has been present in migration policies from the nineteenth century onward. Wicker (2009, 26) describes it as the "golden thread" spinning its way through the different approaches to migrants and refugees in Switzerland. Building on this narrative of *Überfremdung*, the right-wing populist SVP party has been extremely successful since the early 2000s in designing anti-immigration campaigns that continuously nourish a sense that the country is facing a migration crisis. The far right—a stable force in Switzerland's mainstream political landscape—has repeatedly attacked asylum politics by making excessive use of a metaphor of abuse. This metaphor is based on the narrative construction of the figure of the immoral/ undeserving asylum seeker who is leading a good life at the expense of the Swiss taxpayer. Gianni D'Amato (2012, 99) argues that this contemporary figure needs to be read as the direct continuation of an earlier discursive figure that dates back to the nineteenth century, the "immoral pauper" (*liederlicher Pauper*), who, like the figure of the asylum seeker nowadays, was seen to be abusing the goodwill of hardworking, taxpaying citizens. These historical and discursive configurations form the subtext of contemporary integration policies in Switzerland, where the debate has gradually moved from the *right* of refugees and migrants to be included in Swiss society to a *demand* that they must integrate (in other words, assimilate) (Piñeiro 2015, 22–24). What resonates in all these debates is the fear of an imminent crisis: a deep-seated fear that if cultural difference is tolerated, it will inevitably lead to the collapse of Swiss values and to the disintegration of the country's wealth.

The emergence of the figure of the unaccompanied minor needs to be read within these national and transnational politics of crisis. It was born out of an ongoing project of distinction between those who are classified as deserving of protection (the especially vulnerable, such as single women, children, the chronically ill) and those who are not (such as single men, religious fundamentalists, "economic" migrants). While it has helped the young people this book focuses on to receive special treatment, it will become clear how harsh the repercussions can be for those who do not perform according to these ascriptions and thus lose their status of deservingness.

The school forms a crucial domain of societal life that enables us to observe how these highly politicized questions about belonging and nonbelonging, integration and assimilation, crisis and exceptionality are acted out and made sense of in the everyday. Understanding the vernacular ways such interior frontiers are set up, defended, and challenged is of crucial importance. Societal debates about integration, crisis, and otherness cannot be reduced to the discursive level. The ambiguous back-and-forth between innocence and guilt, deservingness and undeservingness, compassion and repression inherent in crisis talk trickles down into everyday interactions. By zooming in on the interactions in classrooms for unaccompanied refugee youth, the book will show how within these deeply contradictory dynamics it becomes perfectly acceptable to implement the harshest measures of exclusion while cloaking them in a language of compassion and inclusion.

TWO COHORTS, TWO COUNTRIES

The book is based on seventeen months of ethnographic research with unaccompanied refugee youth in two German-speaking cantons in Switzerland. The first field site was located in the canton of Bern, where I followed the everyday pathways of eight unaccompanied minors and their extended groups of friends in and beyond the integration classes they attended. In my second field site in Zürich, my focus was on an educational pilot project for unaccompanied refugee youth. I accompanied eight young Eritrean men in a training program developed to foster their inclusion in the Swiss labor market and society. While the first four chapters of the book focus on the youth I worked with in the canton of Bern, the last two chapters are dedicated to the educational institution in Zürich, where Abel and his friends lived.

The decision to include two cohorts of youth and field sites in the book was driven by a couple of ideas. Firstly, this double focus allows me to describe and analyze very different social dynamics. While the field site in Bern sheds light on the ways refugee youth navigate their educational hopes and struggles both in and beyond school settings, the field site in Zürich shows the close grip institutions can have on refugee youths' lives and future opportunities. Secondly, and more importantly, the two field sites enable me to show that the logic of inclusive exclusion permeating the schooling of unaccompanied refugee youth cannot be put aside as the failure of one single education project or the misconduct of individual pedagogues. Given that critiques of the persistence of discriminatory practices in the Swiss education system are routinely stifled by digressions into debates about cantonal differences in the education of refugees and migrants, this is an important point to emphasize. By shedding light on the dynamics in two different cantons, I can bring to the fore the structural inequality underwriting the Swiss education system.

At the time of my research, the two cohorts of refugee youth were between fifteen and eighteen years old. Reflective of the overall arrivals in Switzerland at the time, the majority of them were male and came from Eritrea. That most of the stories presented in the book relate to the experiences of Eritrean youth has to do with the sociocultural composition of the institutions that formed my ethnographic entry point. At that particular moment, Eritrean youth formed the largest proportion of unaccompanied minor asylum seekers in Switzerland, and so it was not surprising that they were the main group I encountered in the youth protection facilities and refugee classes. Despite coming from a small country with a population of about five million, Eritreans form the ninth largest refugee population worldwide. In 2017 the UNHCR counted 486,200 Eritrean refugees, among them an exceptionally high number of young people (UNHCR 2018, 15). In the same year, Eritreans formed the second largest group of unaccompanied minors lodging asylum applications worldwide (49).

The exodus of young Eritreans reflects the collective sense of hopelessness permeating life in a country marked by decades of political turmoil, poverty, war, and violence, leading to a situation of "chronic emergency" (Belloni 2019, 10). In Eritrea, a country marked by centuries of occupation—from the reach of the Ottoman Empire on its coastal region to Italian and British colonization and the annexation by Ethiopia in the 1960s—displacement is not a new phenomenon. The three-decade-long war for independence from neighboring Ethiopia, headed by the revolutionary Eritrean Liberation Front (EPLF), did not lead to the stability and prosperity many Eritreans had hoped and fought for. In 1991 Eritrea became an independent country. Rather than ringing in an era of prosperity, however, independence marked the beginning of homegrown despotism. Eritrea's first and only president, Isaias Afwerki, has ruled the country with an iron fist ever since, installing an elaborate security apparatus that cracks down on any sign of dissent, leading to a militarized state that is frequently characterized as one of the worst contemporary totalitarian regimes on the basis of surveillance, terror, arbitrary incarcerations, and torture (United Nations Human Rights Council 2016).

The youth exodus from Eritrea is linked to the desperate political situation in the country. But as the stories presented in the book will show, it is also inextricably connected to education. In Eritrea, all male and female students in their last year of secondary schooling are sent to the Sawa military facility in the

Gash-Barka region of the country to study for their university entry exam while being trained as soldiers (Müller 2008). This measure was first introduced in 1995, only two years after the EPLF had declared independence from Ethiopia (Iyob 1995). Sawa was established as an institution through which the spirit of the struggle for independence was to be disseminated to successive generations. Magnus Treiber (2018, 53) notes that the EPLF envisaged Sawa as a place through which "the hardship and asceticism of 30 years of war was to be experienced and embodied even after the war was over." While the training camp was initially intended as a temporary measure, the intensification of the border conflict with Ethiopia between 1998 and 2000 led to its establishment as a permanent compulsory scheme. Afwerki used the bloody conflict to justify the suspension of democratic reforms and the establishment of an authoritarian state.

Sawa training camp is a central pillar in the government's "development scheme" that legally obliges all Eritrean nationals of the age of eighteen to become conscripts in the national service (Bozzini 2015). The camp is known for its hardships: despite extreme temperatures, food and water rations are low, and students are punished for the smallest infractions of the strict disciplinary regime. The UN special rapporteur to Eritrea reports that students at Sawa are subjected to various types of human rights violations, including torture, sexual abuse, inhuman or degrading treatment, and corporal punishment (Keetharuth 2014, 12). Dropping out of school to avoid this ordeal is no option because without the national service clearance certificate, young people are denied access to vital things such as food rations, the permit to open a business or bank account, or the right to own a mobile phone (Tekle 2018). The Eritrean state has developed refined techniques of surveillance, mainly through the introduction of documents that have to be presented at one of the hundreds of checkpoints located throughout the country, and these are aimed at cracking down on deserters or people attempting to evade national service (Bozzini 2011). At the end of the training in Sawa, only a handful of students are allowed to continue to higher education. The majority are forcefully drafted into the national service for an indefinite period of time. Throughout their service as conscripts, they receive hardly any pay, often have to perform heavy labor, are not allowed to return home regularly to attend to their families, and are not permitted to hold a passport. The arrival of large groups of Eritrean youth in Switzerland in 2015 and 2016 is connected to the militarization of education in their home country. To escape enforced subscription into the army, many young people flee the country before they are enrolled for the training year in Sawa. But education also propels the migration of Eritrean young people on another level. It is often the hope of gaining access to better educational opportunities that incentivizes them to embark on the long and treacherous journey to countries like Switzerland.

While the experiences of young people from Eritrea illustrate the historically embedded role of education as a key driver for youth migration, the book also gives glimpses beyond the Eritrean case. One chapter details the lifeworld of Thierno, a young man from Guinea—a country that is marked by its own youth exodus. The country has a long history of youth mobility. For many decades, these migratory journeys took young people mainly to neighboring countries in West Africa or to other African countries like Angola, Libya, or Egypt, where they spent a couple of years to earn enough money and prestige to return home and establish their own families. Over the last decade these trajectories have started to shift. The number of young people leaving Guinea to embark on dangerous journeys to Europe has risen exponentially. In 2016 the International Organization for Migration recorded the arrival of 25,000 Guineans in Italy alone, placing the small country of 13 million inhabitants among the nations with the highest migration outflow in Africa (IOM 2019, 1). As in Eritrea, this youth exodus has much to say about the conflict-ridden relationship between the state and youth in a postcolonial society (Engeler 2019).

In the era after Guinea's independence in 1958, youths were seen as an important driver of societal change (Straker 1990). Influenced by socialist future imaginaries, young people formed the key to realizing a state freed of the colonial and traditional baggage that was holding its citizens back. They formed the foot soldiers of President Ahmed Sékou Touré's "demystification program"—an ambitious national reeducation project targeted at eliminating "backward" cultural practices deemed a hindrance to the progressive transformation of Guinea into a modern, cosmopolitan state where ethnic affiliations no longer counted (McGovern 2012). While this focus on youth education enabled a generation of young people in Guinea to gain more autonomy and freedom, the regime did not permit dissenting views. It expected youth to accept the predetermined truths they were exposed to in state education programs (Engeler 2016, 72). Rather than installing a more socially just society, Guinea's three-decade-long experiment with scientific socialism formed the basis for the conflicts that are plaguing the country today. While ethnic clientelism was officially banned, ethnic affiliation continued to inform political actions (Rey 2016), leading to the uneven distribution of power and access to public resources. These dynamics have come to haunt the governments succeeding the end of the socialist regime in 1984. The drastic decline of living standards and rise of poverty caused by neoliberal state policies have led to an intensification of political tensions, particularly between the two largest ethnic groups—the Madinka, who make up about 30 percent of the overall population, and the Fulani, who make up 40 percent. The current president, Alpha Condé, a

Mandinka, violently crushes oppositional protests on a regular basis. In doing so, he attempts to silence accusations of large-scale corruption and the sellout of the country's iron ore resources to international mining companies while the majority of the country lives in excruciating poverty (Human Rights Watch 2019a). Children and young people are disproportionally represented in human rights organizations' reports about the regular police roundups, beatings, and even killings organized by the government's security forces in response to protests (Amnesty International 2018).

Although young people played a crucial role in the establishment of Guinea as an independent country, in the ethnic and political unrest marking the more recent past, youth has turned into a highly politicized social category. This politicization is deepened by the fact that young people under the age of twenty-five currently make up 60 percent of Guinea's overall population (Schroven 2019, 12). Youths thus form a considerable force in the country. Political leaders both count on them for political mobilization and fear them for their explosive potential. In a country where everyday life is characterized by unemployment, poverty, and lack of opportunity, young people find themselves stuck in the category of youth, unable to acquire the social and economic resources necessary to transition into the state of adulthood (Christiansen, Utas, and Vigh 2006). The frustration and anger caused by this enforced stalemate as well as the violent crackdown on the activities of young political activists are the main catalysts of the Guinean youth exodus. Once in Europe, however, young Guineans often discover that their struggle for a dignified life is far from over. Unlike Eritrea, many European states, including Switzerland, categorize Guinea as a democratically ordered country. This classification has a large impact on asylum applications. As Guinea is seen to be safe to return rejected asylum seekers to, unaccompanied refugee youth often fear the arrival of their eighteenth birthday, when their special protection status as children ends.

The detour from the book's overall focus on Eritrea to youth from a country that was placed at the bottom of the hierarchy of asylum in Switzerland enables a highlighting of the structural violence of inclusive exclusion. It helps expose the lasting effects of the ambiguous treatment of youth as both innocent children in need of protection and undesired migrants awaiting deportation: how the structural and symbolic violence emanating from interior frontiers manages to seep into young people's bodies and minds, directing their orientation to the world. Rather than ending the suffering and pain refugee youth have to endure on their migration journeys to Europe, the affectively charged frontiers of belonging they are confronted with in Swiss society form a continuation of the boundaries and borders they have had to contend with.

BRIDGES TO NOWHERE

The entry point into my field site in the canton of Bern was a home for unaccompanied young asylum seekers in the countryside, about an hour's drive away from the capital city. I received access to the home under the precondition that I would find ways of making myself useful, so that I would not disturb the daily routine in the home or become a nuisance to the social workers. I entered the field eager to shed light on the young people's own perspectives and experiences—perspectives that are still vastly underrepresented in forced migration research. There have been many studies focusing on unaccompanied minors' psychological well-being (e.g., Halvorsen 2002; Bean, Eurelings-Bontekoe, and Spinhoven 2007), on the policies and children's rights determining their status (e.g., Bhabha 2007), and on the social work practices and welfare services aimed at them (e.g., Kohli 2006), but little is known about their social worlds. While I was propelled by social scientists' call for more ethnographic research focusing on young unaccompanied asylum seekers' own perspectives (Wernesjö 2012; Heidbrink 2014), I first had to convince the social service providers in Bern of the importance of such a child-centered approach. They were concerned that having an ethnographer present would disturb the routine in the home or pressure the young people into revealing details about their lives that could be used against them. With the support of a crucial member of staff, an open-minded social pedagogue who had just initiated a radio program for the unaccompanied minors living in the care facility, I was able to develop a way of conducting participatory observation that felt more "participatory" and less like "observation." I became involved in the radio project as a volunteer and worked with a group of young people on their stories, which were aired once per month through an independent youth radio station.

The radio project formed an important entry point into the lifeworlds of the young people from Eritrea and Guinea whose stories I focus on in the first four chapters of the book. Through the weekly gatherings, we got to know one another's biographies, hopes, and despairs, and over time the young people were able to better understand my research motives. Once they had acquainted themselves with the idea that I was going to write "a book" about them, as they liked to think about my research project, I extended our meetings beyond the radio setting and joined them in their everyday routes and routines. After gaining permission from the school, I started participating in the reception classes for unaccompanied refugee youth most of the radio group's participants were attending. Over the course of half a year, I alternately visited one of the two classes for unaccompanied minors in a school in the countryside of Bern for one day per week.

When I started my research in the field site in Bern, the young people received access to basic education in so-called internal classes that were located inside the home. These classes were mainly aimed at learning German and did not follow the national school curriculum. After the youth had achieved basic language proficiency, those who were under the age of sixteen were transferred to local schools and included in the public school system. As mentioned before, the UN Convention on the Rights of the Child guarantees the right of every child regardless of their nationality to access compulsory schooling. Yet by the time they had completed the first cycle of German-language classes in the internal school, all of the young people I worked with were older than fifteen and had therefore lost this right. What further complicated their situation was that the Swiss school system is marked by distinct practices of selection (Streckeisen, Hänzi, and Hungerbühler 2007; Hofstetter 2017) that are notoriously difficult for migrants to permeate (Oester, Fiechter, and Kappus 2008). Swiss students are separated according to their skills from the early age of eleven or twelve. Depending on their abilities and interests, they get channeled into either an academic pathway through secondary schooling or a vocational one through an apprenticeship in a trade. Unaccompanied youths aged sixteen or older thus find themselves in a difficult situation, as they have missed the important turnoff point that would have allowed them to access higher education and can also not easily be included in the apprenticeship system (BASS 2016).

When I started my research in Bern, there was no educational strategy for refugee youth past the obligatory cutoff age. In the summer months of 2015, however, when the number of unaccompanied young asylum seekers peaked, the cantonal authorities were forced into action. As public compassion with the plight of the unaccompanied minors soared, many cantons—including Zürich and Bern, where I conducted research—agreed to fund the establishment of so-called integration classes (*Integrationsklassen*), reception classes specifically designed for unaccompanied refugee youth aged sixteen and older. The classes were usually located in existing bridging schools (*Brückenangebote*). These schools are set up as interim solutions for students who have completed mainstream obligatory schooling and have not been able to secure an apprenticeship or a placement in a secondary school. The rationale behind the institutions is to give students who have slipped through the cracks an extra year of schooling to catch up with their peers. Under the guidance of specialized teachers and through work placements that allow them to gain experience in different trades, they are expected to use the school as a bridge to transition into an apprenticeship. Similarly, the integration classes in the bridging schools were set up to prepare refugee youth for their inclusion in the job market.

The two integration classes where I conducted research in Bern were part of a larger educational project in the canton that used the available infrastructure of bridging schools for classes that were specifically aimed at unaccompanied refugee youth. Between May 2015 and 2016, seven such classes were put up across different bridging schools in the canton of Bern. Unlike former education projects that had been solely open to youth with refugee status, this program also enabled young people who were still awaiting the decision on their asylum application to gain access to education. Many of the refugee sector and educational practitioners I encountered celebrated the cantonal authorities' willingness to invest in young asylum seekers' integration as an important step forward. Yet, as will become clear from the young people's stories, these bridging projects that aimed to form a springboard for refugee youths' inclusion into mainstream education in fact created an insurmountable number of new obstacles. Paradoxically, these so-called integration classes, which, as the name implies, are aimed at including refugee youth in Swiss society, start from the premise of the need for separate educational streams in refugee-only classes. Sidelined and stigmatized as problem cases, the young people find it difficult, if not impossible, to make the jump into mainstream educational opportunities. While the teachers and practitioners kept talking about the integration classes in positive terms, framing them as bridges into Swiss society, the young people I worked with increasingly came to describe them as bridges to nowhere.

The experiences of the young people the book zooms in on demonstrate that the focus on the extraordinarity of the unaccompanied minor as a crisis figure provokes not just ambiguous *social* categorizations but also such *educational* categorizations. While their status as vulnerable children in need of protection affords them educational possibilities refugee youths over the age of eighteen do not gain access to, the supposed vulnerability this special status is based on forms a major educational stumbling block. The chapters based on my research in Bern show how the idea of vulnerability comes to be used against the young people, when teachers, social workers, and potential employers base the impossibility of unaccompanied minors' inclusion in the mainstream educational system on their supposed vulnerability. These expectations of vulnerability are at odds with the strong sense of autonomy many of the young people display, which is often sanctioned or pathologized. The result of these developments is the continued educational isolation of the young people. While the bridging schools were initially set up as temporary measures, they quickly turned into something permanent, with some unaccompanied minors spending years in isolated, refugee-only classes. From the sixteen young people I accompanied closely throughout my fieldwork and the about sixty teenagers I got to know more loosely, nobody managed to transition from the separated refugee-only classes to secondary schooling, and only a handful were able to gain access to regular apprenticeships. The majority of the young people remained in the integration classes or in short-term refugee apprenticeships that channeled them into the lowest-skilled segment of the job market. While teachers and pedagogues were quick to put this low success rate on the young people's supposed weak academic performance, this does not explain why other European countries with a high intake of unaccompanied minors from similar backgrounds fare much better. In Sweden, for example, 40 percent of the male and 50 percent of the female unaccompanied refugee youths manage to complete high school by the time they have turned twenty-four (Çelikaksoy and Wadensjö 2015, 17).

The high number of young refugees finding themselves catapulted out of the education system in Switzerland needs to be read against the backdrop of the selective nature of German-speaking school landscapes—a phenomenon that has been analyzed and critiqued by many educational scholars (Haeberlin, Imdorf, and Kronig 2004; Gomolla and Radtke 2007; Söhn 2011). The exclusionary dynamics within the integration classes described in this book thus do not only affect unaccompanied minors. They also form barriers to the educational opportunities of other groups of young people, such as children from lower socioeconomic backgrounds, first- and second-generation migrant youth, or disabled children. Yet while much has been written about the selective nature of German-speaking school systems, little is known about the ways these processes of selection, screening, and locking out work on a vernacular, local basis. Building on the work of anthropologists in Switzerland (Oester and Brunner 2015) and elsewhere (Abu El-Haj 2015; Gilliam and Gullov 2016; Jaffe-Walter 2016) who stress the need for more nuanced knowledge about the ways educational in- or exclusion is produced in everyday actions and interactions, this book aims to shed light on the *intersubjective* nature of these processes.

EVERYDAY UN/DESERVINGNESS

By focusing on the intersubjective ways inclusive exclusion is produced, lived, and made sense of in everyday school life, I build on existential approaches in anthropology that see human existence as inherently relational (Jackson 1998; Lucht 2012; Jackson and Piette 2015). Rather than the search for individual essence, the emphasis lies on "inter-existence" (Jackson 1998, 3)—the ways people actively deal with the dialectics of simultaneously being a subject for themselves and an object for others. Michael Jackson poignantly describes this dialectic as an existential struggle to strike a balance between being a "who" and a "what": "Each person is at once a subject for himself or herself—a *who*—and an object for others—a *what*. And though individuals work, act and speak toward belonging to a world with others, they simultaneously strive to experience themselves as world makers" (Jackson 1998, 8).

It is precisely this existential leitmotif that interests me—how young unaccompanied refugees who find themselves thrown into a highly regulated environment that is not of their making actively deal with this situation and strive to turn it into a world they co-own. However, while the focus lies on the everyday interactions, actions, and "minor" moments of existence (Piette 2015) from which these processes can be observed, it is important never to lose sight of the wider field of forces they occur in. As I turn my attention to the young people's experiences of structural violence, it becomes clear that intersubjectivity should not be misunderstood as a synonym for empathy, harmony, or shared experience. The existential aporias that the logic of inclusive exclusion repeatedly confronts the young people with demonstrate that intersubjectivity works to affirm not just identity and belonging but also difference and alienation (Jackson 1998, 4).

In my previous work I have looked at the continuing importance of emplacement in a world characterized by movement and displacement (Lems 2018). The present book can be read as an attempt to think through the existential predicaments of *being-out-of-place*. As the stories and experiences I zoom in on show, this condition of being-out-of-place is not due to the inescapability of displacement or the impossibility for refugees' being-at-home. It needs to be read against the backdrop of the current sociopolitical climate in Europe, where migrant bodies are marked as problem cases in need of integration, control, or expulsion and are thereby kept them from laying claim to places. Rather than speaking of being-out-of-place as an inherent state of being, I therefore treat it as a condition that is actively made. By weighing migrant subjects up against one another on a scale of un/deservingness, it is not just their right to participate as equal members of society that is at stake but their very right to being-here (*Dasein*). In a social order of things that is based on such a shaky equilibrium, the life of the people placed at the undeserving end of the scale comes to be valued as less "grievable" and more dispensable than that of others (Butler 2009).

Un/deservingness has so far mainly been discussed in relation to the moralization of poverty, inequality, and access to resources in welfare states (Stack 1974; Haney 2003; Kalb and Halmai 2011). While I am interested in the ways states use frames of un/deservingness to justify or depoliticize inequality, I do not treat them solely as techniques of governance or discipline. Rather, I am interested in the ways such ideas move beyond the discursive arena and permeate the everyday, how they turn into "vernacular moral registers" (Willen 2012) that have the power to determine individuals' emplacement within society to a great degree. One of the core questions the book aims to flesh out empirically, then, is how this condition of un/deservingness is made and unmade in the everyday. How are interior frontiers that determine who is allowed "in" and who is to stay "out" set up, defended, and policed? At what point do ideas of un/deservingness come to enter bodies and minds and turn into embodied ways of knowing and

encountering the world? How do they come to permeate biographies and inter-
sperse with individuals' most intimate scripts of self? And what strategies do
young people deploy in response to these powerful mechanisms? By keeping my
focus on the ways these questions play out in the everyday, I put the spotlight on
both the ways young people are turned into "matters out of place" (Douglas 1966)
and the strategies they deploy to challenge and overturn this.

As magnifying glasses of wider societal issues, school settings offer an interesting entry point into a deeper understanding of the ways ideas about un/
deservingness are lived and grappled with on the ground. For while schools are
commonly perceived as places of individual progress, they also represent the
state's attempt at creating ideal, "desirable" citizens. Laura Gilliam and Eeva
Gullov (2016) coined the term "civilizing practices" to describe these dynamics
whereby the state molds young people into the "right" citizens through public
education programs. They show that one consequence of the liberal ideal of
inclusive societies has been the creation of subtle exclusionary practices in multicultural school settings, where migrant bodies come to be marked as problematic and in need of special interventions. Similar dynamics can be seen in the
educational responses to unaccompanied refugee youth in Switzerland. While
humanist, liberal influences force policymakers to think about the education of
this group of young people who live under the direct protection of the state, the
forms of schooling directed at them are driven by distinct practices of exclusion.
Within these settings it becomes close to impossible for the young people to
make the move into mainstream education. If they display too much autonomy,
they run the risk of losing their status as vulnerable/deserving child refugees, but
if they display too little autonomy, they are deemed not fit for public schooling
because of their vulnerability. The chapters highlight how refugee youth from
Eritrea and Guinea come to terms with the deeply ambiguous social realities
caused by their educational isolation in refugee-only classes. This focus on the
everyday makes visible how young people whose journeys to Switzerland were
propelled by a strong hope of upward social mobility through education deal
with an environment that simultaneously marks them as problem cases that
need to be kept "out" and pressures them into proving their deservingness to be
allowed "in." While the emphasis of this book lies on the small and seemingly
banal ways the logic of inclusive exclusion enters and envelops the everyday, it
will become clear that the struggles this paradoxical reality forces the young
people into are by no means innocent, apolitical, or banal. The individual stories
and experiences focused on in the chapters show how the structural violence
caused by the politics of exclusion currently sweeping through liberal, Western
societies plays out in young refugees' most intimate lives, encroaching on their
hopes, dreams, and future perspectives.

EXISTENTIAL APORIAS

Having mapped out the core social and political dynamics playing into the educational pathways of unaccompanied refugee youth in Switzerland and the ambiguous social realities they foster, I can finally return to the troubling questions posed by Abel at the beginning of the chapter. His Post-it note can be read as a powerful testament to the existential aporias the logic of inclusive exclusion creates in young people. Importantly, his note allows for a first glimpse into the ways ideas about educational un/deservingness trickle down into the everyday and bring up key questions about belonging and alienation. To better understand the dynamics that propelled Abel to write the note, however, I need to shed light on my second research site in Zürich and the specifics of the educational project he had been selected to participate in.

In many ways the institution that had initiated this education program can be seen as an extreme manifestation of the dynamics of inclusive exclusion that I have attempted to sketch. Unlike the integration classes in Bern, which were attached to existing public institutions, the second education project I accompanied was based in a private institution that specializes in the social rehabilitation of trouble youth. Located on large, secluded premises in the countryside around Zürich, it offers young men aged between fifteen and twenty-two the possibility of doing an apprenticeship under the strict supervision of social workers, therapists, and legal guardians in lieu of a prison sentence. Because the number of youths classified as delinquent had reduced drastically in the years leading up to the summer of displacements in 2015, the institution faced serious financial issues. When its administrators were looking for alternative options to keep the home and its training workshops afloat, the idea of starting a project with refugee youth came up.

The establishment and justification of this project is inextricably linked to the rhetoric of crisis talk: the management framed its decision to include a group of unaccompanied minors with no history of criminal offense in a correctional facility against the backdrop of the urgent need to respond to the refugee crisis and relieve the overburdened education system. The book's last two chapters will show how, in return for these efforts, they expected a constant display of thankfulness and loyalty from the eight Eritrean young men who were the "chosen ones" to participate in this self-described "integration pilot." If the young men did not comply, or if they questioned their placement in the correctional facility, the social workers cast doubt on their status of deservingness, pitting the unaccompanied refugee youths' behavior against that of the dissocial youth living in the facility. Here the twisted logic of inclusive exclusion reveals itself in full force: amid a sociopolitical landscape that has normalized the seclusion of asylum seekers and refugees, *any* project that opens the door to Swiss society a tiny crack can pride itself on inclusionary, cosmopolitan ideals, even if the project is located in an institution directed at the containment of societal outcasts. It was not only the management and staff working in this institution who failed to see the contradiction between the aim to "integrate" unaccompanied refugee youth and their placement with young men who themselves were located at the very edge of Swiss society. Refugee aid practitioners, legal guardians, teachers, and the responsible authorities all celebrated the project as a best-practice example of integration. The fact that the institution opened its doors to me and that I was generously permitted to participate in virtually all domains of daily life—from the workshops and internal school to the leisure-time activities, excursions, and staff meetings—was only possible because the management was convinced of the project's humanitarian ethos.

On the one hand, the situation in the institution was almost picture-perfect: The boys received intensive German classes in small groups of four. They had secured access to short-term apprenticeships and lived under the supervision of relatively open-minded, friendly social workers. The eight boys were chosen out of 150 unaccompanied minors in Zürich who had been keen to participate. Most of their friends remained stuck in secluded refugee classes or, once they turned eighteen, on their own without access to any form of education. On the other hand, the structures of the institution had been set up for delinquent youth, and no exceptions were made for the unaccompanied young men. This meant that their lives were heavily controlled. From the moment they woke up in the morning to their lunch breaks and the evening checkups—the boys were under constant supervision. Unsurprisingly, the rigid and punitive structure regularly led to outbreaks of rebellion among the dissocial youth living in the facility. Most of them had a history of social abandonment and abuse and had been handed from one correctional facility to the other. So while the eight Eritreans had joined the project full of enthusiasm for the educational opportunities it offered, the other youth saw it as a form of banishment.

On that August morning when Abel wrote the message, he had realized that the educational institution he had come to live in was not the perfect springboard into Swiss society he had imagined it to be upon his arrival. Throughout the two weeks he had spent there, he had been confronted with the suspicious and at times aggressive behavior the young people already living there showed toward the newcomers. He had come to see that he had once again been sidetracked into a place with "problem kids," a place that was out of sync with the reality of the Swiss teenagers attending public schools. His decision to embark on the dangerous journey to Europe had been driven by the idea of gaining access to quality secondary education and its promises of upward social mobility. But while he had managed to make his way to one of the safest and wealthiest countries in the world with a well-established public education system, he found himself stuck in a segregated facility that would only allow him to follow a career in a manual craft and that thereby moved the higher education he had hoped for out of reach.

In a conversation that morning during the coffee break, just before Abel stuck the Post-it note to his chest, he had realized how deep this social and educational isolation went. Marina, the social pedagogue in charge of the refugee boys that morning had told them about the rules regarding the weekends, that they were only allowed to have one visitor per apartment and that she did not want them to start "a habit of inviting all your refugee friends over." While Kibrum and Aaron had been up in arms against these rules, Abel had remained quiet, observing the bickering with a removed, depressed glance. Minutes later, when Abel stuck the Post-it note to his T-shirt, he forced everybody to take notice of the deeply troubling questions that were on his mind. Indeed, his act got him the attention of the shocked social pedagogues, who did not know how to react to his refusal to speak. He spent the next hour working in complete silence.

Later on, when the social pedagogues had left the scene and the trainer sent us to the shed at the other end of the premises for some tools, Abel started to talk. He told me that he felt overwhelmed by the many rules that were imposed on him. He said that he had lived on his own since he was twelve years old, that the social pedagogues treated him "like a child that has to be taken by the parents' hand," and that they wanted to control everything, even the people the youths invited on the weekends. What upset him the most was the fact that they had to hand in the keys to their apartments whenever they went to work, a measure aimed at the dissocial youth to keep them from returning to their rooms when they refused to work. To Abel, the act of handing in his keys felt like an intrusion into his privacy and, more importantly, his capability to move about freely. "What is this here, a prison?" Abel asked. While he had hoped the education project to be a springboard to a better future, he now felt that it was just another form of keeping him out. Rather than using education as a vehicle to move forward in his life, he perceived it as a blockage that kept him from participating in the "real" world and with the "real" society. That his mother had sold all her belongings to pay for his journey to Europe and that now he felt it was impossible to fulfill his promise of making something of himself made his life appear to be at a standstill. As the dramatic message Abel stuck to his chest demonstrates, it even made his life appear dead.

Throughout my fieldwork, I observed the importance the young people attached to education as a way of moving forward in their lives. These hopes of movement through education propelled people like Abel during their dangerous journeys through the Libyan desert and across the Mediterranean. Over the course of the book, I deploy an existential lens to clarify what happens when these imaginaries of mobility clash with the reality of an asylum system that curtails the young people's educational possibilities and opportunities to move forward in their lives. It shows that the prolonged waiting and hopelessness refugee youth are exposed to in Switzerland can be experienced as a form of violence surpassing the violence and chronic uncertainty that led them to leave their home countries in the first place.

ABOUT THIS BOOK

As I turn to the experiences of the young people in Bern, the fundamental questions posed by Abel will continue to resonate in my thinking and writing. While I come back to the Post-it incident only in the very last chapter, when I trace its social afterlife in my field site in Zürich, the questioning of the deep and utter sense of being-out-of-place the note throws up spins its way throughout the book. The existential aporias the logic of inclusive exclusion create are counterpoised by the young people's attempts to move beyond these impasses. Each chapter sheds light on the lifeworld of one young person and on the particularity of their educational pathways. Driven by an interest in the ways the frontiers of belonging are learned, embodied, enacted, and challenged in the realms of the two educational settings where my fieldwork took place, each chapter fleshes out a strategy young people deployed in response to the situations they found themselves cast into. It is important to emphasize that I am not using the notion of *strategy* with the same sense of planning and calculation the term is commonly associated with. The strategies I explore stand for the everyday practices and improvisatory acts that arose in correspondence with the world the young people were moving through (Lems 2016, 326). The strategies are the outcome of intersubjective processes within and beyond the classroom, and they enable the young people to gain a certain degree of control over their own lives. Yet, given the restrictive and disciplining character of refugee politics in Switzerland, these strategies do not necessarily appear in the form of open resistance. In most of the chapters, they appear in the cracks and interstices of social spaces, such as the tireless efforts the young people invest in passing themselves off as "normal" teenagers (chap. 1), "model" pupils/refugees (chap. 2), or poster children of "integration" (chap. 3). Other chapters show the structural violence of inclusive exclusion—how the frontiers of belonging come to enter individual bodies and minds and play out in personal relationships (chap. 4). While these first four chapters are based on my fieldwork in the integration classes in Bern, the last two show the everyday production of un/deservingness in the education institution in Zürich. By paying attention to the clashing expectations the young people and pedagogical staff had of the "integration pilot," I flesh out the ways the logic of inclusive exclusion enters and permeates the education of unaccompanied refugee youth (chap. 5). In the final chapter of the book, I return to Abel's Post-it note to explore the hauntings interior frontiers produce. By looking into the Post-it note's social afterlife, I cast light on the dramatic existential balancing acts the young people have to perform in their striving for autonomy and belonging (chap. 6).

Each chapter aims to accomplish a different conceptual point. While chapter one discusses the normalization of modern ideas about youth and childhood and the ways unaccompanied minors subvert them, chapter two focuses on the ways such ideas enter classrooms and create distinctions between "normal" and "problem" students. Chapter three casts a critical light on the integration paradigm, pointing to the race for deservingness it creates in young refugees. Building on these thoughts, chapter four thinks through the violent nature of contemporary asylum regimes and the destruction it causes in individuals marked as undeserving of protection. Chapter five attempts to conceptualize the paradoxical social and political currents marking the education of marginalized groups and the kinds of abandonment they produce. The book ends with a discussion of the profound existential aporias these dynamics provoke.

Even though the book focuses on the educational trajectories of two cohorts of refugee students, it is not a classic school ethnography. I share with school ethnographers an interest in the routines of school life and the mechanisms of domination and oppression the everyday interactions between teachers and students allow to unveil. This book departs from a school ethnography, however, in that it treats the classroom as one of many domains where the young people negotiate questions of autonomy, recognition, and belonging. While chapters two, three, four, and six zoom in on classroom situations, my ethnographic focus also moves beyond the walls of the educational institutions the youth attended. By focusing on their everyday paths, actions, and interactions, I can detail some of the ways the young people made sense of their situation in spaces that were not controlled by teachers or other authority figures. To describe the profound role of education in the youths' striving for existential freedom, the chapters weave in and out of their life stories. This biographical angle enables me to embed the role of education as a forward-moving force—a powerful idea that propels young people to leave their families and embark on dangerous journeys—in wider histories of hope for progress and modernity. This focus on the particularities of the young people's lifeworlds requires meticulous ethnographic attention to the details of social life as it unfolds in the everyday. It involves a learning process in the ethnographer so that she is able to take note of the small, minor modes of communication and action through which young people negotiate their placement in the world. Often these negotiation processes involve teachers, social pedagogues, or other adult figures. The educators therefore form important supporting characters in this book. I speak of them as supporting characters because, unlike in classic school ethnographies, I do not introduce them as main protagonists. While the chapters give glimpses into their thoughts, doubts, and stories, the focus remains on the young people's perspectives.

Although this book concerns the lifeworlds of a small group of unaccompanied refugee youths and the educational settings they attended, I believe that it has the power to speak for more than the particularity of these empirical case studies. I take my cue from Veena Das (1995, 2006), who has repeatedly insisted that a "descent into the ordinary" does not equal a descent into the banal or apolitical. Societal shifts do not occur on a meta level, hovering above the lives we live in actuality. They play out in the realms of the everyday, where they seep into webs of relationships and form the basis for action and change. The fields of action a descent into the ordinary enable us to uncover therefore do not just attest to the creative means individuals deploy to make the world they inhabit their own. The everyday also forms an arena where crucial political ideas about belonging and nonbelonging are fought out. The stories that follow thus pay testament to more than the immediacy and flux of life as lived by a marginalized group of young people in Switzerland. In paying attention to the small gestures, conversations, murmurs, or silences that form crucial building blocks for the erection or defense of interior frontiers, they unravel the social architecture of the politics of exclusion that is currently sweeping through liberal democracies.

NOTES

1. To protect the privacy of the young people I conducted research with—some of whom are in precarious legal situations—all names are anonymized throughout the book. This also includes the pedagogues and institutions. Details that could reveal their identities have been changed.

Earlier versions of the ideas presented in the introduction have appeared in special issues I coedited for international journals. This includes the special issue "Stuck in Motion: Existential Perspectives on Movement and Stasis in an Age of Containment," which was published in *Suomen: Journal of the Finnish Anthropological Society* (Lems 2019), as well as the special issue "Children of the Crisis: Ethnographic Perspectives on Unaccompanied Refugee Youth in and En Route to Europe" in the *Journal of Ethnic and Migration Studies* (Lems, Oester, and Strasser 2020).

2. The original message in German read as follows: "Ich lebe nicht. Vielleicht tod. Ich bin in Himmel. Lebe ich noch auf dieser Welt?"

3. My translation from German. The original reads: "Die ersten, ursprünglichen und wahrhaft natürlichen Grenzen der Staaten sind ohne Zweifel ihre inneren Grenzen."

4. As the cantonal governments in Switzerland enjoy a great degree of autonomy in the reception of asylum seekers, the treatment of unaccompanied minors can vary greatly depending on the cantons they are allocated to. In late 2015 the consultation of cantonal social directors (Konferenz der kantonalen Sozialdirektorinnen und Sozialdirektoren), the core institution negotiating social questions such as child protection and education between the cantonal and federal level, gathered to establish recommendations regarding the treatment of unaccompanied minors (SODK 2016). It signaled a push for a unified approach to the housing, supervision, and education of unaccompanied minors so that underage refugees will be guaranteed the same level of protection, regardless of the canton they are allocated to.

ONE

—ᴍ—

ON DOING "BEING NORMAL"

FUN STORIES

In early June 2015 I made my first visit to the home for unaccompanied minor asylum seekers in the canton of Bern. I was there to meet Thomas, the home's pedagogical leader. He was working for a social enterprise charged with reorganizing the housing and supervision of unaccompanied refugee youth throughout the canton according to EU and children's rights standards. After negotiations with the organization, I was allowed research access to the home via the radio project Thomas had initiated several months earlier. That morning he was going to introduce me to Thierno, Nuba, Omar, Jamila, and Lula, the five young people from Guinea, Tibet, Somalia, and Eritrea who had been producing radio stories so far. At the time of my first visit, the institution was one of the two in the canton that had been set up specifically for the housing and supervision of underage unaccompanied asylum seekers. The home I was permitted access to was the largest one, with about fifty young people living there at the time. The "center" (*Zentrum*), as the staff and young people called the place, was located in a former agricultural boarding school in a small village about an hour's train journey away from the city of Bern. The building was on top of a steep hill above the village. Surrounded by herds of grazing goats and cows, it gave view to the stunningly beautiful surrounding valley with its luscious green meadows. On a clear day one could see glimpses of the high Alpine mountain ranges in the far distance. But most of the young people living in the home did not indulge in the tranquility of its surroundings. The remoteness of the location and the difficulty of affording regular public transport trips to Bern on the meager monthly allowance they received made many young people feel stuck and isolated there.

Thomas appeared from the office and welcomed me. He said that he had been just about to go to the school building next door to prepare for his class and invited me to sit in on the lesson. That way he could introduce me to the young people and I would have the chance to explain to them my research and participation in the radio project. As we walked to the school, Thomas said that over the past year, he and his colleagues had been feverishly working on an education program for unaccompanied minors. Up until that point there had been no coordinated effort in the canton to enable young unaccompanied asylum seekers' access to even the most basic education, such as German language classes. Thomas was eager to change this. In the first months after their arrival, the young people were scheduled to attend one of the two internal classes in the building next door. The focus was on teaching German and getting the young people used to a school routine so that they would be ready for transfer into an integration class in one of the cantonal bridging schools as soon as possible.

The school building was cold and damp, the bare concrete walls making it appear like a monumental workshop rather than a school. Its former use as an agricultural education institution spoke through the abandoned machinery and workbenches located on the ground floor. Thomas told me that in winter they had been struggling with the cold and that some kids had to wear gloves and hats in class. "But you know, beggars cannot be choosers," he said, hinting at the fact that he was happy they had been able to gain a majority of votes in the cantonal parliament for the financing of the education program at all. Several months later, after five hundred unaccompanied minors had been allocated to the canton, and as the organization Thomas worked for was desperately looking for buildings to establish new homes, I learned that the centers' frugal appearance was no accident. The organization was very careful in their choice of houses. To avoid feeding into right-wing narratives of asylum seekers living a luxury lifestyle on the backs of Swiss taxpayers, they intentionally chose homes that were old and in isolated locations. The shaky equilibrium of un/deservingness forming the basis for the reception and schooling of the unaccompanied minors—an equilibrium so well expressed in Thomas's saying that beggars cannot be choosers—was seen through the bleakness of the internal school building. One of the classes was based in a large room that practically formed a hallway into the second classroom. The two classrooms were poorly equipped with old wooden desks and chairs reminiscent of photographs from schools in the 1930s. As we entered the room where Thomas was teaching that morning, I noticed that some of the young people had written their names on the furniture with waterproof markers. The crinkled names and sayings the students from Swiss farming families had engraved into the wood decades ago were in the process of being overwritten by new names and sayings. "Mohamed" was written in capitals across the length of one desk, "Naima and Aisha best friends 4ever" in the corner of another.

Thomas installed a portable projector to show his students a documentary about the history of migration in Switzerland. He explained that he was planning to watch short sequences of the film and discuss the themes and new words the students had been able to identify. As I would observe in the two hours I sat in on Thomas's class, as well as during the countless hours he would allow me to participate in his classes in the months that followed, he was an exceptional teacher. Thomas did not see teaching as a top-down business whereby the students had to passively consume his knowledge or incorporate predetermined truths. He recognized the skills and ideas the young people had brought with them and was genuinely interested in learning from them. A socially and politically engaged pedagogue in his midthirties, he had a deep interest in experimenting with unconventional ways of teaching and learning. Opposed to the hierarchical ideas of education marking the public schools where he had started his career as a teacher, he saw the job as a pedagogical coordinator of the home for unaccompanied minors as a means of escaping the oppressive atmosphere of mainstream education institutions.

Thomas had put in a good word for me with his boss and colleagues and taken it upon himself to accommodate my aim of conducting participant observation largely because he wanted to gain a deeper understanding of the young people's experiences in the Swiss education system. He hoped the insight would ultimately allow educators to develop new, more inclusive pedagogical approaches. But he had also been interested in my suggestion of deploying storytelling as a means of working with the young people. When I met with his organization to talk about the possibility of gaining research access to the homes, I had introduced the idea of deploying life storytelling, a research tool I had had positive experiences with in my previous work with Somali refugees in Australia (Lems 2018). I explained that my emphasis would not be on the collection of biographical data about the young people but on the social processes involved in the act of telling stories. I talked about the research value of storytelling, explaining that because of its intersubjective nature it has the ability to shed light on the teller's hopes, imaginings, and ambitions and also on the reality of being part of a wider world that often contradicts and shatters these hopes (Jackson 2002). In research with unaccompanied young asylum seekers, acknowledging these dynamics was crucial: in the asylum procedure, creating particular and accepted narratives of oneself is a survival strategy—a dynamic that was likely to play into my research setting and that had been mentioned many times in the literature on research with unaccompanied refugee youth (Adams 2009; Chase 2010; Ní Raghallaigh 2013). I explained that rather than attempting to undercut these strategic representations or force the young people to patch their complex biographies of displacement into a coherent whole, I wanted to deploy storytelling as a means of gaining insights into the ways young people actively made sense of their situation and reworked their experiences.

Thomas had taken an interest in this approach because it resonated with some of his own ambitions for the radio project. The idea had grown from his search for alternative, more practice-based methods of learning German. He was convinced that radio was an excellent tool for young people to practice their conversation skills. He believed that the act of hearing their own voices through the recordings provided them with feedback on their use of sentence structure and pronunciation without a teacher correcting them from top down. Taking charge of topics that interested them and finding means of communicating those topics to others also allowed the young people to think beyond the often-simplistic stories presented in German language textbooks. But besides these pedagogical advantages, Thomas had seen in the radio project the emancipatory potential of storytelling. Through the project, he hoped to create an arena for the young people to express, reflect on, and share their experiences. He hoped that my participation would enable him to emphasize this aspect of the project more strongly. As the numbers of unaccompanied minors arriving in Switzerland and his organizational duties were growing steadily, he had not been able to dedicate the time and attention necessary for such stories to emerge.

In the course of the radio group's first gatherings, Thomas's eagerness to provide a platform for young refugees' voices was palpable. His enthusiasm for the project was infectious and attracted many newcomers to the group. But these first meetings also revealed a major paradox: although Thomas had initiated the project with the idea that the young people would use the radio stories to reflect on the reality of being an unaccompanied minor in Switzerland—an outcome he believed to be educational not just to the young refugees themselves but also to the Swiss audience listening to their stories—that was not the story the participants wanted to tell. I realized this during a gathering in the summer of 2015, when Thomas was trying to convince the group to participate in an event on the plight of unaccompanied minors organized by a charitable organization in Bern. He imagined the young people participating, telling their stories, and producing a radio report about the event. When he introduced the idea to the young people, their reaction was anything but enthusiastic. Jamila, a sixteen-years-old girl from Eritrea, was the most vocal in rejecting the idea. She rolled her eyes and made a dismissive gesture with her arm. "Oh god, that's boring," she said. I asked her to explain why she thought it was boring. "Always all these refugee stories—in the media and everywhere I go. It's too much." Thierno, a seventeen-year-old boy from Guinea, agreed with her. "If I come to this event, the least I need to get for it is a Rivella," he said, referring to a popular Swiss soft drink we all knew he enjoyed. Thomas laughed, answering that he could buy him a drink before the event. Thierno raised his claims. "And what about something to eat?" he asked, adding that he would come, but only if Thomas made sure he would get something decent to eat and drink. By now Jamila had completely withdrawn from the conversation and was immersed in her smartphone. When Thomas explained the details of the event, she suddenly turned toward me: "You know, I want to do a fun show for the radio. Something *fun*." I asked Jamila what qualified as a "fun" story. "Fun stories," she explained, were "normal" stories—stories anyone could tell, stories that would be recognized by other young people, particularly Swiss youth.

In the pages that follow, I take Jamila's experiences as a point of departure to inquire into the "fun," "normal" stories she liked to tell. A focus on the stories that she deemed interesting enough to be heard by others, as well as those that were not, makes visible the "normality" the young people envisioned their Swiss audience to represent and the ways they used their stories to mimic and gain access to that "normality." That focus will allow us to unravel the broader processes of normalization that determine whether somebody is accepted as part of society or barred access to it. If we are to develop a more nuanced understanding of the logic of inclusive exclusion marking contemporary European reactions to migration, we need to take seriously the small, seemingly banal everyday processes whereby some people come to be taken for granted as part of a naturally shared "ordinariness" while others are excluded from this unspoken normality. Jamila's experiences demonstrate the everyday strategies the young people deployed to write themselves into the communities of ordinariness they had been excluded from. This shared sense of ordinariness plays a crucial role in understanding the ways exclusionary ideas of belonging seep into educational settings, where they are used to justify the separation of students marked as out of the ordinary.

EVERYDAY POLITICS OF ORDINARINESS

Jamila's insistence on telling a fun story rather than dwelling on her exceptional status as an unaccompanied minor reflects the wider dynamics I encountered in the radio group. While Thomas had initiated the project expecting exceptional stories to emerge, the young people wanted to use radio as a tool for escaping the status of exceptionality they were relegated to as unaccompanied minors and refugees. The stories they wanted to tell revolved around seemingly mundane themes such as (predominantly North American and mainstream) pop stars, Hollywood blockbusters, their teachers' hobbies, or the local soccer team. And the stories often did not involve their own voices but were mainly told by playing music clips in which other people voiced themes that were of importance to them.

What Thomas had envisaged as an emancipatory tool—the feedback of their own voices through the recordings—made most of the participants feel uncomfortable as it confronted them with their broken German, thereby making them stick out as "strange" or "different."

At first glance, the radio stories we produced did not seem to offer any insights into the young people's experiences. Yet as time went by, I came to see their insistence on creating a picture of themselves as "normal," "ordinary" teenagers as testimony of their struggles for emplacement in Swiss society. The everyday politics of ordinariness formed a crucial basis for understanding the exclusionary dynamics the young people were up against at school and in daily life. It enabled me to look beyond ordinariness as taken for granted, as a condition that simply or naturally *is*. For although much has been written about processes of othering, we know very little about the everyday construction of a shared normality those processes are based on. Michel Foucault (1977) has famously described how modern institutions exert disciplinary power and social control through tactics of normalization that make certain behaviors appear "natural" and others "abnormal." In analyzing the normality Jamila aimed for, I am more concerned with the question of how these tactics play out on an everyday, intimate level. In his later writings, Foucault (1997) admitted that much of his work had been preoccupied with technologies of domination, thereby overlooking the vernacular modes through which processes of normalization entered individuals' bodies and minds. Shortly before his death he became more interested in what he described as "technologies of the self." He started to explore the extent to which feelings, thoughts, and desires are not unfiltered states of being that simply overcome people but powerful tools that allow them to "effect, by their own means, or with the help of others, a certain number of operations on their own bodies and souls, thoughts, conduct, and way of being, so as to transform themselves in order to attain to a certain state of happiness, purity, wisdom, perfection, or immortality" (Foucault 1997, 225).

Foucault was interested in the history of sexuality and the ways ideas of "normal" and "abnormal" sexual behavior regulate individuals' innermost desires and feelings. He attempted to uncover technologies of the self by analyzing historical texts from the early and late Roman Empire. While Foucault's work offers a fruitful point of departure for analyzing the everyday politics of ordinariness, from an anthropological perspective this also necessitates a move beyond his emphasis on the interpretation of discursive practices. It requires exploring in more detail how ideas of "normality" actually enter people's lives and thoughts in day-to-day encounters. How does something or someone become accepted as normal? How do people *make* normalness; how does it look, feel, or sound? And how does normality fold into individual lifeworlds?

In thinking through these questions, I take my cue from a wonderful essay by the sociologist Harvey Sacks (1984). He argues that normality is not a natural state of being we can take for granted. Instead, he emphasizes the hard work people have to invest to appear ordinary—an act he aptly describes as "doing 'being ordinary.'" Being ordinary, he points out, is "the way somebody constitutes oneself, and, in effect, a job that persons and the people around them may be coordinatively engaged in, to achieve that each of them, together, are ordinary persons" (Sacks 1984, 415). Being an "ordinary" person is thus not a state of being that simply and straightforwardly *is*. To get to that point involves fastidious work, a constant preoccupation of *doing* "being ordinary" (Sacks 1984, 414).

Guided by these ideas, we must look into the ways young refugees actively worked toward a sense of being an ordinary—or, as they preferred to describe it, a "normal"—person in correspondence with an environment that constantly marked them as inordinary. When looked at as something that is actively produced in the realms of people's day-to-day encounters, normality turns out to form an essential building block in the formation and defense of interior frontiers of belonging. Gaining insights into the everyday production of ordinariness is therefore important in obtaining a deeper understanding of the social dynamics propelling the logic of inclusive exclusion. To do so, I first need to shed light on the dynamics in Switzerland, whereby the unaccompanied minor was turned into a figure marked by exceptionality. Next, I zoom in on Jamila's lifeworld to evaluate how these expectations of exceptionality clash with the young peoples' desires of being "normal" teenagers. Her experiences make visible the precarious social and emotional work going into doing "being normal."

REFUGEE STORIES

For the radio groups' participants, a banal, unexceptional life was a luxury they did not possess. By virtue of their specific humanitarian status, they were treated as exceptional cases in need of special protection, intervention, and care. Almost every aspect of their lives in Switzerland—from their placement in the youth shelter to their status as asylum seekers or their attendance at separate refugee classes—marked them as inordinary youth. Jamila's opposition to "refugee stories" grew from this public fascination with unaccompanied minors' exceptional, "abnormal" childhoods. The charitable organization's round table about the plight of unaccompanied minors was just one of many such events taking place that summer. Swiss newspapers, online outlets, and television programs were full of images and stories of the hundreds of thousands of refugees making their way to Europe. When the idea that Europe was dealing with a refugee crisis took hold—a crisis that, it should be emphasized, was no longer seen as one of people forced to leave behind their countries because of violence, war, or chronic uncertainty but as a crisis of the European countries that could no longer keep the movements of displaced people at bay (Carastathis et al. 2018, 5; Lems, Oester, and Strasser 2020)—the figure of the unaccompanied minor came to occupy center stage. As stories about the plight of tens of thousands of refugee children traveling the dangerous flight routes on their own made their way into the media, the figure of the unaccompanied minor rapidly turned into a representative of the human dimension of the crisis. While adults' motives for seeking asylum in Europe were routinely questioned, the unaccompanied child refugee formed the purest of all victims. Depicted mainly through their perceived vulnerability and innocence as children, unaccompanied minors were not seen as responsible for their own actions. They were seen as victims of a cruel adult world, a world that they were not responsible for and that they needed to be protected from.

The "refugee stories" Jamila referred to bespeak this public obsession with unaccompanied minors as exceptional child figures. At the time, the Swiss public was hungry for more detailed knowledge about these children, leading to countless public events featuring their stories. The unaccompanied minor as an extraordinary child figure appeared again and again in the Swiss media coverage about the refugee crisis. In the summers of 2014 and 2015, when the numbers of unaccompanied minors seeking asylum increased significantly, all major Swiss newspapers as well as most local media outlets picked up the story of unaccompanied minors in Switzerland. Overall, these reports were sympathetic to the plight of the young asylum seekers, depicting them as a highly vulnerable and deeply traumatized group of children in dire need of help. In this vein, in August 2014 the tabloid newspaper *20 Minuten* published an article entitled "Seeing Children Suffer like This Is Very Moving." A year later, in August 2015, the newspaper *Aargauer Zeitung* published a feature article entitled "The Youngest One Is Only 10: Trauma and Dreams of the Refugee Minors." The *Neue Zürcher Zeitung* published a feature carrying the simple but expressive title "Alone, Young, Traumatized."[1] The media coverage emphasized the young people's vulnerability, loneliness, and sadness, their shocking experiences of abuse and violence on the migration routes to Europe, and Switzerland's responsibility for taking care of these children and offering them "normal" childhoods. Where adult asylum seekers were routinely depicted in terms of the burden they put on Swiss society, described with metaphors such as "overcrowding"[2] or "asylum alarm,"[3] in these initial months of crisis talk, unaccompanied minors came to be depicted almost exclusively in terms of their vulnerability as children.

The fixed idea of unaccompanied minors seeking asylum in Switzerland as innocent *children* is curious, given that the majority of the young people arriving at the time were between the ages of sixteen and eighteen. That unaccompanied minors were so strongly connected to ideas of dependency, victimhood, and infancy has much to do with the channels through which this figure entered the public discursive arena in Switzerland. It made its way into this arena via the policy and child advocacy sphere, where unaccompanied minors had been mainly talked about in terms of children's rights. The broader public in Switzerland had not been aware of unaccompanied minors as a specific category of asylum seekers before their emergence as crisis figures surrounding the events of 2014 and 2015. However, the crisis figure had been distinct in professional spheres for at least a decade, where it took shape in ways that came to influence the public imagination.

The 1989 UN Convention on the Rights of the Child was the first body of international laws to attend to this particular figure. It clearly states that until the age of legal adulthood, host states are responsible for the protection of unaccompanied minors' best interests regardless of their nationality or visa status (UNCRC 1989, article 22). Although Switzerland is a signatory to the UN Convention on the Rights of the Child and refugee organizations have repeatedly emphasized the importance of implementing child-specific forms of protection (Netzwerk Kinderrechte 2002; Terre des Hommes 2009), it took more than a decade for the specific situation of unaccompanied minors to gain more widespread attention by politicians and nongovernmental organizations (NGOs) in Switzerland. This gradual awareness of the unaccompanied minor as a distinct child figure was linked to broader developments in Europe. In 2008 the European Commission's core body for statistics started to collect data on unaccompanied minors seeking asylum in the EU. By this time, the unaccompanied minor as a specific legal and humanitarian category had started to take shape in EU policy discourse. Children's rights experts, NGOs, and policymakers started to evaluate and compare the reception and integration of unaccompanied minor asylum seekers throughout Europe (EMN 2010). The 2011 EU Qualification Directive, determining harmonized protection measures for asylum seekers across EU member states, laid down uniform standards for the supervision, reception, and protection of asylum seekers categorized as unaccompanied minors (Council of the European Union 2011). In its periodic review of the implementation of the UN Convention on the Rights of the Child from 2014, the UN called on Switzerland to address the lack of child-appropriate infrastructures and procedures for unaccompanied minor asylum seekers in some cantons (UN 2015, 2–3). These international and local debates allowed the figure of the unaccompanied minor to take shape in Swiss professional and policy discourse. Similar to the media coverage in 2014 and 2015, in these professional debates unaccompanied minors appear as traumatized and hyper-vulnerable child figures that are positioned outside the realms of what is thought to be a "normal" childhood (Wernesjö 2012, 504).

On the basis of the moral, legal, and political responsibility to protect children's right to a carefree childhood, the figure of the unaccompanied minor as a child victim calls for intervention.

To provide a better understanding of the "refugee stories" Jamila had been so vocally opposed to and the normality she was attempting to represent instead, I need to spell out in more detail the ideas of "normal" or "deviant" childhoods underpinning these dynamics. As Susan Terrio (2008, 878) poignantly puts it, unaccompanied minors raise fundamental questions about what constitutes a "normal" childhood and what deviance from that norm means. As "matter out of place they intensify the preoccupation with normative conceptions of the 'good' child, the 'proper' family, and the 'right' upbringing" (Terrio 2008, 878).

NORMAL CHILDHOODS

The figure of the unaccompanied minor as an exceptional child category is inextricably linked to dominant Western ideas of childhood. While children's rights and child-saving discourses tend to normalize childhood as a time of dependency and vulnerability that needs to be protected and that every child has a right to, this idea is neither universal nor self-evident. By studying how people in various parts of the world classify young people, anthropologists and sociologists have long shown childhood to be a socially and culturally constructed category that can vary dramatically depending on the context (e.g., Mead 1928; James and Prout 1990; Bucholtz 2002). Furthermore, the idea of childhood has not been stable in Western societies either. The notion that childhood is a specific developmental stage separate from that of adults only emerged in eighteenth-century Europe. Prior to this, the notion of childhood as we know it today did not exist. Children were depicted as miniature adults, or often even as embodiments of human savagery and sinfulness (Aries 1962). From the beginning of the eighteenth century, these narratives shifted to debates about the innate innocence of children. They came to be seen as beings in need of special attention and care. As tabula rasas that knew nothing about the world, children depended on the family environment and school to prepare them for their transition into adulthood. Sharon Stephens points out that while the idea of a protected childhood was first only available to affluent families, the practices and notions surrounding this new figure came to spread throughout society: "In time, a vast network of institutions—ranging from the nuclear family to school, health and legal systems—contributed to the generalization of childhood, at least as an ideal, throughout Western society" (Stephens 1995, 5).

The normalization of the idea of childhood as a space of innocence and vulnerability is linked to the child-saving discourses that came to permeate European and North American societies in the nineteenth century (Fassin 2011a, 179; Heidbrink 2014, 65–70). Justified by the need to protect children from ill treatment, abusive work conditions, and delinquency and to ensure their "proper" upbringing into morally correct adult citizens, the state received an ever-growing degree of control over the lives of young people. The types of children whose childhoods it sought to protect through these institutions, measures, and laws were clearly demarcated. They were deviant children, young people from working-class, migrant, or (in the case of the US) African American backgrounds, who did not fit in with the bourgeois ideal of "normal" childhoods.

The focus on children's rights initiated the birth of a range of expertise on children and childhood, with a specific focus on children's own (or "best") interests. However, the normalization of childhood as a time freed of responsibilities went hand in hand with narratives about inordinary children or childhoods in crisis. Discourses of lost, stolen, or abandoned childhoods have become dominant narratives in the Western world. In these stories, childhood appears to be "threatened, invaded, and 'polluted' by adult worlds" (Stephens 1995, 9). The centrality of the links between childhood and innocence in Western thought hinges on the strict division between the state of adulthood and childhood. The division between "pure" or innocent children and "polluted" or spoiled adults is of crucial relevance in contemporary humanitarian discourses, where children are frequently depicted as the worthiest victims because they are untouched by politics and innocent of war and violence (Malkki 2010, 62). Vanessa Pupavac (2001, 97) sees the figure of the child as the quintessential integrative myth of our times. Acting instinctually and removed from politics, it promotes a new international ethical order. "In these circumstances, it is the child, not the politicized adult, who becomes advanced as the agent, or rather the focus, of social change" (97). Marking particular migrant bodies—such as the unaccompanied minor—as innocent can thus be seen as a response to a contemporary urge to secure spaces of purity that are untouched by the contamination and corruption characterizing the world of adults (Ticktin 2017, 578).

While the quest for innocence has enabled unaccompanied minors in Switzerland to receive a degree of attention, compassion, and care adult asylum seekers do not receive, these classifications of deservingness are based on shaky grounds. Miriam Ticktin (2017) has convincingly argued that the quest for innocence displaces politics and thereby erases the structural and historical causes of inequality. She points out that in its conceptual history, innocence appears again and again in terms of the absence of knowledge or experience, thereby calling into life specific moral categories that give rise to binary oppositions such as deserving/undeserving or innocent/guilty. Ultimately, these oppositions justify the distinction between different human types. "Innocence has worked to produce the idea of a deserving humanity, one that can escape the compromised and often-corrupt nature of political life." (Ticktin 2017, 579)

These child-saving ideas played a crucial role in the formation of the unaccompanied minor as an extraordinary child figure in Switzerland. Throughout the summer of 2015, unaccompanied minors came to be depicted as the most deserving refugee category on the basis of the idea that as children they were innocent about the political and societal conflicts leading to their displacements and that there was an urgent need to reinstate the childhoods they had lost. But although their characterization as innocent victims secured them a position on top of the scales of un/deservingness, this came at a high cost. In order to maintain the "façade of innocence" (Ticktin 2016), the young people had to silence their deeply complex biographies, erasing any sign of political activity, opinion, or autonomy. While their journeys to Europe attested to a great degree of agency, once they were labeled unaccompanied minors, they were expected to shed these personas and take on the characteristics of apolitical and submissively thankful child victims. This child victimhood discourse has become so powerful that it has permeated institutional contexts, where unaccompanied minors are consequently *demanded* to display signs of trauma, vulnerability, or victimhood to gain access to resources. As unaccompanied young asylum seekers can only obtain permission to stay if they fulfill the benchmarks of the refugee and children's rights regimes, they are forced to perform their status as child victims in front of institutions and social workers. These "strategic performances" (Adams 2009, 160) directed at passing the "test of innocence" (Ticktin 2016, 257) often form the core basis for claims to legitimacy within the asylum system. Innocence thus forms a currency with which unaccompanied minors can gain access to resources, such as housing, education, or the permission to stay.

Europe's repressive asylum regime depends heavily on the distinction between innocent/deserving and guilty/undeserving refugee figures, but those labeled innocent can never think themselves safe. Ticktin (2017, 584) stresses that the figure of the innocent child victim is not stable: "The innocent sufferer can never be isolated for long enough to keep it uncorrupted by history or context." The twisted logic of innocence becomes apparent in the backlash against unaccompanied minors that followed the initial phase of compassion in Switzerland. The obsession with child victims was gradually replaced by anxious stories about potentially dangerous or bogus refugee youth. As innocence gave rise to guilt, the young people lost their categorization as children—and with it, their right to a normal childhood. Needless to say, these "normal" childhoods had never been open to everyone. Feminist and postcolonial scholars have long shown Western ideas of childhood to be heavily gendered, racialized, and riddled with class differences (Scheper-Hughes and Sargent 1998; Comaroff and Comaroff 2005;

Bernstein 2011). While child-saving narratives proclaim the right to a carefree childhood for every child in the world, they have always run alongside narratives of children deviating from this norm as inherently risky. Public outbursts of compassion for "lost" or "stolen" childhoods colluded with outbreaks of "moral panic" (Cohen 1972) about the same groups of young people endangering the social order. The figure of the innocent child thus goes hand in hand with child figures marked as "abnormal" and potentially dangerous: the street child, the child soldier, the young delinquent, the unaccompanied minor—all these figures show how quickly innocent child victims can morph into potentially dangerous subjects that need to be brought under the tight control of the state.

The unaccompanied minor as an exceptional child figure is thus marked by ambiguity. While this figure embodies the ultimate child victim, it simultaneously cannot escape its deeply political entanglements. Although it calls for protection, it cannot shed its heightened sense of agency. While it appears to be innocent of the violent world it escaped, it can never entirely rid itself of that world. And even though it cries out for a space in the protected realms of childhood, it always also forms a threat to it.

In the radio meeting, when Jamila voiced her refusal to contribute to the plethora of refugee stories circulating in the Swiss public sphere and claimed the right to tell "fun," "normal" stories instead, she spoke up against all these ambiguous categorizations—as a "traumatized" refugee, a "lost" child victim, a "vulnerable" woman, a "problem" student—that worked to catapult her outside the shared sense of normality Swiss young people in her age seemed to be part of so straightforwardly. As I got to know her better, I came to see how deep this longing to be included in a community of ordinariness went and how strongly the systems of care and education she had been channeled into worked against her wish to be a "normal" teenager.

NORMAL STORIES

When I first met Jamila, she was sixteen years old and had arrived in Switzerland about eight months earlier. During the first radio group meeting, she stuck out because of her self-confidence and outspokenness. While the other girls participating in the group tended to retreat when the boys' discussions became louder, Jamila did not have a problem with making herself heard. She immediately attached herself to me, telling me that she needed a "normal person" to talk to. She spoke fluent English and was glad to have found someone she could talk to in a language she understood well, allowing her to briefly escape the burdensome German she was struggling to come to terms with. While she described me as a normal person, she made it clear that, in her opinion, the people she was forced to live with day in, day out in the home for unaccompanied minors did not qualify as normal. At the center, she kept her distance from the other Eritrean young people and often told me that she felt that they did not understand her, that she had nothing in common with them.

For the first few months of the radio project, I did not know much about Jamila's background. Although she was very tight-lipped about her personal story, she was one of the most committed participants in the radio group. During the tumultuous summer months of 2015, many other young people withdrew from the project because of the chaos and unpredictability that ruled their daily lives. Despite all this, Jamila was determined to keep working on radio stories. Her productions during these months were not so much stories as music shows with very brief spoken intermezzos in which she announced the songs. To get her to record the spoken parts was hard work, as Jamila felt extremely uncomfortable hearing herself struggling to speak in German. The final straw was an interaction with Marianne, the elderly lady who was responsible for supervising the young volunteers in the youth radio station that aired the groups' stories once per month. One afternoon, as we were finalizing Jamila's half-hour music show, Marianne approached me to complain about the undisciplined behavior of some of the young refugees who had joined the studio for summer internships. She was angry that they kept showing up late for appointments and that the supervisors in the center did not bother teaching them what responsibility entailed. I tried to explain to Marianne that the young people's everyday lives were marked by a high degree of uncertainty and that even simple things like receiving a bus ticket to get to the radio studio involved complicated bureaucratic balancing acts. But my attempts to explain the situation did not convince her. In the end, she turned to Jamila abruptly, calling on her to have her story finished by three o'clock that afternoon. "In clean German, please" (*in sauberem Deutsch*), she emphasized, adding that the young refugees needed to work harder on their pronunciation so that their stories were understandable to others. Marianne's emphasis on the clean use of the German language embarrassed Jamila. It implied that the way she spoke was dirty or unclean. It made her feel as if all her attempts at creating "normal" stories through her music shows had been in vain. The moment Jamila opened her mouth, Marianne's remark suggested, she outed herself as being beyond the norm. Jamila's reaction highlights how unsettling it can be when the seemingly most banal features allowing us to interact with the world are lacking. When people have to learn a new language, they do not just have to memorize new words or grammatically correct ways of putting together sentences. They have to learn an entirely new repertoire of engaging with the world.

After the conversation with Marianne, Jamila refused to continue doing the voice-overs for her shows in German. "I don't like the German language," Jamila told me. "I don't feel at home in it." She begged me to do the voice-overs for her.

As I sensed how deeply unsettling the feeling of not being at home in a language was for her, we came to the agreement to produce bilingual shows. We recorded her voice in English, and I did the translations in German. After the incident, the dynamics of our collaboration changed. Our meetings often revolved around stories Jamila would have loved to make, rather than actually making them. She would have loved to make stories focused on what she described as "crazy people"—young people with exceptional and "fun" hobbies, such as storm chasing, capoeira, or volcano climbing. One such "crazy person" she was particularly fascinated with at the time was the US pop star Rihanna. During our meetings, Rihanna's song "American Oxygen" was on repeat, and Jamila played the video clip for me again and again. In the song, Rihanna depicts the American dream from the perspective of immigrants, celebrating the endless possibilities the country offers, depicting it as a place where anyone can make it. As the video clip shows migrants traveling on rubber dinghies, the lyrics refer to a young girl hustling in the midst of the ocean. Rihanna directly addresses the refugee girl by encouraging her that "you can be anything at all. In America, America."[4]

The aspirational tone of the video clip and the fact that Rihanna herself had managed to transform from the daughter of a crack addict in Barbados to an American superstar moved Jamila deeply. The "you can do it" attitude of the song resonated with her own ambitions. It was precisely these kinds of characters she was eager to represent in her radio stories. All the characters she wanted to include in her stories were unique and carefree, people who enjoyed pushing their luck. They were winners and heroes, people who had found acceptance through their extraordinary choices. The "normal" stories Jamila wanted to tell reveal the slipperiness of the notion of normality. The heroic youth figures she was interested in show that being a "normal" teenager actually also entails the opportunity of being different or exceptional—but in a way that is socially accepted as part of "ordinary" teenage experience.

At first, I was struck by Jamila's insistence on creating fun stories and her refusal to acknowledge the very difficult situation she was in. She was still awaiting the result of her asylum application, and she felt unhappy in the home for unaccompanied minors, where the other Eritreans increasingly treated her as an outsider. As a member of the Muslim Bilen minority in Eritrea who had grown up in Sudan, she was somewhat odd to the Tigrinya-speaking and Christian Orthodox majority of the Eritrean unaccompanied minors, most of whom were also male. In interactions within the radio group as well as in school, she was careful not to display any sign of weakness. In an attempt to produce a picture of herself as a "normal" Swiss teenager, she distanced herself from the other young Eritreans' "embarrassing" behavior that made them stick out as "different," such as listening and singing to Tigrinya music in public spaces, speaking or laughing out too loudly, or wearing the "wrong" clothes. In the bridging school she started to attend in August 2015, she often refused to participate in class, putting up a defensive attitude toward the teachers. The pedagogues were having trouble dealing with her oppositional stance, interpreting it as a sign that she was struggling to adapt to school routine and its set of rules. When we talked about her problems in the integration class, however, Jamila explained that she did not see the point in going to school if it was not a "normal" one. She said that she had attended a good private school before she came to Switzerland and that she was bored in the bridging school, that the quality of the education she received there was bad, that it felt as though she was just wasting her time there. Just like her use of German, her eagerness to distance herself from other Eritreans, and her controlled way of acting, clothing, and speaking to avoid sticking out, Jamila's refusal to engage in class was propelled by her urge to be a "normal" teenager.

Over the months that followed, I received insights into Jamila's lifeworld and into the dynamics underlying this urge. In the midst of the chaos marking the summer of displacements of 2015, most other young people struggled to keep up a routine and come to the radio group meetings. The majority had been moved into new forms of accommodation and had trouble adapting to the continuous change in supervisors, teachers, and roommates. With the participants spread over different homes, guest families, or shared houses in the canton of Bern, it became difficult to arrange a meeting place and time. Over the course of the summer, Jamila was also transferred to a new accommodation, a youth home supervised by the Swiss child protective services. Although she was now living in a small village at the other end of the canton, she was keen to continue our meetings. The same day she had moved into her new home, she called me, asking about the next meeting. During the summer months, when the radio project came to a halt, Jamila and I continued meeting and working on (or discussing) radio stories. Our one-on-one catch-ups were important to her, as they allowed her to escape the new, unfamiliar situation she found herself in yet again, in a new home with new supervisors and roommates. In the absence of the other young people, she was able to let her guard down and speak to me more openly. As we hung out by the river in Bern, in cafés, or in the living room of her new house, she started to tell me more about her life. It was only by getting to know more details about Jamila's lifeworld that I could place her insistence on doing "normal stories"—and indeed on *being* normal—in an experiential context.

JAMILA'S STORY

In many ways, Jamila's decision to migrate to Europe can be seen as a means of gaining access to the idealized versions of childhood that she had never been able to experience herself but that she had been exposed to through the global circulation of images about the carefree teenage normality young people in Western countries seemed to enjoy. She had decided to attempt the dangerous journey on her own, without the consultation or consent of her parents. This decision had not been driven by an immediate threat to her life, or by economic and political uncertainty, but by a deep desire to live in a country where she could be a "normal" teenager.

Jamila had never qualified for an "ordinary" childhood. Because of her complicated family history, she had always stuck out as extraordinary. This became clear as she told me about her upbringing. On a rainy afternoon in October 2015, Jamila and I met in the café of a large department store close to her new home. The place was impersonal and not particularly cozy; at that time of the afternoon, only a few other people were sipping on their coffees. Every few minutes there was an announcement through the speakers, advertising the newest products or items on sale. But somehow the place worked well for us. The fact that we could sit on our own and nobody would interfere or listen in created an environment in which we could talk freely. We took our cups of cappuccino and tea to a table by the shop window. While we were talking, we observed the movements in the street in front of us. As we took to our places, we talked about Jamila's educational aspirations, about how she had changed her plans. She told me that while in Sudan she had always wanted to go to college, but she had realized that she would not be able to realize this plan in Switzerland. I asked her what she would have studied in Sudan. Jamila said she always wanted to become a secretary. "But a secretary for a big company," she said. Jamila added that, anyway, that would have been her only chance because in Sudan you can only find work if you know somebody. "My only chance would have been to work with my father, well, my second family, you know?"

Jamila threw in this detail about her second family as if it was an unimportant sidenote. However, from the way she looked at me, waiting for my reaction, I noticed that it was of importance to her. She had always been reluctant to talk about her family. Even though she mentioned her father, a businessman, a lot, I could never make sense of her family situation. I did not understand why, having been raised in a wealthy family with a private school education, Jamila had made her way to Europe on her own. The things she had told me so far were contradictory. I asked Jamila why she called them her second family, whether her mother had divorced and remarried. "No, no, they just took me and raised me," she said. After this, I did not have to ask any more questions. She told me the entire story of her upbringing.

Her mother, an Eritrean who lived in Sudan as an unregistered refugee, had been unable to look after her. Her father had left soon after she was born, and as her mother needed to work night shifts in restaurants to make a living in a country where she did not have a permit to stay, she did not know what to do with her small child. A wealthy Sudanese family her mother was working for at the time then offered to adopt Jamila. They sent her to private school and treated her like a daughter. For a long time, Jamila did not know that they were not her real parents, but when she was about eight years old, she was introduced to her biological mother, and she subsequently spent her time moving back and forth between her real and adopted family. Jamila said that as she grew closer to her biological mother and grandmother, things became difficult in her stepfamily. "Everything was complicated, you know," Jamila said, adding that she found it hard to explain to somebody else. She told me that when she got to know her real mother better, she started to question the Sudanese traditions she had been raised with. She was struggling to accept the strict "Arab rules," as she called them. She said that when she was younger she had been happy and treated well in her stepfamily, but when she grew older she was expected to obey and respect her stepfather unconditionally. "But I didn't like it," she said. She explained that she had become accustomed to Eritrean culture through her real mother and grandmother and did not want to accept her subordinate position as a girl in Sudanese society, particularly in regard to her education. While her stepfather pressured her to end her schooling and get married, Jamila wanted to achieve more than that. She was dreaming of a university education. Because the Sudanese family could protect Jamila from the regular police roundups targeting Eritrean refugees who did not have regularized status in Khartoum, her mother insisted that she should stay with them. She was afraid that if Jamila left the family, she would lose the possibility of attending school and become part of the extremely precarious Eritrean workforce in Sudan or, even worse, be deported to Eritrea. The increasingly tense situation at home, as well as her exposure to young Eritreans traveling through Sudan in search of a better life, contributed to Jamila's decision to embark on the dangerous journey to Europe.

Unlike other young Eritreans, who often went on the journey together and fended for one another in groups, Jamila was on her own. In Europe, she hoped, she would be able to receive a better education and lead a self-determined life. Importantly, she hoped that in Europe she would gain access to the happy, "normal" childhoods she had seen in the music clips and TV shows she liked to watch with her friends. She had not anticipated the difficulty of the journey and of receiving access to higher education as an asylum seeker. She had also not anticipated the sense of guilt she would feel toward her two families. She had made the decision to leave Sudan without their permission, thereby putting them in a difficult situation when people smugglers contacted them to request a large sum of money once she was in Libya. Now Jamila felt that she could only save face with her family if she demonstrated the value of her decision to migrate by showing great educational success. Yet that proved to be tricky in the Swiss school landscape. Aged sixteen, she was above the cutoff age for obligatory schooling, and thus it became very difficult for her to gain access to higher education. Being relegated to the integration class of the bridging school, where teachers prepared her for a future in such job branches as elderly care or hairdressing, did not just mark her as a problem case in need of specialized schooling in Switzerland. It also marked her as "other" to her friends back in Sudan who were completing their high school degrees and preparing applications for college. A few weeks before the meeting in the coffee shop of the department store, Jamila had told me that she had stopped communicating with her friends back home because she felt embarrassed about her lack of educational success.

The afternoon when Jamila told me her family story, she said that she never told it to anybody else because it made her look strange. She was afraid that people would not understand her, that they would think she was "weird." It was from these many layers of being inordinary—within her family, within the Eritrean community, within the country she grew up in, and as an unaccompanied minor asylum seeker in Switzerland—that Jamila's desire to be a "normal" teenager grew. Sitting in the café, she said that she had never imagined ending up in that situation. "You know, when I went to school in Sudan I had refugees from Syria and other countries who were put in my class. I found them weird, sometimes we laughed at them, and I thought that I never wanted to be like them." She gave me an ironic glance. "And look at me now. Now I am in the same situation. Now I am the strange person, the stranger [Ausländer]." I asked whether that was how she felt—like a stranger. "I just want to be normal," she replied, "but here I am not." Looking out the café window onto the gloomy streets, Jamila sighed. "Sometimes I don't even know if it's good to be here," she said. Then, as if to convince herself, she backpedaled: "I know it is good for my future to be here."

CLAIMING TEENAGE NORMALITY

Reading the radio stories Jamila chose to tell against the backdrop of her deep-seated experiences of exclusion creates a different perspective on her insistence on telling "fun" stories or on being "normal." The teenage normality she wanted to transport through her stories was the normality she was simultaneously struggling to gain access to. This struggle, Jamila's biography suggests, did not only begin once she set foot on Swiss soil. Through the global circulation of images of youth cultures, she had formed very clear ideas about what a "good," "proper" youth should be like prior to her departure—ideas that would finally propel her to leave Sudan and embark on the journey to Europe. Like many of the other young people I encountered during my research, Jamila had not left just to escape the many pressures she was under in a country where she had no legal right to stay. Her decision to leave was also a decision to actively claim access to modern Western ideas of childhood—ideas that held the promise of freedom, personal progress, and upward social mobility. She had hoped that her decision to migrate would enable her to experience the carefree teenage normality she felt so far away from amid her complex social reality in Sudan. Being exposed to the normative benchmarks of what a "good," "proper" youth should be like, she actively sought the means of achieving those ideals for herself.

In her work with female migrants from Mexico and El Salvador in the US, Sarah Horton (2008) found globally circulated imaginaries of ideal childhoods to be a core migration incentive. The women she worked with had left behind their children, in the hope that a migration to the US would ultimately enable them to provide those children with carefree childhoods (Horton 2008, 927). The "lost" childhoods the migrants tried to free their children from were marked by adult responsibilities and difficult living environments. They deviated from the "rapidly globalizing norm of childhood as a protected, safe stage of human development set apart from the sphere of labor and of instrumentalized relationships" (930–31). Yet, while parents often argued that they had migrated "for the children" (927), their expectations clashed with the realities of a restrictive labor migration and border regime that effectively prolonged the separation from their children. In a similar vein, Jamila had decided to leave Sudan to escape her "problem" or "lost" childhood. Rather than waiting for adults to change her situation, she had made this decision on her own. However, she had not anticipated that as an unaccompanied minor in Switzerland she would once again end up marked as different from the other young people, as a problem case in need of special intervention. Jamila's experiences demonstrate the ambiguous ways the logic of inclusive exclusion permeates the unaccompanied minor as an exceptional child figure: while normalized ideas of what a "proper" childhood should look like had enabled Jamila to gain access to special channels of protection and care—and ultimately led to the asylum court's decision that she should remain in Switzerland indefinitely to protect her from her "abusive" stepfather—the very same channels ultimately marked her as too different to be allowed access to mainstream schools or youth culture.

On yet another level, the contrast of the story Jamila told me in the café and the "normal" stories she wanted to produce in the radio project also has a lot to say about the interplay of stories that are designed for the public and those that are aimed at more intimate, private settings. In conceptualizing this interplay, I find Michael Jackson's (2002) engagement with the work of Hannah Arendt ([1958] 1998) helpful. Arendt does not treat stories as a simple matter of creating *either* social *or* personal meanings. Instead, she describes storytelling as a subjective in-between in which private and public interests intersect. Building on Arendt's work, Jackson (2002, 12) emphasizes that storytelling occupies a crucial social function. Through telling stories, humans gain a sense of existential reciprocity, the feeling "that one's being is integrated with and integral to a wider field of Being, that one's own life merges with and touches the lives of others." Importantly for anthropologists deploying storytelling as a method, however, Jackson is circumspect about equating storytelling with a kind of psychological resolution or a form of relief. Rather, he highlights that stories can also work to exaggerate differences and do violence to the tellers, particularly if they do not find an audience that is willing to listen (11).

The idea underlying the radio project, as well as many other participatory storytelling and creative arts projects, that giving refugees a space to perform their stories is cathartic, needs to be critically examined. The young people I worked with were forced to perform narratives of vulnerability and trauma from the minute they arrived in Switzerland. Rather than using the space of the radio to perform their stories, they longed for a space where they could escape such pressures. The young people's refusal to tell their personal stories through the radio project forced me to confront the question *for whom* such projects are actually cathartic—for the audience or for the performers. While the young people were forced to perform their biographies as tragedies again and again, they were not allowed to walk off the stage at the end of the night and shed the invented personae. Rather, they were expected to *live* the tragic stories they performed.

In the radio project, the shifting boundary between private and public was of crucial importance. Through the medium of the radio, the young people chose to tell stories they hoped their Swiss counterparts would be able to hear. Rather than talking about their exceptional life stories, they mimicked very specific portrayals of Western teenage normality that they could not experience themselves but that they hoped their Swiss audience would recognize. Jamila's continuous attempts to perform, embody, and simply *do* normality show the hard social and emotional work involved in being "normal." To pass as "normal," individuals have to learn and enact the linguistic, social, and behavioral codes that constitute ordinariness in a given context. While this ordinariness can only be achieved by learning how everybody else does it, access to this knowledge is not distributed equally. Sacks (1984, 415) stresses that people who do not have access to this knowledge are excluded from being ordinary. For people like Jamila, the act of doing "being ordinary" is thus riddled with problems. In order to be accepted as "normal," the young people have to learn, internalize, and perform the small, everyday social codes that would allow them not to stick out as "other." In doing so, they have to contend with long genealogies of racialized scripts in Switzerland that determine who can or cannot lay claim to this ordinariness (Fischer-Tiné and Purtschert 2015).

Jamila's tireless efforts to produce a sense of normality—for example, by distancing herself from other young refugees, hiding her language deficiencies, acting cool and removed, or imitating ideas of youth presented in the music clips she watched—show how hard young people like her have to work to learn, understand, and inhabit the codes of normality. In effect, she was not just mimicking teenage normality. She was actively working on her innermost feelings, in an attempt to manipulate and change them the way she wanted to be and feel. Arlie Hochschild (1979, 561) coined the term "emotion work" to capture the "act of trying to change in degree or quality an emotion or feeling." The term refers to the effort people invest in getting to this point, rather than to the actual achievement. She argues that failed efforts of emotion work are still important points of departure for social theorization, as they allow us to grasp the ideal formulations guiding the effort. Importantly, the term suggests an active understanding of feeling. Building on Hochschild's work, Veronika Siegl (2018, 64) argues that the efforts people invest to act and behave in specific normative ways need to be seen as "technologies of alignment." By adopting essentializing ideas about "natural" behavior or states of being and appropriating these through their acts, emotions, and bodily behavior, people adapt to hostile environments that leave little room to act.

The young people's attempts to mimic normalized ideas of youth could easily be misunderstood as acts of conformation to dominant white and middle-class narratives of childhood or teenagerhood. Yet the communities of ordinariness the young people aspired to should not too easily be discarded as banal or insignificant. The longing to be a part of such communities speaks of a deeply existential urge of being significant to others, of having one's social existence reciprocated by one's surroundings. Hochschild (1979, 568) argues that we should consider displays of emotion as forms of social exchange. The use of certain gestures or displays of feeling is often linked to the people it is directed at—it is the gesture we believe we owe to oneself or the other. This exchange takes place on the basis of a shared understanding of entitlement: "Any gesture—a cool greeting, an appreciative laugh, the apology for an outburst—is measured against a prior sense of what is reasonably owed another, given the sort of bond involved. Against this background measure, some gestures will seem more than ample, others less" (568).

The "normal" stories Jamila and the other young people wanted to produce should not be read as mere signs of their powerlessness and inability to find acceptance. Their stories were directed at an imagined audience of Swiss teenagers. By attempting to mimic and perform teenage normality, they were hoping to instigate a social exchange through a language of cultural and symbolic codes they believed their counterparts to understand.

The emotional and social work invested into becoming part of a community of ordinariness speaks of an existential striving to be heard and seen by one's environment, of having others take notice of and respond to one's existence. In the context of research with Ghanaian undocumented migrants in Naples, Hans Lucht (2012) coined the term "existential reciprocity" to capture people's reciprocal engagement with their environment. It pays tribute to "the entire field of symbolic exchange relations amongst the constituents of the human life-world, sustaining individuals and bringing them into existence" (Lucht 2012, 102). These exchange relations do not just take place on abstract, superordinate levels, such as the society, the economy, or the state. They play a determining role in people's everyday engagements with the world, a world they continuously sound out for responses. Lucht suggests that while people often choose to migrate in search of practical improvements, they also seek an existence in an environment that interacts with them. As such, migration is often driven by the hope of gaining a sense of existential reciprocity, of "regaining a sense of direction and recovering one's life from a discouraging future" (96).

Jamila's story shows the immense efforts the young people invested in order to be seen and heard by their surroundings. It also shows the violence inflicted on migrants thrown into the midst of unresponsive social environments, in which their presence goes unnoticed. While Jamila's story only marginally alludes to education, I believe that it still forms an important point of departure for thinking through the social, emotional, and existential consequences of schooling refugee youth in secluded classes that amplify their status as abnormal child figures and students. But Jamila's story also sheds light on the small, everyday strategies the young people deployed to wriggle themselves out of this status of exceptionality. Her story shows how young people came to demand a place in Swiss society by actively laying a claim on the "normal" childhoods promoted by the protection regimes they were subject to.

THE STRANGENESS IN US ALL

Having spent so much time thinking through the efforts the young people invested in passing off as "normal," I want to end on an ethnographic sidenote that turns all these ideas on their head again. Despite the slight detour the note requires, I believe it is important to include it as it demonstrates that with all the struggles involved in gaining a sense of existential reciprocity by enacting normality, the young people also acknowledged the opposite tendency inherent to the human condition: an irreconcilable sense of alienation and estrangement from the world. Interestingly, it was Jamila who voiced this idea in the most pronounced way. While she had been so adamant in her striving to be a "normal" teenager, interested in "fun" stories, in one particular moment she troubled all these efforts by suggesting a human condition that was characterized by a deep sense of alienation from the world.

The moment occurred during a meeting of the radio group in October 2015, when several recently arrived young people had joined and started to participate on a regular basis. The interaction I am referring to occurred between Samuel, a seventeen-year-old Eritrean who had arrived in Switzerland only weeks before, and Jamila. Samuel was trying to explain the radio story he wanted to produce, but he was struggling to find the right words to do so. "I have said it before," he said. "I want to understand the world; how did the world get to the level it is now?" Noticing the other young people's puzzled looks, I added that Samuel had talked about this idea the week before, that he wanted to understand how one world can be so different depending on where you are, how life in Eritrea can be so different from life in Switzerland, and how Africa came to be so poor while Europe was so rich. Jamila laughed. "Hmm, yeah, great story," she said ironically. I suggested that we might have to look into history to find an answer to this difficult question. Jamila sighed. "You can't find it there," she said assertively. Samuel did not agree. "Yes, you can find it there," he said. "But how?" I asked, wanting to see how the group thought we could tackle this question, where we could start looking for answers. "This is really difficult," Jamila responded. "For a long time, I have been searching where the people came from and even today, I don't know. Because there are people who say that humans are not from the earth but that they're from somewhere else. That's why people get sick and have to go to hospital because they are not okay here." I asked Jamila where she believed people originated from if not from the earth. "If you look at it properly, it might really be that way," she said. "I mean, if we really belonged here, we wouldn't be sick or feeling bad so often. We need a lot of protection in order to be okay here [on the earth]. I am just saying this because I am interested to understand where people are from, but until now I don't know." Jamila paused for a moment, thinking about it. "When I went to sixth grade I learned a lot about humans, but all the explanations came from the Quran, and that is a little bit like . . . fantasy. Some things that have to do with religion are a bit like fantasy for me." Returning to the question of whether humans were really all alien to life on the earth, she sighed. "Yes, and I still don't know whether it is this way or not."

This brief interaction has much to say about the deeply troubling effects of exclusion and inequality. It suggests that the repeated treatment as "different," "weird," or "problematic" throughout her childhood and time in Switzerland made Jamila question whether the kind of normality she longed for actually existed. All the struggles she had encountered made her wonder whether humans simply did not belong to the earth, whether they had accidentally been dropped in the wrong reality. Her thoughts made her investments in being a "normal" teenager look in vain, as the entire human condition was characterized by a state of alienation that could not be overcome. At the same time, the scenario she introduced loosened the burden on her to act according to predetermined social rules to find acceptance and belonging. If all humans are essentially alien to the world they live in, the sense of displacement she had been grappling with her entire life was not unique to her. It was a condition that engulfed humanity as a whole and that she shared with every single human being relegated to life on this planet.

NOTES

1. *20min.ch*, "Kinder so zu sehen, berührt schon sehr," August 12, 2014, http://www.20min.ch/schweiz/news/story/10552556; *Aargauer Zeitung*, "Der Jüngste ist erst 10: Trauma und Träume der minderjährigen Flüchtlinge," August 7, 2015, https://www.aargauerzeitung.ch/aargau/kanton-aargau/der-juengste-ist-erst-10-trauma-und-traeume-der-minderjaehrigen-fluechtlinge-129420571; *Neue Zürcher Zeitung*, "Jung, allein, traumatisiert," November 20, 2015, https://www.nzz.ch/schweiz/allein-jung-traumatisiert-1.18649459.

2. *SRF.ch*, "Überfüllte Asylunterkünfte in der Schweiz," July 8, 2014, https://www.srf.ch/news/schweiz/ueberfuellte-asylunterkuenfte-in-der-schweiz.

3. *Berner Zeitung*, "Kanton Bern löst Asyl-Alarm aus," July 26, 2014, https://www.bernerzeitung.ch/region/kanton-bern/Kanton-Bern-loest-AsylAlarm-aus/story/18847229.

4. The official videoclip of Rihanna's song can be watched on her YouTube channel, accessed January 21, 2020: https://www.youtube.com/watch?v=Ao8cGLIMtvg.

TWO

—⚊—

THE MODEL(ED) PUPIL

DAY OF ENCOUNTERS

In June 2015, just a week after my first visit to the home for unaccompanied minors, I got to know Meron. While not a member of the radio group at the time, he came into focus through his inescapable presence, pulling me into a dialogue from the moment he entered the room. A communicative sixteen-year-old with a distinct interest in analyzing and discussing everything that was going on around him, he could not be overlooked. I first noticed Meron as I was sitting in on a lesson in the internal school. Thomas had asked me to assist the radio group in producing a report about a special event taking place in the youth shelter that day. With teachers from a school close by, he had organized a *Begegnungstag,* a "day of encounters," to foster a dialogue between unaccompanied minors and Swiss youth of the same age. The teachers from the local bridging school had been keen to initiate this encounter to provide their students with a deeper understanding of the reality of asylum-seeking youth. They believed that the experience of walking in refugees' shoes would compel them to see cultural diversity with different eyes. As this particular school was going to open two integration classes for unaccompanied minors after the summer break, the event was also envisaged to prepare the Swiss students for the arrival of a large cohort of youth with a refugee background. The day of encounters was based on the idea of a school swap. In the morning about fifteen students from the bridging school visited the home for unaccompanied minors, participated in a lesson in the internal school, and were guided around the house. In the afternoon, twenty-odd refugee youth accompanied the Swiss students to their school, participated in a lesson, and played a friendly game of soccer with them. The Swiss students were to produce a photo report about the things they had seen and learned during the day, while the radio group was producing a fifteen-minute radio report about the visitors in the center.

That morning, as the Swiss students entered the internal class, there was a tense silence. An unspoken boundary seemed to be cutting its way through the room, visible through the seating arrangements. While the refugee youth were all crammed up in one corner of the room, the Swiss students and their teachers automatically chose the seats at the other end. The Swiss students' lack of enthusiasm for the experiment was palpable. They looked bored and annoyed, much as do many student groups dragged into museums by teachers to learn about "culture." The students' reaction to the day of encounters reveals the problematic nature of such projects of "reverse inclusion" (Slee 2011, 117–18). It depicts the manyfold ways the logic of inclusive exclusion has come to permeate educational settings. While the teachers who had organized the project saw it as a politically progressive attempt to make students experience the difficult reality of youth who because of their status as asylum seekers were labeled as "problematic" by the wider public, the encounters it entailed were steeped in unequal relations that were never openly addressed. As Roger Slee (2011, 118) points out, the problem with such projects is that they are often based on an understanding of tolerance that does not set it in relation to unequal power dynamics or make visible the structural violence of being at the margins of society. He likens such activities to a neoliberal "feel-good" approach to cultural diversity that deflects from the minutiae of racism and exclusion that migrant or other marginalized youth are confronted with in everyday life. The project day in the home for unaccompanied minors was based on such convoluted ideas of inclusion. What was intended to form a bridge between Swiss and refugee youth turned out to fortify the young refugees' sense of being out of the ordinary, of having been turned into pitiful symbols of deviant, "problematic" childhoods.

When Thomas announced the first exercise of the day, both guests and hosts expressed their dislike. To illustrate the difficulty of attending classes in a foreign language, the refugee students were to teach their Swiss counterparts some words of Tigrinya, the language spoken by the majority of the unaccompanied minors in the home. Thomas asked Lula, a shy sixteen-year-old Eritrean girl, to be the teacher. Lula was mortified by this unexpected task. She protested, saying that she had only started to learn German a few months ago and that she did not know how to talk to "the Swiss." Others jumped to her defense, arguing that Thomas needed to pick somebody else, somebody who could master this task better. Most of the young people in the room had never spoken to a Swiss person of their age before. They believed that the important task of communicating with this group should go to someone who could represent them in a clear and dignified way. As they were discussing who this person could be, Meron entered the scene. Within a split second he was in the spotlight, captivating the room with his witty and well-versed remarks. In exceptionally good German, he expressed the groups' discontent over Thomas's choice. Half-jokingly, he said that he himself would have been the more obvious candidate for such an important task, especially as he had been the top student of Thomas's class in the internal school and the best student of his cohort in the school he had attended in Eritrea. While most of the other refugee students in the room lacked the self-confidence to approach their Swiss peers, Meron was keen to speak to them.

In the hours that followed, I observed Meron's eagerness to communicate with the Swiss guests. As the refugee youth followed instructions to take their guests on a guided tour through the house—an awkward undertaking marked by shameful silences and uneasy interactions—he quickly turned into the tour guide. He made sure to show the Swiss students every corner of the house, from the more fun public areas, such as the computer or television room, to the rather gloomy spaces, such as the bedrooms, shared bathrooms, and basement. He patiently responded to the at times very forward questions the Swiss guests had about the cleanliness of the shared bathrooms, the cleaning roster, the separation between boys' and girls' floors, the shared bedrooms, and the welfare money they received. While many of the young people living in the center lacked the linguistic and social grammars to enter into a dialogue with their Swiss peers, Meron displayed a great degree of social versatility. He had not just learned German well enough to strike a conversation but also picked up some of the habitual gestures, phrases, jokes, and behavioral patterns Swiss young people used in everyday interactions. As established in the previous chapter, these phrases, gestures, and jokes are by no means innocent or banal. They are the arbiters of a shared sense of ordinariness. In everyday situations, seemingly miniscule things like these can decide a person's social inclusion or exclusion.

Again, Meron's ardent zeal to be accepted as "normal" should not too easily be written off as a desperate act of compliance. Over the last decades, and under the influence of thinkers such as Michel Foucault, social theorists have developed important critiques of the "regimes of the normal" (Mitchell 2014, 1) that force marginalized youth to make themselves "fit" by asserting their sameness with dominant groups (Yuval-Davis 2006; Slater 2015). While these calls for nonnormative politics of belonging are crucial on an intellectual and political level, they tend to overlook the fact that in everyday life young people marked as different often actively lay a claim on being ordinary and strive for inclusion in mainstream society. Edmund Coleman-Fountain (2016, 768) therefore stresses that scholars need to take more seriously the gap between marginalized people's lived experiences of belonging and social theories of difference. He argues that "while the desire to contest hierarchies of privilege and reframe difference is important," it is equally important to recognize that the aim for many youths marked as different is "not to create alternative spheres of living, or refuse existing social arrangements, but to open up given material and social arrangements" (768). In his study with gay and disabled young people, he found that while many were critical of the discriminatory practices they were subject to, they refused to base their identities solely around difference. Instead, many young people actively worked toward a sense of sameness with mainstream society. In a similar vein, Meron's devotion to mimicking, performing, and embodying social codes of ordinariness can be read as both a deep desire for recognition by asserting sameness and an active attempt to twist existing social norms. For unaccompanied refugee youth like Jamila or Meron, who find themselves at the edge of Swiss society, marked as problem cases and deviant children, the struggle for acceptance contains continuous existential balancing acts between achieving a sense of sameness and striving for the inclusion of difference. Meron confronted me with the need to develop a deeper understanding of the role of these balancing acts in the young people's struggles for access to education. These balancing acts contained the ability to react to a social environment that was riddled with contradictions and uncertainties. For Meron, it contained the ability to navigate the fine line between being a *model* and *modeled* pupil—between being an enthusiastic and fast learner in charge of his own future and getting caught up in a web of ascriptions, expectations, and hurdles that forced him onto pathways that were not of his choosing.

EXISTENTIAL BALANCING ACTS

The term *model pupil* is not my choice for characterizing Meron. It was the way Thomas introduced him to me on the day of encounters, and it was the term I would hear social pedagogues, supervisors, and other youth use in relation to him time and again. When the students were gathering in the kitchen for tea and cake, Thomas approached me to ask how the guided tour had been. I told him about the important role Meron had taken as a guide and translator between the refugee and Swiss students. Thomas was not surprised. "Meron is a success story (*Erfolgsgeschichte*) of integration," he said. He added that he was a "model pupil" (*Musterschüler*) who had learned German in record time. Meron had stuck out as such an exceptional student in his class that Thomas had decided to sign him up for the integration class in a local bridging school as soon as the pilot project started. Having attended the beginners' level for a few months, he was to be transferred into the advanced integration class after the summer holidays. To be admitted to the advanced level, students typically had to attend the beginner's integration class for at least a year. That Meron would be allowed to go there after such a short time marked him as extraordinarily talented. Meron, Thomas explained, was one of the few exceptional cases one did not have to worry about. There was no doubt that he would succeed in following his educational ambitions and building a future in Switzerland.

Although Meron was introduced to me as an exceptional model pupil, I soon came to learn the complex dynamics underlying this label. From our very first conversation, Meron made me realize that for an unaccompanied minor in the Swiss school system, the label *model pupil* did not necessarily open the doors to more educational opportunities or to the trouble-free future Thomas had alluded to. At the end of the guided tour, when the young people retreated to the foosball table in the common area, Meron approached me. He wanted to know more about the radio project, and about who I was. After talking for a while, I asked Meron whether he was going to attend the local bridging school after the summer holidays. The question agitated him. He made a dismissive gesture. "Nobody here tells me what I can do," he said. When I asked what he would like to do, Meron responded that he had always wanted to study medicine but that everybody kept telling him that he could not get there because it required him to attend secondary schooling. He said that he had been sent to a bridging school without being consulted about his educational ambitions. He had only realized in retrospect that the bridging schools focused on vocational rather than academic training. The supervisors in the home had not reacted to his pleas to explain to him what he had to do to attend secondary schooling. Relegated to the lowest educational track, he was even struggling to find an apprenticeship. "I don't understand how it [the school system] works," Meron said. "They don't tell me anything here."

Over the months that followed, as Meron became a key participant in the radio group, I gained deep insights into the immense importance he attached to education. Behind the facade of the ambitious, vigorous model pupil was a deeply entrenched desire for personal transformation through education. To fully understand the complexity of the existential balancing acts Meron had to perform in the stretch between being a model and a modeled pupil, one must comprehend the innermost hopes and expectations he had attached to education as a project of self-making.

Meron was the fourth of six children who grew up in a well-respected family in a small town in the Eritrean highlands. Until the Afwerki regime expropriated a large proportion of his father's possessions, he had been a prosperous trader who had built his success on the money he had saved as a migrant laborer in Saudi Arabia in the 1990s. His father was an important religious and moral authority, and people from across the region consulted him for advice in the settlement of disputes. While Meron's older brother and sister followed in his father's footsteps and entered Christian Orthodox training, he had always shown more interest in academic questions. His parents had encouraged his educational ambitions from an early age, ascribing to him the role as the thinker in the family who would make it to college in Asmara. So when attending the local school in his hometown, Meron had invested much effort in being a model pupil. He had been a diligent learner, adamant about staying within the top group of students. The Eritrean public education system is structured in a highly competitive way. Every student is ranked within their class, and the most successful students receive prizes or are promoted to the next level (Treiber 2018, 53). Meron had worked hard to keep his excellent ranking to meet the requirements for higher education. Yet because of the links between the education system and the military regime in Eritrea, this goal became unattainable. As for all other teenagers in Eritrea, the compulsory military training year in Sawa was inevitable and the chances of gaining access to higher education afterward was dwindling away.

Whether somebody is drafted into the army after completing the year in the Sawa training camp or is permitted to transition to higher education largely depends on connections to government officials or family background. When Meron was thirteen years old, his father was imprisoned for pursuing business activities that were not approved by the regime. With his family stigmatized as oppositional, he knew that the chance of being drafted into the army rather than being allowed to pursue an academic career was high. Even if he had been allowed to continue higher education, he would have had to apply his skills in the service of the Eritrean nation after completing his studies. Meron observed many young people from his town and school disappearing overnight. To escape the year in Sawa and conscription into the unlimited national service, which leaves Eritrean youth without any options for upward social mobility and paralyzes their possibilities of achieving a social status as self-determined adults, many Eritreans opt for migration from a very young age (Hirt and Mohammad 2013). Milena Belloni (2020, 337) points out that the youth exodus from Eritrea is linked to the long-term social disruption, economic deprivation, and political oppression that have created a situation where crisis is no longer a temporary interruption of normality but an ongoing everyday reality. This difficult reality pushes young people into a social and existential dead end, where they are caught "between the constraints of the government's developmental policies and the social pressures to 'become adult'" (337). In this situation, they come to perceive migration as the only option for achieving a viable life.

Like tens of thousands of other young Eritreans, Meron decided to leave the country when he was fourteen years old. Without consulting his parents, he made his way to Ethiopia, where he stayed in a refugee camp for six months. When he realized that life in the camps was marked by severe hardships and that gaining access to higher education was not possible there, he started to weigh other options. From an internet café in Ethiopia, he meticulously researched the various school systems in Europe. The fact that Switzerland appeared as one of the countries with a good public education system and that many Eritreans had gone there before him propelled his decision to leave Ethiopia and embark on the dangerous journey to Switzerland.

Meron's eagerness to be a model pupil was thus not just linked to his situation in Switzerland. It was intimately interwoven with his personal history and with a social obligation he felt to live up to his own and his family's expectations. Like most of the other young Eritreans I encountered, Meron had not discussed the option of going to Europe with his family first. He had simply embarked upon the journey, thereby confronting his parents with a very difficult situation when they suddenly had to raise thousands of dollars to ensure his passage out of Libya. In her research with Eritrean refugees en route to Europe, Milena Belloni (2016) found this to be common practice. Knowing that they would force their parents into a moral impasse if they openly asked them to fund their potentially fatal border crossings, Eritrean youth often leave home without consulting their parents first. Belloni (2016, 52) notes that the decision to keep their departure unknown even to close family members needs to be seen as a demonstration of respect. By making the decision to embark on the dangerous migration journey autonomously, the young people try to protect their parents from self-blame in case something goes wrong.

While Meron's parents never held his decision to leave unannounced against him or requested that he send money back home, he often talked about the need to prove that their investment in his future had been worthwhile. As I got to know him better, I came to see that Meron's efforts to perform, embody, and finally *be* a model pupil were motivated by a deeply entrenched desire for education as a means of moving forward in his life. This forward movement was a crucial way of living up to his family's expectations, and it formed the basis of his self-understanding. To move forward and socially upward in Switzerland, however, he continuously had to push the boundaries he found himself confronted with, resulting in difficult existential balancing acts between these entrenched hopes and expectations and the reality of an education system marked by the logic of inclusive exclusion—a system interspersed with invisible roadblocks and unspoken hurdles.

THE EDUCATIONAL LADDER

Soon after my first encounter with Meron, he became part of a cluster of eight young people forming the heart of the radio group. First he observed the group's doings for a while, dropping in and out of activities and commenting on the radio shows that had been aired, until one day he announced that from then on he was going to come to the meetings every week. This was just after the chaotic summer months of 2015. Thomas had secured a new gathering place for the group in a church community house in Bern. The decision to shift the meetings from the home for unaccompanied minors in the countryside to the city of Bern was driven by the changed circumstances. With the arrival of hundreds of unaccompanied minors over the summer months, the young people had been dispersed across the canton, making the city the easiest middle ground for everybody to reach.

Like many of the other participants, Meron decided to join the radio group partially because it offered an opportunity to escape the overcrowded situation in the home and explore the city. Although he enjoyed discussing ideas for possible radio stories within the group, he did not show much enthusiasm for actually leaping into action and producing them. This resembles the overall dynamics I encountered. Once the meetings had shifted to the community house and stabilized around a core group, they transformed into a space for private rather than public stories to emerge. While the decline in coproduced radio stories meant that the project lost its original footing, this change in direction did not halt the sharing of stories. The protected realm of the radio group away from the home for unaccompanied minors and beyond the reach of supervisors, teachers, or legal guardians allowed for private, more intimate stories to appear.

From the day Meron announced that he wanted to become a fixed member of the radio project, he started to use the weekly meetings as a space to discuss his worries and frustrations about his school situation. In November 2015, when the newly consolidated radio group met for the first time, he approached Thomas immediately after entering the room. He told Thomas that he urgently needed to talk to him. When Thomas asked what he wanted to talk about, Meron answered that it involved "problems at school." Instead of waiting for Thomas's response, he started to explain his problem with a great sense of urgency. He said that he could no longer accept his head teacher's behavior, especially his insistence on doing one work placement after the other. One of the core components of the integration classes' curriculum was the gathering of work experience. The refugee students had to identify possible companies, call them, and ask whether they would let students participate in their work routines for a few days. These *Schnupperlehren* (trial apprenticeships)[1] are an established educational measure in Switzerland. Teachers hoped that they would not only give the young people insights into various job fields but ideally also pave the way to an apprenticeship contract. Meron explained that it was becoming impossible to find companies that were willing to take him on and that he did not see any use in this exercise as it did not lead him anywhere. The placements he had been able to secure so far had not been in job fields that interested him. On top of that, they had not led to an apprenticeship offer. When Thomas responded that he could not do anything about it, that Meron had to do what everybody else in the class had to do, Meron started to complain bitterly about his head teacher, Mr. Schmid. He described him as a "strict and angry man." "Every morning when he comes in, he first likes to fight with someone for half an hour," he said. "I am always looking at him nicely so that we don't get into a fight." Meron fluttered his eyelashes, impersonating how he was feigning his support for the teacher to avoid becoming a target. Thomas admitted that Mr. Schmid could be difficult at times. Meron agreed. He said that the same afternoon, the teacher had spent half an hour lecturing the class about how bad Eritreans in Switzerland were, saying that 80 percent of them did not have a job. "And all of us, we just went like this," he said, mimicking how the students had leaned back in their chairs, closing their eyes and ears. "Are we in school or doing politics?" Meron asked.

Meron's description of his teacher's use of racial stereotypes and his question of whether it was appropriate to turn the classroom into a space for political battles struck me. His remarks made me curious about what was actually going on in the classroom. In the weeks that followed, the importance of comprehending the classroom dynamics became even more apparent. During our weekly meetings, Meron kept bringing up his discontent with the integration class and his teacher. One of his main worries was the pressure he was under to do a short-term apprenticeship (*Eidgenössisches Berufsattest*—EBA). These apprenticeships are aimed specifically at youth who do not meet the language or educational skills for the more demanding four-year apprenticeships (*Eidgenössisches Fähigkeitszeugnis*—EFZ). While the EBAs offer migrant youth with little prior schooling or educational deficits the opportunity to catch up to a working level of German, they also relegate them to the lowest qualified job sectors. With the heightened importance of specialized skills, the chances for people without higher qualifications to gain employment have decreased significantly in Switzerland, meaning that access to full EFZ apprenticeships is a crucial precondition for refugee youths' inclusion in society (Gonon et al. 2006; Imdorf 2010). Yet such apprenticeships are always tied to businesses willing to take on and finance trainees. Swiss education scholars have pointed out that in these selection processes, young people from migrant backgrounds are significantly disadvantaged (Haeberlin, Imdorf, and Kronig 2005). The insecure immigration status of many unaccompanied minors exacerbates these difficulties, as businesses often perceive investing in the training of a young person who might have to leave the country again to be too great a risk or will not take the bureaucratic hurdles to receive the cantonal permission to employ asylum seekers or young people on temporally limited humanitarian visas.

Meron had quickly grasped the danger of getting caught up in this downward spiral and was desperately trying to find ways out. Yet he was walking a fine line: the integration class was his last opportunity to access public education. If he had not secured an apprenticeship at the end of it, he was in danger of tumbling out of the system altogether. So while Meron did not want to be pressured into the lower-tiered apprenticeships, he was painfully aware of the difficulty of gaining a full apprenticeship with the temporally limited humanitarian permit he had received and without Swiss school certificates. A few weeks after the conversation with Thomas, he showed me a road map of the Swiss educational system that his teacher had handed out in class. The map depicted a pyramid of the different levels of education after obligatory schooling. Pointing to the bottom of the pyramid, Meron explained that this was where the refugee apprenticeships and bridging schools were situated. I asked him where he would like to be on this pyramid if he had the choice. "But I cannot do it, there is no way," he responded, giving me a depressed look. I asked him to explain it to me anyway. He said that he wanted to become a doctor. "But I cannot," he hastened to add. Pointing at the schedule again, he said, "To become a doctor you have to go to the very top. Look at me, I am at the bottom."

The sense of disillusionment inherent in Meron's descriptions of his educational opportunities started to preoccupy me. How could it be that someone continually referred to as a model pupil characterized himself as someone occupying the bottom of the educational ladder? Why had he come to think of his dream of becoming a doctor as something so unattainable that he even kept himself from uttering the possibility? And why was there no way for him to transition into secondary schooling? Given the high level of German he had acquired within the year he had spent in Switzerland and his obvious educational ambition, I found it hard to understand why the teachers would not support him in achieving more than a lowly qualified apprenticeship. While the refugee youth practitioners I encountered during my fieldwork kept talking about the integration classes in positive terms, framing them as bridges into society, the young people I worked with described them in much more ambiguous terms. As Meron's statements show, they increasingly came to question the premise of the idea of "integration" the classes they attended were based on, which, they felt, did not entail the opportunity of becoming an equal part of society but rather their relegation to the lowest end of the social ladder.

In order to fully understand the discrepancy between these intermingling narratives of inclusion and exclusion, I had to move my research beyond the realms of the radio group. After gaining permission from the bridging school Meron and three other participants were attending, I therefore started to sit in on their lessons. It was only by accompanying Meron to school and getting to know his teacher that I came to grasp the full extent of the interior frontiers he was up against and the at times impossible existential balancing acts they confronted him with.

A MAN OF PRINCIPLES

The bridging school Meron attended was located in a small town close to Bern. At the time, the school housed two integration classes attended predominantly by unaccompanied refugee youth, as well as two "regular classes" (*Regulärklassen*) attended by students who had previously been schooled in the Swiss mainstream system. While the "normal" or "Swiss" classes, as the young people described the regular classes, were placed on the upper floor of the building, the integration classes were at the bottom level. Besides this physical and linguistic separation between "regular" and "irregular" classes, the two integration classes were divided into beginners and advanced, a system that was extended by further segmentation within these classes, as the teachers divided the students into groups according to their skills. These various crisscrossing levels of separation marking the integration classes created an informal "map of limits" (Hilt 2017, 593–94) the students had to pass in order to be included in more advanced levels, with a short-term apprenticeship (EBA) forming the highest goal.

When I started to participate in Meron's class, I quickly grasped the omnipotent role of the short-term apprenticeship and the complete silence surrounding other educational options. Although the young people had German, math, and English classes, most of their energy went into writing CVs, researching and contacting businesses, doing work placements, or working in the school's wood or metal workshops. The fostering of practical skills thus took precedence over the enhancing of academic knowledge. Mr. Schmid, the head teacher, had made it his mission to use the year the young people spent in his class to help as many of them as possible transition to a short-term apprenticeship, which, he believed, was the most feasible educational option available to them.

When I had approached the school about the possibility of conducting research in Mr. Schmid's class, I had been prepared for a setback, especially after the negative stories I had heard about him. But he had welcomed my participation unconditionally. He saw this exchange as an opportunity of demonstrating the important work he and his colleagues were doing in the bridging schools. He was passionate about the value of apprenticeships, and he frequently defended the bridging schools against their bad reputation. When Meron had located himself as hopelessly stuck at the bottom of the educational ladder, he had grasped a much-debated misbalance permeating dual education systems (Arens 2007; Ditton 2007; Quenzel and Hurrelmann 2010). The division between academic and vocational tracks for young students in German-speaking countries has often been criticized for its tendency to channel people into particular careers according to their class backgrounds rather than merits and for its creation of hierarchies and hurdles that make it difficult for young people to switch from a vocational track into higher education (Becker and Lauterbach 2004; Becker 2009). Historically, the bridging schools have been heavily stigmatized as melting pots for "problem" students—predominantly from lower socioeconomic and migrant backgrounds—who are derailed and incapable of staying within mainstream educational tracks (Del Percio and Duchêne 2014, 197). The bridging schools thus did not carry a stigma only for the refugee youth. It also affected the attending Swiss students, who were struggling to overcome being labeled as school failures for not having managed to secure an apprenticeship, or as troublemakers who did not deserve a placement within the public education system. To a certain degree this social stigma even spilled over to their teachers, who had a lower income and less public funding available than secondary school teachers did. In our attempts to bring to the fore the logic of inclusive exclusion that young people like Meron were grappling with in the Swiss school system, it is therefore important to keep in mind that this logic is not solely a product of the immigration regime. It is inherent to the very schools they attended.

Like many other teachers, Mr. Schmid himself had been socialized in the apprenticeship system. Before switching careers to become a vocational teacher, he had been trained as a metalworker and was passionate about Swiss craftsmanship. He saw practical training as a key motivator for disadvantaged youths' inclusion in society. He was convinced that performing manual labor and learning to take responsibility in the workshop helped young people from difficult backgrounds to overcome mental barriers and traumatic experiences. When he had heard about the pilot project for unaccompanied minors in the bridging schools around Bern, he had been so keen to participate that he had given up the position as head of a vocational school he had held for many years. A stern, straightforward man in his midfifties, Mr. Schmid had been interested in taking up this new challenge in the last years before his retirement to help refugee youth find a footing in Swiss society. He believed that the approach he had developed over the years, which he liked to describe as "firm but fair" (*hart aber herzlich*), would be beneficial to adolescent refugees who had often spent years without adult guidance or school routines. Mr. Schmid was a man of principles, and as such he firmly believed that it was not his job to coddle the unaccompanied refugee youth. His job, he liked to tell his students, was to prepare them for the harshness of the "real world" that was awaiting them outside the protected walls of the school.

Mr. Schmid was deeply preoccupied with the ways European societies were going to deal with the socioeconomic consequences of the refugee crisis. He saw it as his educational mandate to lead the young refugees attending his class toward "integration." In his opinion, this "integration" could only work via their inclusion in the labor market. To get there, however, they needed to acquire a range of skills he believed they were lacking. Like the other teachers in the bridging school, he was convinced that the separate schooling was inevitable because of the young people's grave deficiencies that needed to be overcome before they could enter mainstream schooling or the higher-qualified apprenticeship streams (EFZ). How little he thought of his students' skills became apparent in a conversation we had one afternoon, when he showed me the class list and told me that although they were only three months away from the end of the school year, out of the twenty-five students in his class only four had been able to secure a short-term apprenticeship. He said that for those students who had not yet reached the age of eighteen, this probably meant that they had to do another year in one of the integration classes. I asked him why, when he was teaching the advanced class, none of his students would enter secondary schooling in the next year. Mr. Schmid told me, "It would be impossible to keep them there. Their German and educational levels are simply too low." Seeing the surprise on my face, he added, "I know this might be the kids' dream, but I strongly believe that the Swiss educational system should not bend for them. If we let them enter the regular school system, it will lower the educational standards for everyone."

In describing the young refugees as burdens that, if allowed to enter mainstream schooling, risked bringing down the entire system, Mr. Schmid deployed a "language of contagion" (Anagnostopoulos 2006, 18) I was to hear teachers use to justify the segregated schooling of refugee youth again and again. It goes hand in hand with a deeply entrenched deficit view of refugee background students that links the need for lower-tiered tracks to their educational shortcomings. Education scholars have critically examined the tendency of Swiss educators to base their pedagogical decisions on deficit-centered assumptions about migrant children entering the school system (Kronig, Haeberlin, and Eckhart 2000; Del Percio and Duchêne 2014). The underlying belief is that refugee and migrant children have weak educational backgrounds and that the schooling they received in their home countries does not qualify them for the advanced Swiss education landscape. This tendency has been well documented for various migrant groups entering the school system, from the children of Italian and Portuguese guest workers in the 1970s (Eigenmann 2017) to the children of refugees from the former Yugoslavia in the 1990s (Schader and Hoti 2006) and the African and Middle Eastern youth today. Teachers' negative attitudes often have little to do with existing educational gaps. Rather, they tend to mark migrant children as "problematic" before they even have the chance of proving themselves (Kronig, Haeberlin, and Eckhart 2000, 15).

Although these dynamics have been known and discussed in the community of Swiss educators for a long time, in the integration classes they proved to form a major hurdle that was almost impossible for refugee students to overcome. In the conversation following his statement, Mr. Schmid explained to me that he did not even believe his students were fit to enter the apprenticeship system. To prove his point, he pulled out a book that teachers in the vocational schools for higher-qualified apprenticeship training worked with. He showed me a number of examples, such as a description of how to do a presentation, or a self-assessment test. As he read out the texts, he stopped along the way, commenting on how impossible it would be to get the refugee youths to understand such complex tasks. He said that he had a responsibility toward the teachers from the vocational schools, that he could not send them kids with such low German language skills. Again, the use of language competency as a marker of differentiation and educational segregation is a well-documented practice in Switzerland. In their research in integration classes for newly arrived migrant youth in the French-speaking part of Switzerland, Alfonso Del Percio and Alexandre Duchêne (2014, 199) found that teachers often used language deficiencies as a tool to justify young people's continued exclusion from mainstream education. This tendency was exacerbated by the fact that young people's previous schooling in countries teachers perceived to have inferior education systems often turned into a further stigma (204). Teachers used the young people's educational upbringing in schools in African countries as a means to justify their automatic selection for the lowest educational tracks. Despite the prevailing discourse of equal opportunities for everybody, teachers assessed the young people's educational competencies mainly on the basis of their cultural backgrounds (204). These examples show that the logic of inclusive exclusion did not appear out of the blue. While the European refugee crisis formed a particularly fertile ground for it to grow and expand, the seeds for the ambiguous placement of refugee and migrant youth within and yet outside the Swiss school system were sown a long time ago.

Similar dynamics were at play in Mr. Schmid's class. In viewing the unaccompanied minor student as a figure riddled with problems, he homogenized the diversity in the educational backgrounds of his students. All of the young people attending his class had received prior schooling, and the majority had in fact very solid, if interrupted, educational biographies. While some students were still struggling with German, others, like Meron, were advanced and complained about the low academic demands in the integration classes. Despite this diversity in backgrounds, the teacher treated them all as if he had to start from scratch by teaching them what going to school actually entailed (see Hilt 2016). Here, the young people's perceived educational deficiencies melded with a sense of cultural shortcomings. Our conversation about the language problems led to a long-winded monologue in which Mr. Schmid complained about the lack of self-initiative displayed by the refugee youths. He mainly linked this to their refusal to interact with the Swiss students from the regular classes in the bridging school, arguing that it proved the fact that "the Eritreans" or "the Afghans" liked to stick to themselves and had no genuine interest in integration. Rather than seeing the wider sociopolitical context—such as the schooling of refugee youth in separate refugee classes—that made the young people's efforts to get to know Swiss peers impossible, the teacher searched for the fault in the students themselves, scolding them for sticking to themselves and sabotaging his "integration" efforts.

Mr. Schmid believed that because of these cultural shortcomings the refugee youths needed to be instructed on how to behave in the Swiss school system before they could be included in the mainstream. As a result, he put much emphasis on what he perceived to be particularly "Swiss" values he believed the refugee students were lacking, such as punctuality and tidy appearance. The "Swiss" values he described are reminiscent of the moral incitements for the education of lower-class youth by pedagogues trained in bourgeois institutions, including an emphasis on the correction and control of students' behavior, motivation, and hygiene (Dovemark and Beach 2016, 184). Mr. Schmid regularly accused the students of turning the classroom into a "pigpen" (*Saustall*) and made a point of randomly inspecting their folders for tidiness and order. He believed that these were small but important measures to lead the students toward a deeper cultural understanding of life in Switzerland. As a man of principles, he was convinced that his main task as an educator was to help the young people integrate into a system of values that was alien to them. Toward the end of our conversation that afternoon, he said that it was "very difficult, perhaps even impossible, for these kids to learn the Swiss democratic values." On the basis of all these perceived cultural and educational deficiencies, the teacher believed that it was impossible for his students to become part of a mainstream class any time soon.

BOUNDARY WORK

By accompanying Meron to school, I came to see the many hurdles he was up against in his quest for education. The interactions in the classroom revealed the boundary work performed by his teacher. The term *boundary work* has been used by social scientists to describe the vernacular processes whereby individuals or groups come to draw lines between self and other, inside and outside (Lamont and Molnar 2002; Wimmer 2011). These practices of boundary drawing often go unnoticed, as they do not make use of openly exclusionary language or acts of expulsion. Often, these boundaries are drawn in quieter, much less obvious ways, hidden behind a veil of benevolence, tolerance, and compassion (Jaffe-Walter 2016, 33). I find the metaphor of boundary work useful to expose the experiential reality of the interior frontiers Meron was up against and for the dissection of the logic of inclusive exclusion these frontiers were based on. While Mr. Schmid saw his firm-but-fair approach as a crucial means of helping refugee youth adapt to Swiss society, it created distinct lines between good students worthy of quality education and deficient students in need of special educational measures. Beneath the surface of the seemingly benevolent language of "help" and "integration" permeating the everyday school setting Meron was moving through, historically ingrained narratives of Swiss (white) supremacy come to the fore. They speak through Mr. Schmid's emphasis on the cultural and linguistic shortcomings of his students, his belief in the unquestionable superiority of the Swiss education system, and his efforts to educate the refugee students into "proper" Swiss standards of cleanliness and order. The conceptions of race and cultural difference reverberating through these actions need to be understood as the fundaments and catalysts of interior frontiers.

When deploying the term *race* as an analytical category, I must clarify the angle I am coming from. Because of its central role in Nazi ideology, scholars studying processes of exclusion in German-speaking contexts have been wary of the terms *race (Rasse)* or *racism (Rassismus)* (Gingrich 2004). Although in the Anglophone world *race* has become a widely accepted notion to capture the sociopolitical practices through which people from particular backgrounds are excluded, stigmatized, and marginalized, in the German language any use of the term *Rasse* immediately casts doubt on the writer's political motivations. The term has never moved beyond the cruel biologically deterministic features it acquired in the 1930s, when Nazis created hierarchies of human races. After the Second World War, the notion of *Rasse* was banned from public conversations in the German-speaking world. Unlike *race*, *Rasse* is no longer used in relation to human beings but merely for the classification of animal species. While I do not intend to rewrite the use of the term *Rasse*, I agree with the suggestion that migration scholars can no longer afford the blanket refusal to address questions of *race* across Europe (Balibar 1991; Markom 2014; De Genova 2018). It is important to recognize the different etymologies of the term. Yet it is equally important to recognize the ways certain categories—such as immigration, integration, or cultural difference—have come to be used as substitutes for the notion of race (Balibar 1991, 20). The "racism without racists" (Bonilla-Silva 2006) emerging from this scenario is no longer based on open expressions of aversion against people with particular physical markers. It has transformed into more subtle forms of structural violence, contempt, and humiliation against people and groups stigmatized not as biologically but as culturally "other."

In a belated postcolonial turn, Swiss historians and cultural theorists have recently started to dismantle the prevailing narrative that because of the absence of official colonial ties, Switzerland is absolved from discussions of structural racism (Purtschert, Lüthi, and Falk 2014; Fischer-Tiné and Purtschert 2015). While Swiss people often like to see their country as a *Sonderfall* (exceptional case) in terms of its position in Europe and humanitarian tradition (Kaufmann 2011; Wimmer 2011), scholars have begun to draw the outlines of a racialized social and national order (Lavanchy 2015). Not only does the country prove to have enjoyed strong economic involvement in colonial endeavors, but these historical colonial entwinements have set in motion a range of cultural practices based on racial differentiation, exploitation, and stereotyping, which because of the myth of noninvolvement have widely been left unexamined (Purtschert 2015; Michel 2015). In conversation with these important debates, I deploy race as an analytical category to shed light on the ways narratives of Swiss (white) supremacy and exceptionalism play out in everyday boundary work. Rather than framing the boundaries Meron found himself confronted with in his struggles for education solely through the prism of exclusion or marginalization, it is important to widen the focus and look at the ways these dynamics are linked to distinct Swiss practices of racial othering. His head teacher's fears of the unbridgeable cultural differences Switzerland faced because of the arrival of refugees from African countries and their need for reeducation to "fit" into the superior Swiss system show that, in everyday school settings, frames of un/deservingness do not just serve to distinguish between worthy and unworthy students. In justifying hierarchies of humans, they serve as crucial tools of racial differentiation.

These frames of racially based un/deservingness are not abstract concepts or ideas. The boundary work underlying the erection and defense of interior frontiers should not be reduced to the discursive, structural level alone. While studies of race and education have been dominated by social constructionist perspectives, Gardner Seawright (2018, 914) makes an important observation when he argues that there is an urgent need to complement these findings with phenomenologically driven perspectives that can show the ways "socially fabricated racial constructs come into existence through experience." From a critical phenomenological perspective, race remains a social construct, yet it is conceptually broadened, in that it is looked at as a material and lived condition of social reality (Alcoff 2006; Ahmed 2007). Phenomenological approaches to race in education studies thus look at the intersection of everyday experiences and structures of white supremacy. They stress that individuals' worldviews cannot be reduced to the intellect or the mind but that they are constitutive of the relational and existential conditions of the world we inhabit (Seawright 2018, 918). To emphasize the lived, experiential quality of racial differentiation and segregation, I have kept my focus on the details of specific interactions and discussions in the context of Meron's lifeworld. Without taking away from his remarkable ability to act and react within this restrictive environment, I believe it is important to make visible the significant impact silent or hidden interior frontiers can have on young peoples' sense of self-worth and on the educational possibilities opened or closed to them. Given the impalpable, hidden ways interior frontiers are erected and defended and the grave impact they have on current politics of belonging, it is of immense importance to expose them as existing and "real" social actualities.

Just how ambiguous boundary work is became apparent in the regular outbursts of anger I witnessed in Mr. Schmid's class. While the teacher himself saw these outbursts as a side effect of his firm-but-fair approach—that is, the need to "help" the students by rebuking them for behavior that might get them into trouble in the "real" world—the young people experienced them as another measure that brought home to them their insufficiency. These outbursts were a constant topic of discussion among the students, leading to endless anticipations and strategizing to prevent the next one. The first time I observed such a moment was on a Monday morning not long after I had started research in the school (also see Lems 2020). Mr. Schmid was discussing the students' progress in finding work placements. He was disappointed about the lack of effort he believed they showed in sourcing a company willing to take them on. As the discussion progressed, the teacher talked himself into a rage, scolding the class for their lazy attitude. "With quite a few of you I have the feeling that you haven't made any progress," he said. "It's like you haven't moved forward at all since you arrived in Switzerland. It's like you don't want to learn anything, as if you are just sitting out your time here." Tapping into a familiar Swiss narrative of refugees as lazy good-for-nothings who are just sitting out their time on the taxpayers' money, the teacher held against the students the sense of stagnation their prolonged exclusion had created. Rather than acknowledging the fact that many of the young people struggled to find apprenticeships because of structural discrimination in the labor market, their immigration status, and the stigma attached to this form of schooling, he searched for fault in the students themselves. In refusing to acknowledge that their struggles were linked to wider sociopolitical questions, the teacher held them responsible for their own exclusion.

The students did not passively accept the teacher's hurtful remarks. Several of them protested, attempting to explain the difficulties they encountered, including limited internet access, which complicated the search for suitable companies, and the lack of businesses willing to take them on. Yet these objections left the teacher even more infuriated by the absence of thankfulness the students displayed for the opportunity they had been given. "You are all coming to school out of your own free will," he said. "Some of you might think that this school is not the right thing for you, that it doesn't meet your expectations. Then you just have to leave the school and do something else."

Given the young refugees' lack of access to any other form of schooling, the teacher's suggestion that it was up to them to either accept their exclusion "out of their own free will" or do something else was indeed insulting. It perfectly demonstrates the paradoxical dynamics inherent in the logic of inclusive exclusion: deployment of positive, liberal vocabulary of free will and self-responsibility is used to justify a grammar of exclusion.

Moments like these happened repeatedly. Mr. Schmid continually complained about the students' lack of thankfulness, thereby calling into question their deservingness of the educational opportunities that had been given to them because of their special status as unaccompanied minors. One morning, when the teacher entered the class early and found that the students were talking too loudly, he again complained about the "pigpen" they were creating. Going into another outburst of anger, he yelled at the students: "You seem to believe that you can do whatever you want here." It was palpable that Mr. Schmid's "here" did not refer to the classroom but to the country at large. Moments such as these made clear the place he believed his students to occupy in Swiss society, his belief that they should not be allowed to *do whatever they want here*. Similar to the dynamics described by Thea Abu El-Haj in a multicultural school setting in the US, Mr. Schmid located his students outside the boundaries of Swiss national belonging. To him, his students were "living, eating, and learning in someone else's country, and this guest status required respect" (Abu El-Haj 2010, 266). By constantly reprimanding the young people for not being thankful or respectful enough to their Swiss hosts, he effectively banished the right to utter critique. Mr. Schmid abruptly ended any conversation in which the students expressed distress over their mistreatment in public or discrimination in the apprenticeship market by telling them, "Life isn't fair, I have never argued otherwise." In doing so, he created a blanket of silence around the interior frontiers the young people were up against. His firm-but-fair approach turned out to emphasize the firm over the fair end of the equation. The negative pedagogy that he claimed would prepare his students for the harsh reality of the real world was mainly a preparation for the young refugees to take their allocated place at the bottom of the social and racial ladder (Abu El-Haj 2010, 245; Lee 2006).

SOCIAL WORK

By accompanying Meron to school, I came to see the complex everyday balancing acts he had to perform between the impulse of being a self-determined model pupil and the danger of becoming a pupil modeled by forces that were out of his control. He was acutely aware of this predicament, and he invested all his energy into finding ways out. With his usual sense of clarity, Meron dissected the situation from different angles and finally came to the conclusion that the only possible way to escape his educational downward spiral was to do everything in his power to exit the integration class. In a discussion about education with other participants of the radio group, he argued that it was "useless to attend a class with an *I* in front of it," thereby hinting at the *I* marking the two integration classes in his school. When I asked Meron to explain why he believed that these classes were useless, he responded, "The *I* stands for one thing only: foreigners (*Ausländer*). When I am looking for an apprenticeship nobody is interested in someone like me, from a foreigner's class." The conversation revealed the stigma he attached to the classes that were marked with an *I* as well as the stigma society at large attached to migrants subject to integration measures. Meron feared that the *I* on his school report would haunt him forever, as it immediately revealed the fact that he was not going to a "normal" school.

Yet Meron was aware that he could not openly voice his critique of the integration class, as this would turn Mr. Schmid—the most crucial educational advocate with the power to open or close new doors—against him. One afternoon, as we were walking to the train station after a gathering of the radio group, he told me that he had had an appointment with his legal guardian to talk about his school situation. He had told him that he was receiving little academic training in the bridging school and that the lack of biology and chemistry subjects severely complicated his aim for further education in the medical sector. After this conversation, the legal guardian had initiated a meeting with Mr. Schmid. "He didn't tell him about biology, he told him that I thought this school wasn't good for me," Meron said, giving me a distraught look. "That was bad for me, very bad." Meron said that his legal guardian had never done anything for him. "The only time I met him was then and he made things worse for me," he explained. He told me that while Mr. Schmid never confronted him directly, he gave him hidden messages. In front of the entire class, he had nodded in Meron's direction and said, "Well, I now know that some of you are not happy with this school." He added, "Perhaps I need to tell them how unhappy I am with some of the students." This incident shook Meron deeply. It made him realize not only that he could not count on his teacher's support if he was vocal about his critique of the integration class but also that he could not turn to his legal representative, who, by definition, should be working in his best interests.

In an attempt to adapt to these parameters, Meron changed his strategy. He put his plans of achieving a high school diploma on hold. Instead, he started to invest all his energy into a new project: receiving the head teacher's approval to make the transition from the integration class to one of the regular classes within the bridging school. He hoped that a certificate that did not have an *I* attached to it would enable him to at least gain access to a full, four-year apprenticeship, rather than the lower-qualified two-year apprenticeships the teacher was pressuring him and his classmates to apply for. To persuade his teacher, Meron switched his behavior from a critically engaged student to a quiet and extremely well-organized pupil who put all his efforts into being able to read and quickly react to his teachers' demands. He invested an enormous amount of energy in learning and perfecting the social and linguistic codes that would enable him to speak and act in the idealized "Swiss" ways his teacher promoted in class. This involved mimicking his teacher's expressions, learning when to be quiet to avoid sticking out, and internalizing unwritten rules about how to or how not to move about in class and in public spaces. In performing these versions of a "normal," nondescript Swiss model youth, he hoped to gain the teacher's trust. In our weekly gatherings, Meron spoke openly about his struggles and voiced pronounced critiques against Mr. Schmid, often by performing brilliant parodies that entertained the entire group. Yet, he was careful never to reveal his thoughts to anyone outside this protected circle of friends. In our conversations, Meron made it clear that he did not believe that he would be able to achieve his goals by openly attacking the interior frontiers he encountered. For him, the only way of combatting the exclusionary dynamics he was up against was by thwarting the underlying idea of nonbelonging. By learning the silent, everyday codes of shared ordinariness people used to justify his exclusion, he hoped to be able to stun them into a defeat, thereby provoking a collapse of the interior frontiers.

Similar to the status of ordinariness Jamila was working toward, achieving the label of a model pupil worthy of educational advancement involved continuous social work. The "work" I am referring to here does not necessarily entail the physical or mental exertions in exchange for payment that are commonly associated with the term. The kind of work I am aiming at is closer to Hannah Arendt's ([1958] 1998) use of the term. She describes work as a deeply social activity that lays the foundations of human experience by actively constructing a world we coinhabit. Unlike the solitary activity of labor, which is focused on the production of things that allow humans to stay alive but that do not have any importance beyond the "recurring cycle of its own functioning" (Arendt [1958] 1998, 115), the products of work "guarantee the permanence and durability without which a world would not be possible at all" (94).[2] Building on Arendt's understanding of the term, I see work as an activity of world making that encompasses social, existential, and emotional capacities. In the context of young unaccompanied refugees such as Meron, this kind of work involves the ability to identify, surpass, or thwart countless invisible hurdles to actively create a world of permanence they can coinhabit rather than a world that merely permits their functioning as individuals.

While this capacity to work toward a world shared with meaningful others is a crucial human feature, it is important not to romanticize these processes of world making. This becomes apparent in the desperate acts of compliance Meron had to perform to achieve the status of a student worthy of educational advancement. At a time when education is seen as a costly public good that should not be wasted on "problem" students or noncitizens, the social work I am aiming at also includes repetitive cycles of negotiating, performing, and satisfying the criteria of educational deservingness.

In Meron's case, the immense social work he invested in his educational advancement entailed mixed results. On the one hand, his change of strategy paid off. At the end of the school term, he was the only unaccompanied minor Mr. Schmid promoted to the regular class. After one more year in the regular class, he managed to secure a full, four-year apprenticeship in plastics engineering. Teachers, supervisors, and other youth see this as the ultimate proof of his virtue as a model student and continually hold him up as exactly the success story of integration Thomas had alluded to when I first got to know him. Compared to that of his classmates, Meron's trajectory can indeed be described as a success story. By the end of the school term I attended, only a handful of students had secured a short-term apprenticeship (EBA). The majority of the refugee youth had to spend one, often even two more years in one of the segregated integration classes before they found a short-term apprenticeship or transferred to the *Triagestelle* (triage office), a measure of last resort for youth past the obligatory schooling age who are in danger of slipping through all the educational nets. On the other hand, Meron's success story is riddled with layers of concessions, self-denials, and disappointments he is still struggling to reconcile with the hopes and dreams that propelled him to leave behind his family and friends in Eritrea.

As I am writing, Meron is twenty years old and in the third year of his apprenticeship. While it fills him with pride that he has managed to successfully master this technically demanding training, he simultaneously mourns his unrealized dream of becoming a doctor. To avoid disappointing his parents, who, he argues, would not understand the Swiss apprenticeship system or his training with manual factory labor, he evades their questions about his current life in Switzerland. When he calls, his father always asks him about school, inquiring about the level of education he is receiving, and Meron always responds affirmatively, saying he is going to school every day. Throughout the five years he has spent in Switzerland, he has never revealed to his family the difficulties he has encountered in the Swiss school system. Just as he never told his family about other major blows he experienced on his journey to Europe, like his imprisonment in Libya, where he was forced to spend months working in slave-like conditions, he believes that telling them about the difficulties he is encountering in Switzerland would not be fair. Opening up about these questions one afternoon at the end of a radio group meeting, Meron told me that he does not like to verbalize his worries as doing so puts emotional pressure on others. Given the difficult situation his family in Eritrea face and the little they would be able to do for him, he believes that sharing his problems with them would just add another worry on top of their already troublesome lives. "That's why we Eritreans don't like to tell each other if we are feeling bad," Meron said, hinting at an unspoken social obligation toward the loved ones migrants leave behind. "It just makes the others feel bad about not being able to help."

This inability to reveal to his family the nuances of his daily life in Switzerland and the person he has become is painful. So painful, indeed, that it has made Meron avoid phone calls from home. This deeply felt pain reveals yet another set of boundaries he has to deal with—the inescapable distance arising between those who leave and those who stay behind. Those who have stayed behind hold an image of Meron he has had to twist to the point that it has turned into something entirely new.

As painful as this process of adaptation has been, Meron's story also reveals humans' capacity to deal with the insurmountable obstacles they encounter. It involves continuous existential balancing acts that shift between active attempts to make the world one's own and usurpation by that world. Meron's story reveals the human condition that never sees us reach the point where we are completely at one with ourselves, always torn between the different forces pulling and pushing us in directions we might have never intended to take. Yet his story also shows the ways we never slavishly submit to the world we are thrown into. Meron's struggles for education reveal the hard social work he had to invest to keep up the fragile existential balance between being a modeler of his own future and being modeled into a future determined by others.

NOTES

1. The German verb *schnuppern*, which the word *Schnupperlehre* derives from, literally means "to sniff." The idea behind these placements is thus for young people to get to know or "sniff out" potential job markets.

2. Like *work*, Arendt uses the term *world* in a very particular way. She does not see the world as being identical with the earth or with nature but as being a "human artifact," related to "affairs which go on among those who inhabit the man-made world together" (Arendt [1958] 1998, 52). Thus, the world is an in-between space that relates and separates humans at the same time. It is the space that physically lies between people but also the space out of which their worldly interests arise. These interests, she emphasizes, really ought to be thought of as *inter-ests*, as things that lies between individuals and have the capacity to bind them together. Yet while the world joins people together as communities, it also separates them as individuals (see Arendt [1958] 1998, 182).

THREE

—⚊⚊—

THE POSTER CHILD OF
INTEGRATION

THE RADIO-LESS RADIO GROUP

By spring 2016 the radio project had evolved into a new shape. The group remained open to new participants and frequently had visitors drop in and out of
the gatherings. Unlike in the previous months, however, it now consisted of a core
of eight youth who attended regularly. They came from diverse social and cultural
backgrounds, had been in Switzerland for varying amounts of time, and lived in
different youth shelters across the canton. Despite these differences, they developed strong ties with one another. In the institutions they moved through, social
interactions were often marked by mistrust and suspicion—not only between the
refugee youth and their supervisors but also among the youth themselves. The
unstable nature of the scales of un/deservingness marking Swiss asylum politics
also made itself felt in the homes for unaccompanied minors, where it created
unspoken hierarchies of winners and losers. Contrary to these dynamics, the
participants of the radio group came to tie their sense of affiliation to an unspoken
obligation to stand up for one another as friends and team members.

The sense of communality the young people attached to their membership in
the radio group was remarkable, given that some of them barely shared a common
language and that the prospects for their asylum cases differed widely depending
on their countries of origin—a gap that caused much resentment among various
groups of asylum-seeking youth. The heart of the radio group included Jamila,
Meron, Samuel, Lula, and Ella from Eritrea; Thierno from Guinea; and Yusuf
and Abdi from the Somali minority in Ethiopia. At the time, they were between
sixteen and seventeen years old, with the majority nearing their eighteenth birthday. The threat of falling outside the protection net reserved for asylum seekers

categorized as unaccompanied minors thus loomed large over the group. While Jamila, Lula, and Meron had received a temporary protection visa, all the other participants were still awaiting the outcomes of their asylum applications.

The insecurity of their immigration status and the fear of turning eighteen before having completed the asylum procedure preoccupied the young people deeply. In hindsight, I believe that the nagging sense of uncertainty permeating their lives was a core factor leading to the radio group's new, radio-less shape. In the face of the all-encompassing asylum decision and the other major hurdles the participants had to overcome, the sharing of intimate worries and anxieties took precedence over the production of radio stories. And yet these weekly conversations were not entirely quotidian. In many ways they resembled the discussion formats of editorial board meetings. Often inspired by something they had experienced, read, or seen on television, the young people suggested topics they wished to discuss with the group. These themes ranged from mundane, everyday questions, such as the best way of registering a mobile phone without a permit to stay in Switzerland permanently, to more complex ones, such as the latest political developments in their home countries, the wave of antimigrant sentiments in Europe, or their educational struggles. I sometimes interfered by asking questions or was pulled into the discussion as an adult with deeper knowledge about the Swiss system. But it was mostly the young people themselves who set the tone for these conversations. The themes discussed in our weekly meetings could have made for thought-provoking radio stories. Yet they turned out to be too laden with personal meaning to fit into clear-cut story lines. The young people did not place the political questions they discussed in a removed discursive sphere that could be separated from their own lives. They found it impossible to unlink the personal and political, making it difficult to turn our conversations into radio narratives that could be shared with a wider audience. As Thomas had largely left the day-to-day coordination of the radio group to me, I decided not to interfere with these dynamics. Rather than forcing the young people to produce radio stories, I followed their lead, allowing the project to take on its new shape.

Besides the difficulty of disentangling private and public stories, the move away from producing radio pieces was also driven by the need for a space that allowed for the formulation and circulation of social critiques. Expressions of discontent were virtually banned from the institutional and public spaces the young people were moving through. To avoid tipping the fragile equilibrium of un/deservingness, the youth were always required to act as humble, grateful, quiet guests. This shaky equilibrium was based on the unspoken premise that the Swiss people were hosts to the refugee visitors and had the power to determine the rules of their own "house" (Gullestad 2002, 54). The "guests" had to constantly display thankfulness for and deservingness of their hosts' generosity. The pressure not to upset this uneven host-guest equilibrium included the unspoken obligation to take on the hosts' customs, while precluding the guests' capacity to question or critique them. As pointed out in the previous chapters, this pressure led some young people to do everything in their power to make themselves invisible and blend in. Yet Meron's and Jamila's stories also hint at the continuing importance of spaces that enabled them to speak up against these disempowering dynamics.

Spaces of respite were of crucial importance for the young people's capacity to restore a sense of agency and muster up the courage to develop responses to the interior frontiers they faced. This became particularly clear to me during a conversation between Meron and Samuel. One afternoon in early spring, only the two of them had showed up for the radio meeting.[1] They were very talkative that day, eager to share their thoughts. Samuel kicked off the debate by stating that if he were to receive a negative decision on his asylum application, it would not bother him. He would simply pack his bag and go somewhere else. He said that this would not be much of an effort for him as the Swiss had made him feel as if he should be somewhere else anyway. "Look, I can stay here, and I am happy to work and learn and do everything they [the Swiss] want me to do," Samuel said. "But do they really want me here?" He fortified this statement by telling us that he would never bring his parents here, even if the authorities allowed him to do so. Meron shook his head. "You're crazy, man," he exclaimed. I asked Samuel why he would not bring his parents to Switzerland. "How can I explain this to you?" he asked, struggling for words. "Look, when I am in Eritrea I am rich, right?" By describing himself as "rich," Samuel, who came from a farmer family in the Eritrean highlands, did not refer to his economic background. Rather, he was talking about the feeling of being surrounded by meaningful others, of having the sense that his social existence was reciprocated by the people he lived among. Samuel explained that when he was in Eritrea he was a "rich" person because people there knew him, he belonged to a family, and other people cared about him. "You see? And here in Switzerland I am poor because nobody wants me to be here." Samuel said that he did not want his mother to be treated like a "poor" person and that this was why he believed she would be better off remaining in Eritrea than coming to Switzerland.

Samuel's story and the question of whether people in Switzerland really wanted them to become a part of society initiated a discussion between him and Meron about the small, everyday things that made them feel out of place. "It's true, they don't want us here, right?" Meron asked me. I returned the question by asking him what made him feel that way. Meron explained that he gathered it from the way people treated him in public spaces, like train stations, parks, or shops. He said that people often stared at him and made him feel bad. Without saying a word, simply by looking at him, they made him feel as though he should not be there. "You know how often I enter a shop and the shopkeeper stands right behind me the entire time, making sure I don't steal something," Meron said. Samuel agreed. He told us that the same thing happened to him in his local supermarket on a daily basis. One of the shopkeepers there kept following him through the entire shop every time he went to buy something. It was the closest and cheapest shop to the accommodation he shared with other refugee youth, so they went there almost every day. Samuel said that although the shopkeeper knew them by now, she did not leave them alone. She kept on following Samuel and his friends—always at a distance, never directing a word at them—from the minute they entered the shop to the moment they left again.

Samuel said that he could not accept this kind of behavior, and so the last time he went to the shop, he had had his own response in store. When he was waiting at the cash register, after having been followed by the shopkeeper the entire time, he waved at her, asking her to come over. He told her to have a "good look" into his pockets to make sure he had not stolen anything. By unmasking the shopkeeper's racist behavior in front of the other customers waiting in line, Samuel successfully managed to flip around the embarrassment she had exposed him to. He assured us that this was not the end of it, that he already had the next maneuver in store. The next time he went to the shop, he announced, *he* would be the one to look for the shopkeeper. Rather than waiting for the woman to start shadowing him and unnerving him with her stare, he would actively seek her out. He would politely invite her to accompany him around the shop, all the while commenting on each piece he added to his basket.

On listening to Samuel's plan of revenge, Meron was shocked. Samuel's loud, confrontational tactics did not at all resemble his own strategy of quiet immersion. "That's not good, Samuel," Meron insisted. "Why do you have to say anything to her at all?" Samuel responded that he could not keep quiet when people treated him like that, that he could not stand it when people behaved as if he did not have the right to be there. He continued to present several more incidents in which he had confronted people about their racist or prejudiced behavior. Meron cringed at Samuel's accounts. "You have to calm down, man," he said. "You cannot say these things to a Swiss person." Samuel laughed, admitting that he knew it did not make sense to try talking to racist people because they usually refused to engage in a conversation with him. Despite knowing this, he said that he could not keep quiet if he felt he was treated unfairly. "You know, I have this problem, I get angry when people mistreat me," Samuel said.

That afternoon, Samuel and Meron told many more stories about the small, intangible things that made them feel as if they did not have a right to express their own thoughts and personalities but were merely accepted as silent, obedient guests in Switzerland. While these stories did not necessarily show openly racist behavior, they revealed the small, everyday actions through which the young people were kept from laying a claim to the place. They also revealed the dramatic existential balancing acts the youths had to perform between the pressure to conform to the roles and expectations reserved for refugee "guests" and the desire to lead a self-determined life. They had developed different strategies of juggling these opposing poles. While Meron invested all his efforts in circumventing or thwarting interior frontiers by mimicking and internalizing social codes of ordinariness, Samuel could not silently accept the unequal power relations underlying these unspoken codes. Rather than looking for ways to sneak around interior frontiers, he believed in the need to call out their architects and expose their exclusionary motives.

The small conversation snippet between Meron and Samuel shows the ways the young people remodeled the radio project into a space that allowed them to identify and critique the many facets of inclusive exclusion confronting them in everyday life. In doing so, they could develop and test out responses to the stumbling blocks that were the outcome of this logic. Taken together, these blocks formed the fundament of the interior frontiers pervading the social space of Swiss society. These frontiers have the usually unspoken purpose of separating groups and individuals deserving membership in a unified "us" from a "them" that must be kept out. The "us" of frontier assemblers sees itself in the role of the host holding the ultimate right to determine the rules and arrangements of his or her "own" place, including the power to stipulate migrant guests' appropriate roles and positions within it. The conversation between Samuel and Meron shows that the young people did not silently accept their status as guests who had to patiently await the hosts' judgments about their worthiness. Each in their own way, they developed strategies of responding to these exclusionary dynamics, be it by feigning sameness or by claiming their right to otherness. Yet, as I was to see when I accompanied Samuel into the integration class, these responses had to be deployed with extreme carefulness. In an environment marked by shaky equilibrium between hosts and guests, any unconsidered utterance of critique risked tipping the balance irreversibly.

THE WEIGHT OF THE WORLD

Samuel joined the radio group in the autumn of 2015, only a few weeks after his arrival in Switzerland. He took an interest in the activities of Thierno, Ella, and Meron when they were documenting the second "day of encounters" between students from the home for unaccompanied minors and the local bridging school. Because of the dramatic increase in the numbers of unaccompanied minors arriving in Switzerland and the heightened public attention this had created over the summer months, the teachers had decided to repeat the event. This time around they were supported by a local refugee advocacy group that coordinated the day's activities and held an information session in which they presented some facts about the causes and effects of refugee movements worldwide. Once more, the teachers' and advocates' well-meant intentions did not manage to undo the deeply uneven relations underwriting the event. The interactions between the two student groups were again marked by problematic exchanges, in which the project tapped into historically ingrained practices of racial othering by turning the home for unaccompanied minors into a kind of "human zoo" (Purtschert 2015). To encourage a conversation between the two groups, the teachers and advocates had scheduled interview sessions in which the Swiss students had to ask the refugee youth questions about their lives in Switzerland. In the interactions arising from this activity, the unaccompanied minors were confronted with a disconcerting speechlessness on the part of some Swiss students who did not know how to relate to them or with unfiltered expressions of pity about their situation from others. Both reactions amplified their position as extraordinary problem children who could not be spoken to on equal terms. The inquisitive questions directed at them by one Swiss student—a young man who repeatedly voiced his reservations about asylum seekers' true motives for choosing to come to "his" country—even exposed them to open hostility about the rightfulness of their stay in Switzerland.

Samuel, who was attending the internal school to learn German at the time, was part of the refugee student group scheduled to participate in the exchange. Like most of the others, he did not show much enthusiasm for the activities. Rather than partaking in the program, he attached himself to the members of the radio group. He was new to the home for unaccompanied minors and did not know many other young people. But he had befriended Ella, a confident young Eritrean woman who had just joined the radio group. She had arrived in the center several months before him and was more familiar with the ins and outs of the place. As I was to learn in the weeks that followed, Samuel and Ella already knew each other from before. They had met in a Libyan desert town when the groups of young Eritreans they were traveling with teamed up to protect one another from the robberies, rapes, and kidnappings that were the order of the day. Samuel had stuck out as he "lost the plot," as Ella put it, and "went berserk" at the blows and insults they received from local militias who, armed to the teeth and high on drugs, pressed them for money. When Ella recognized Samuel on his arrival in the center, she had felt responsible to keep him company and help him understand the new universe of regulations he had been thrown into.

During the day of encounters, when the radio group was recording the event, Samuel curiously observed their work, inquiring about the audio recorders and suggesting questions they could ask the people they interviewed. As he had only just started to learn German, he mainly spoke in English or had Ella translate for him from Tigrinya. Despite the language barrier, he seamlessly inserted himself into the group's activities. Toward the end of the morning session, when Thierno announced that he had to leave, he automatically handed his recorder to Samuel, asking him to take over his job. From then on, Samuel showed up at the weekly meetings, interacting with the other young people as if he had always been there.

Like Meron's, Samuel's participation in the radio project was not so much driven by an urge to produce radio stories but by the need for exchange. He was a proud and serious young man, eager to get to the bottom of questions that moved him. This eagerness was visible in the stubborn persistence he displayed in discussions. Be it in the radio group or at school, he refused to let go of questions if he was not satisfied with the answers he had received. This tendency became apparent when he attended a radio gathering for the first time. That afternoon Thomas had come to tell the group that he had taken several months of leave of absence because the summer months of turmoil had left him exhausted. Like many of his colleagues from the social enterprise he worked for, he had come within an inch of a burnout and needed time to unwind. Thomas wanted to use the last meeting he would attend for a while for a roundtable discussion in which each of the young people presented themes that moved them and that could form the basis for a radio story. When Samuel's turn came, his answer to the question of what interested him was as definite as it was mysterious. "I am interested in how the world came to the level it is at now," he said in English. As we were all struggling to understand this deep and complex question, Thomas asked him to explain it a bit more. "I want to understand the world," Samuel said assertively. Still puzzled, Meron asked Samuel to explain again in Tigrinya so that he could translate it into German. Samuel responded that he wanted to understand the state of the world, that he wanted to look into history to understand how we had come to the point we were at now.

Samuel's fascination with fundamental questions concerning the human condition quickly earned him the nickname "the philosopher" within the group. When we returned to his question in successive radio gatherings, it became clear that the state of the world he was inquiring into was interspersed with inequalities. The unequal distribution of power, wealth, and knowledge in the world preoccupied Samuel deeply. Having experienced the oppression and poverty marking life in Eritrea as well as the dehumanizing treatment of migrants in Libya, he questioned the basis of Switzerland's wealth and abundance. His urge to understand the world was driven by an interest in understanding the histories of domination and exploitation that had brought him and the other young people from the radio group to the position they were at now, as refugees and "guests" in one of the wealthiest countries in the world—a country that jealously guarded its prosperity and continually emphasized its power to determine the legitimacy of their being there. Samuel was deeply troubled by the compartmentalization of the world into first- and third-world countries and refused to accept the idea that the vast disparities in wealth and lifestyle between Africa and Europe could be explained solely through economic or political factors. His experiences as a migrant had awakened in him the latent knowledge that these differences were based on historically entrenched hierarchies of race and power.

By accompanying Samuel to the integration class, I came to see the difficult existential balancing acts he had to perform to act on this knowledge without upsetting the fragile equilibrium of un/deservingness. In a social environment in which interior frontiers are hidden behind a veil of inclusionary language and refugee youth are routinely demanded to display thankfulness for the "help" they receive, any attempt to expose the unequal power relations lurking underneath the surface of benevolence needs to be carefully thought out. In openly display-ing criticism or questioning the status quo, the young people risked being seen as having committed the cardinal sin of ingratitude. They knew all too well the grave repercussions such a characterization could entail, ranging from restricted access to educational resources to the real danger of having to exchange their status as tolerated guests for that of expelled outsiders.

The pages that follow zoom in on these dynamics. Guided by Samuel's experi-ences, I intensify my inquiry into the social work involved in the young people's attempts to balance the fundamental human urge to act on the world against the powerful forces pulling them back. While the previous chapters showed the role of mimicking and performing a sense of sameness as a means of gaining access to educational resources or social acceptance, Samuel's story sheds light on the complex and multilayered strategies the young people deployed to contest the "re-gimes of the normal" (Mitchell 2014) governing the Swiss educational landscape. I first turn to two important biographical moments in his life. The re-narration of events Samuel emphasized as critical turning points allows one to contextualize his urge to understand and act on the world. It also allows one to highlight that the young people's experiences of inclusive exclusion in Switzerland need to be embedded in wider personal and collective histories of exclusion. The interior frontiers they encountered on entering European shores merged with the violent border-protection mechanisms they had been confronted with as migrants and refugees en route to Europe. In a second step I return to the integration class to continue my project of exposing the social makeup of these interior frontiers. I make visible how ideas of integration came to be used as means of determining the young people's level of social and educational un/deservingness, thereby turning seemingly well-intended measures of inclusion into further obstacles.

In detailing the ways Samuel came to simultaneously contest and strategically use the ideas of integration the classes were based on, I will show that the young people did not passively accept their assignment to the role of silent, dutiful guests who did not have the right to speak up. His story highlights the immense resourcefulness and creativity the young people displayed in walking the fine line between compliance and resistance.

TWO TURNING POINTS

Samuel's urge to formulate a critique of the order of the world and his own subordinated position within it had grown out of the things he had witnessed and lived through growing up in Eritrea and living as a migrant in Libya. He often talked about the deep impact these experiences had left on him, how they had shaken him to the depths of his being. While he used the radio group meetings to engage in debates with the others, he also used them to tell us stories about his life. More than anybody else in the group, he expressed the need for an audience responsive to these accounts, particularly in the first months after his arrival, when he was still digesting his journey to Europe. Because of his vivid descriptions, his remarkable skill to depict the details of social life and the often-enthralling plots, I could write an entire book based on Samuel's narratives. Yet the fragile division between stories aimed at the public and those designed for more intimate settings precludes the rendition of many of these stories. I have therefore chosen to refrain from retelling Samuel's experiences in the confidential and detailed tone he told them. As some of these experiences played a crucial role in the ways he came to respond to pressures to conform and because these responses had long-lasting effects on his educational pathway, I have decided to instead sketch the contours of two "critical events" (Das 1995) that fundamentally changed his view on the world. Such personal biographical turning points are crucial catalysts in the young people's struggles for education. Without looking at the entanglement of Samuel's past and present states of being, I would only be able to render an insufficient depiction of his struggles for recognition in the classroom.

Samuel had grown up in an extended farming family in the Eritrean highlands. His father had been away on national service duty for most of his childhood, so they barely knew each other. But Samuel often spoke tenderly about his mother, who had shouldered the task of keeping together the family and farm on her own. He also enjoyed talking about his oldest brother, who had been a father figure to him. Like Samuel, his brother had been an excellent student, and he supported his ambitions to achieve higher education. The most important person in Samuel's life only appeared in his accounts almost a year after he had joined the radio group, as the mere mention of his name pained him. It was

Samuel's twin brother, whom he had left behind in Eritrea. The two of them had grown up sharing everything with each other, but because of the abrupt nature of Samuel's departure, he had not even been able to say goodbye. In a memorable phone call home when Samuel was in Libya waiting for his passage to Italy, his twin brother had told him that he would never be able to forgive his sudden disappearance. By embarking on the journey to Europe without attempting to take his brother along, he had severed the tie that had been connecting them from childhood on.

Like most of the other unaccompanied refugee youth I got to know, Samuel decided to leave Eritrea because of several factors. The actual act of leaving had been caused by a sudden intensification of events that left him no other choice. Together with three friends from his village, Samuel had been caught in a restricted mountainous area that was known to have gold reserves. They had sneaked into the area without a permit to try their luck digging for gold. After they were intercepted by military guards, they were taken to a local prison, where they were kept without a trial or information about the length of their sentence. Together with other political prisoners, they had to perform heavy labor. One afternoon, when they were ordered to work at the edge of a forest, Samuel and some inmates managed to escape into the surrounding mountains. As a return home would have endangered not just himself but his entire family, he headed for the Ethiopian border.

While this dramatic succession of events had been the immediate cause for Samuel's decision to leave Eritrea, he had already been considering the option some time before. Like in Meron's and Jamila's cases, Samuel's decision to migrate had also been propelled by the hope for a better education. Reflective of the historically entrenched idea of education as a means of progress and upward social mobility in Eritrea, Samuel saw educational advancement as the most important way to socially and economically advance his family (Riggan 2013). He had witnessed the disappointment of his older brother who, despite having been an excellent student delivering top marks in his final exam, had not been allowed to continue to higher education. As the authorities had found the intellectual ambitiousness of this young man from a rural peasant background to be suspicious, he had been forcefully drafted into the army and was now performing tedious tasks as a guard at one of the local checkpoints. After this frustrating experience, Samuel's brother had instilled in him the idea of leaving the country before he was in his final year of school. "When this happened to him my brother came to me, he said, 'Look, you have to stop learning, stop trying to get good marks because it's useless, absolutely useless,'" Samuel said, recounting the conversation one afternoon as we were walking to the train station. When I asked whether his brother had given him the advice to go to Europe, he responded, "I asked him what to do and he said, 'What advice can I give to you? I cannot tell you to go to Europe.'" After this conversation, Samuel had started to consider leaving the country.

Samuel's flight story shows the complex, multilayered factors playing into processes of displacement. While the "refugee crisis" has led to an intensification in public efforts across Europe to distinguish between "real" refugees fleeing political persecution and migrants whose movements are purely driven by the economic hope of improving their living standards, the lived reality of people on the move is much more complex. Like most of the young people I encountered throughout my fieldwork, Samuel did not describe his decision to migrate solely as a reaction to the oppressive political situation in Eritrea. Rather, he had also been drawn toward this decision because of the radical transformation of self and personhood he believed a migration to Europe would offer. This quest for transformation through migration should not be thought of as an individual project. As Paolo Gaibazzi (2019) has shown in the context of aspiring young Soninke migrants in the Gambia, migratory projects are often driven by the hope of maintaining and regenerating kinship ties. Paradoxically, migrants' acts of leaving are thus often linked to the hope of restoring relationships at home. In a similar vein, Samuel's decision to migrate to Europe in search of a better education was linked to the hope that he could improve the living conditions of the family members he had left behind. In studying phenomena such as migration, we should therefore not overlook the importance of the intersubjective dimension of mobility projects, because as Gaibazzi (2019, 36) puts it, "migration is not solely about the destination but also about entangled destinies." If the word *displacement* is to capture the experiences of young people like Samuel, it needs to be thought of as an active process that involves elements of choice and circumstance as well as force.

After his escape, Samuel headed toward the Ethiopian border on foot, always on the alert for military checkpoints. After he had crossed the Mereb River demarcating the border between Eritrea and Ethiopia, he met a group of young people from his region who were planning to go to Europe. He joined them, and over the next six months they traveled together, first through Sudan, where they took up labor jobs to finance their onward journey, and then through Libya. Libya formed the second crucial turning point in Samuel's life. During the five months he spent there, he witnessed terrible scenes of exploitation and abuse and was subject to dehumanizing treatment he had never before imagined to be possible. "We lived without water, without food, without air, without anything," Samuel said, struggling for words to describe the situation he had found himself in. "I don't know, it's very difficult, how could I explain that?"

The human rights violations committed against African migrants in Libya are well documented (OHCR 2018; Human Rights Watch 2019b). Over the last decade, the central Mediterranean route via Libya has turned into the core entry point for African migrants and refugees trying to reach Europe. The European Union has reacted by turning the conflict-ridden country into its extended border zone. The dominance of narratives of a refugee crisis threatening the social and cultural order of things in Europe justified the installment of violent bordering practices and a politics of deterrence toward African migrants on their way to Europe (De Genova 2017; Gaibazzi, Bellagamba, and Dünnwald 2017; Andersson 2019). Through joint maritime control operations on Libyan shores and the criminalization of rescue activities in the Mediterranean performed by nongovernmental human rights organizations, Europe has outsourced its responsibility to deal with African refugees to a country with no refugee law or asylum system. Since the 2011 uprising that ended Muammar Gaddafi's forty-year rule, competing factions and clans have been fighting over control in Libya. The violent conflict, chaos, and collapse of the rule of law have created an extremely dangerous environment for migrants and refugees seeking to use Libya as a springboard to Europe. The list of human rights abuses documented by the UN Support Mission in Libya and the UN Human Rights Office describes scenes of horror. They range from inhumane conditions, starvation, and exploitation in shelters set up by people smugglers to killings, rape, forced prostitution, arbitrary and indefinite detention, torture, and forced labor in Libyan immigration detention centers, some of which have been set up with the funds from European migration management projects (OHCR 2018; Global Detention Project 2018).

Like most of the young people in the radio group, Samuel had been subject or witness to many of these cruelties. In his accounts of that time, he described the weeks he spent camping in the desert town with Ella's group as a turning point in his life that permanently altered the way he perceived the world. While he had first dealt with the situation by trying to become invisible to Libyans, one evening something "snapped" inside him. When a group of Libyan gunmen entered their makeshift camp and insulted them by kicking some of the young people who were sleeping on the ground, describing them as lazy donkeys and requesting their money, he could no longer remain silent. He "freaked out," as Ella described it one afternoon when the topic came up again. He kicked and yelled abuses at the stunned militia members. "You should have seen me," Samuel said, laughing. "They had insulted us as donkeys and I had turned into an out of control animal." The repercussions for this show of resistance were grave. Samuel was taken away by the militia and reappeared only weeks later. Ella said that she and the other young people had been convinced that he would never return.

As much as he enjoyed describing this moment of resistance, Samuel chose to remain silent about the time he spent in captivity. However, he explained in detail that the militia had not managed to break his will. From then on, Samuel explained, he had had "the problem" that he could no longer react to discriminatory acts with detachment. The experience awakened in him an urge to understand the correlations between his own situation and historically entrenched structures of discrimination. While he did not fully grasp the complex web of power relations feeding into the mistreatment of migrants in Libya, the role of EU border policies, and the histories of colonialism, he perceived the general state of agony encountered by migrants in Libya as a message of unwelcome from Europe. The Italian philosopher Federica Sossi (2006) argues that Europe's spatial tactics of fortressing itself against undesired people has created a situation where migrants and refugees feel national borders in their bodies long before they ever set foot on European territory. I would add that more than the existence of physical borders, they sense the presence of interior frontiers. They *feel* them while traversing inhospitable deserts on foot or jammed together in trucks; they *feel* them while locked up in inhumane detention camps, forced to live like animals; they *feel* them in the blows they have to endure again and again; and they *feel* them in the way death has become an everyday companion to their journeys (also see Lems 2018, 110).

It would be wrong to assume that the hellish conditions stemming from Europe's politics of externalization manage to break migrants' will to resist. Samuel's story shows that, even in the most desperate situations that seem to leave no room for maneuver, people refuse to submissively accept their fate. Jean-Paul Sartre ([1943] 2003) famously noted that to be human means to be conscious and, as such, ultimately to be free. Building on Heidegger's idea that humans are thrown into a world that is not of their making, he argued that once in the world, people always make choices, no matter how limited their options might be. In exercising this existential freedom, they actively decide what a human being should be. Man, Sartre (1956, 290) put it, "first of all exists, encounters himself, surges up in the world—and defines himself afterwards." In a similar vein, Samuel did not slavishly submit to his subjugation in a hostile world interspersed with boundaries set up to keep him out. The night when he kicked and insulted the Libyan gunmen, he had not just chosen to stand up to his mistreatment. That act had also heralded a new conception of himself and of the order of the world he had been thrown into. Rather than waiting for others to approve of his existence, Samuel decided to do everything in his power to achieve the life *he* believed he deserved.

This profound human will to freedom is frequently ignored in academic debates about un/deservingness, where migrants, asylum seekers, or welfare recipients are depicted as victims to an all-encompassing system judging their social worth. But Samuel's story shows that people subject to this symbolic type of violence have their own ideas of the lives they deserve. In his case, an extreme situation designed to break his will achieved the opposite. It spurred his determination to overcome the treacherous hurdles ahead of him, cross the Mediterranean on a boat that nearly capsized, and, once in Italy, continue his journey across the entire country without a cent in his pocket, making his way to Switzerland to apply for asylum. Even though he was exhausted and sick, he was determined to reach Switzerland as he knew that he had better chances of gaining access to education there than in Italy, a country plagued by economic crisis. Because of the Dublin Convention, which determines that refugees have to remain in the first European Union member state they set foot in, Samuel had to invest a considerable amount of effort into developing strategies that allowed him to evade Italian police controls after he was rescued from the boat close to Sicily. His migration tactics mirrored the journeys of the majority of the young people I met throughout my fieldwork, all of whom had chosen to evade Italian border control mechanisms to make their way to Switzerland, where they hoped to gain access to the kinds of futures they believed they deserved.

In recent years, a growing number of researchers have come to describe the ways migrants collectively appropriate spaces through their disobedient mobility patterns as "the autonomy of migration" (Papadopoulos and Tsianos 2013; De Genova 2017). They argue that academic discussions have been so preoccupied with the emergence of violent border practices intended to ward off fortress Europe that they have overlooked the ways migrants subvert these physical and bureaucratic hurdles and continue to cross borders on a daily basis. In doing so, migrants contest the dehumanizing politics they are subject to and actively exercise their freedom of movement. This autonomist perspective on migration therefore urges to shift the emphasis toward the "acts of desertion from the regimes of subordination and subjection that migrants objectively repudiate through their mobility projects" (De Genova, Garelli, and Tazzioli 2018, 242). I share with the proponents of this approach the conviction that we need to move beyond the deterministic focus on control and power mechanisms marking many social science accounts of Europe's migration regime by laying the emphasis on the subjectivities of migrant mobilities. At the same time, I believe that we need to be careful not to induce the deeply troubling experiences refugees and migrants have to endure in order to subvert Europe's exterior and interior frontiers with a sense of political pathos or "hope against all odds" (Kleist and Jansen 2016, 378). Samuel's interactions with the teachers in the integration class that I turn to will show that this striving for autonomy should not be reduced to simplistic ideas of resistance or speaking truth to power. At a time that is marked by choreographed "spectacles of crisis" (De Genova, Garelli, and Tazzioli 2018, 240), refugees have turned into the main targets of nationalist and reactionary populist movements. Such an environment severely restricts their possibilities of openly expressing critique or defying control without risking their future projects. Zooming in on the at-times-contradictory strategies Samuel deployed to work against his subordination within this hostile social environment will show that acts that appear to be overly compliant at first sight may turn out to be carefully considered strivings for existential autonomy and freedom.

PERFORMING INTEGRATION

In August 2015, when Samuel arrived in the Swiss border town of Chiasso and lodged his asylum application, he knew that he had not yet won the battle. Even though he had managed to make his way to Switzerland without being intercepted by the Italian border police, the most complex hurdle still lay ahead of him: the struggle to obtain refugee status and create a future for himself in Swiss society. Several weeks after his arrival, when he joined the radio group, he told me about the pressure he felt, saying that he could not stop worrying about his future. Although the immigration authorities had categorized Samuel as an unaccompanied minor and transferred him to the youth shelter in Bern, he was acutely aware that time was working against him as he was turning eighteen in a few months. He worried that the fact that he would be treated as an adult for the most important part of his asylum procedure—the second asylum hearing—would deplete his chances. He was also anxious that he might not be permitted to attend school after he turned eighteen and that he would be transferred into mass accommodation for adult asylum seekers, where he would not even have access to German language classes. While unaccompanied minor asylum seekers receive favorable treatment as long as they are categorized as children, these entitlements are often everything but certain. The majority of the unaccompanied refugee youth in Switzerland are at the cusp of the legal age of adulthood,[2] and as has been documented in other European countries, authorities frequently use time as a tactic of immigration control (Allsopp, Chase, and Mitchell 2015). In Switzerland this means that unaccompanied minors are often strategically aged out so that the decisive phase of their asylum procedure is postponed until after their eighteenth birthday, when they no longer enjoy a special protection status and can be deported or detained without much further bureaucratic ado (Leyvraz 2017; Schweizerische Stiftung des Internationalen Sozialdienstes 2016, 14).

With all these uncertainties, Samuel was gripped by a state of nervousness. When we walked to the church community house for the radio group gathering, he told me that since his arrival in the home for unaccompanied minors he had barely slept a night. Too big were the challenges that lay ahead of him and too strong the compulsion to act as quickly as possible to overcome them. Driven by this urge for action, Samuel attempted to make progress in as many areas of his life as quickly as possible. This particularly showed in the enormous energy he invested into gaining access to education. By learning German and catching up on school subjects as fast as he could, he hoped to convince his supervisors and teachers that he was ready to be transferred from the internal school to one of the integration classes before his birthday. Samuel had been told by some of the other young people that the cantonal authorities usually permitted unaccompanied refugee youth who had reached the legal age of adulthood to stay within the school system if they had been enrolled before their eighteenth birthday. Determined to achieve this goal, Samuel leaped into action, dedicating every free minute to learning German, often by spending hours in the public library, where he had access to the internet and could look up language learning and education websites. He also started to meet regularly with Mr. Ronald, an older Swiss man from a Protestant church community who had volunteered to act as a language buddy for refugee youth living in the center. Samuel actively fostered this relationship as he believed that the closeness to an adult who was familiar with the Swiss education system would offer much-needed guidance. Indeed, the language proficiency he gained in the one-on-one sessions with Mr. Ronald and the friendship they developed turned out to be important door openers. After he had spent only two months in the internal school, his supervisors agreed to sign him up for an integration class.

In January 2016, when I started to conduct research in the integration class he attended, Samuel had already moved on to the next step in his whirlwind plan to secure his future in Switzerland. Having been enrolled in the bridging school, he tried to use the integration class as a springboard to an apprenticeship. While Samuel's journey to Europe had been propelled by the dream of higher education, he changed his plans soon after his arrival in Switzerland. Having realized how difficult it would be to achieve secondary schooling in the restricted Swiss asylum and education landscape, he changed tactics and started to pursue an apprenticeship in a trade. He did so by using the *Schnupperlehren* to find a company willing to take him on as a trainee. For many of the students in the integration class, these trial apprenticeships posed a great challenge. As pointed out before, migrants and refugees are significantly disadvantaged in the Swiss apprenticeship system. Because of their insecure immigration status, youth like Samuel who are still in the midst of their asylum procedure are even more at a disadvantage. Samuel, however, did not fear this task. Having learned about the crucial role of the *Schnupperlehren* in the curriculum of the integration classes, he started to tackle this challenge as soon as he learned that he had been enrolled in the bridging school. With the help of Mr. Ronald, he used the Christmas holidays to research and call countless businesses. Before his first day at school in January 2016, he already had three trial apprenticeships lined up.

Samuel's eagerness to secure an apprenticeship in a trade and his swift decision to give up on his dream of higher education need further unpacking. In the conversations and discussions during the radio group meetings, it became clear that the change in his future plans was not driven by a sudden interest in learning a trade or a passion for craftsmanship. Samuel opted for this educational pathway because he believed that an apprenticeship in a trade would form an important bonus in his second asylum hearing. With his eighteenth birthday and the end of his special protection status as a child looming, he did everything in his power to remodel himself into a trustworthy, well-integrated adult. Samuel knew that his performance in the second asylum hearing was of the utmost importance because this interview would form the basis for the decision about his immigration status by the Swiss State Secretariat for Migration (SEM). During the hearing, applicants have to present a consistent and credible narrative convincing the SEM caseworkers that they are worthy of protection by the Swiss state. How this worthiness is determined is subject to intense public debate in Switzerland. In 2016 two investigative journalists from the newspaper *Tagesanzeiger* caused a stir when they published the result of the analysis of 29,263 decisions on asylum cases by the Swiss Federal Administrative Court. They found that judges supporting conservative or right-wing parties were disproportionately more likely to reject asylum seekers' claims for protection status than were moderate or left-leaning judges (Rau and Skinner 2016).[3] Likewise, scholars studying the asylum deter-mination practices of bureaucrats in Switzerland (Affolter, Miaz, and Poertner 2019) and other European countries (Jubany 2011; Fassin and Kobelinsky 2012) have shown these choices to be marked by conflicting moral impulses. Judges and bureaucrats dealing with asylum applications are concerned with reaching just, fair decisions that are in line with the Swiss National Act, the Federal Act on Foreign Nationals, and the 1951 Refugee Convention (Affolter, Miaz, and Po-ertner 2019, 268–69). But they are not immune to politically induced sentiments and stereotypes, and their decisions are often also based on personal values and moral judgments. In her ethnographic research with asylum officers in the UK, Olga Jubany (2011) found that their actions were driven by a set of unwritten rules informed by a general culture of disbelief. Propelled by the impulse to protect "the system" from fraudulent claims, many officers saw it as their main task to distinguish the accounts of deserving, "real" refugees from the tales of undeserv-ing, "fake" refugees. They established the level of un/deservingness in asylum hearings through a range of subjective criteria, such as the applicants' countries of origin, gender, appearance, or display of emotions.

While the principles guiding asylum bureaucrats in their decision-making processes are neither institutionalized nor openly spelled out, they circulate among refugee communities in the form of rumors or words of advice on how to satisfy the parameters of deservingness. In the conversations between the young people, "integration" emerged as the most important means of achieving this goal. During my visits in the home for unaccompanied minors, I noticed that the notion of integration was omnipresent. It was one of the first German words many young people learned, and it formed a core topic of discussions, in school as well as in private conversations. Given the countless ways integration permeated everyday talk and life, it is not surprising that Samuel came to grasp its importance so soon after his arrival. In the weekly gatherings, I noticed that the other young people gave him advice on how to best display his integration efforts to succeed in his asylum hearing.

A brief conversation between Meron and Samuel, which occurred one spring afternoon when the two of them were discussing their educational aspirations, is a case in point. During this exchange, Meron reinforced Samuel's decision to concentrate on finding a company willing to take him on as a trainee rather than pursuing his academic interests. "This will help you in your second interview," Meron said. He was convinced that if Samuel were to secure an apprenticeship, "they will give you better papers because they want to keep you here." Samuel agreed. He believed that the most feasible way to secure his future in Switzerland was to perform his integration efforts. This state of "integration," he was sure, was best achieved by showing his willingness to become a diligent, honest, and well-behaved blue-collar worker who would not become a burden on the Swiss welfare system. When I asked Samuel whether he no longer considered completing secondary education an option, he responded, "Annika, I love going to school and learning. I would like to go to university. But here in Switzerland they really like you when you work, so I have to find work instead."

INTEGRATION WORK

Samuel's effort to strategically portray himself as a poster child for integration did not occur in a vacuum. It echoed narratives put forward by the teachers in the bridging schools that promoted integration as an ideal, final goal for the refugee students attending their classes. Mr. Müller, Samuel's class teacher, described integration as his core educational mandate. During a coffee break, as we were speaking about the great degree of social engagement his job required, he said, "I would say that the vast majority of my work is not teaching German. It is integration work."

Mr. Müller was in his fifties and self-identified as a liberal, open-minded, and concerned Swiss citizen who was critically opposed to dominant right-wing populist narratives about refugees. He had previously worked in a project that provided basic education to young asylum seekers with high chances of being rejected. He had been attracted to the educational project in the bridging school because he believed it to be more clearly directed toward the integration of young people into Swiss society—a positive approach he had been missing in his former position, where the emphasis lay on the return of refugees to their home countries. Because of his years of experience in teaching refugee youth with little German language skills, Mr. Müller had become the main teacher responsible for the beginners' integration class. Like Mr. Schmid, the head teacher of the advanced class, he directed his integration efforts predominantly toward nonacademic skills, such as orderliness, enunciation, courtesy, punctuality, and demeanor. Like his colleague, he believed that proper "integration" was only possible if the young people became part of the Swiss job market. Mr. Müller's "integration work" was therefore guided by the attempt to assist his students in acquiring the cultural skills he believed to be necessary to find a company willing to offer them short-term apprenticeships. The option of secondary education did not occur in these pedagogical plans. While Mr. Müller did not support Mr. Schmid's firm-but-fair approach, he shared with him the underlying assumption that the young people needed to overcome a vast array of cultural and linguistic deficiencies before they would be fit for inclusion in the Swiss education system.

The idea that the refugee students were so culturally different that they needed the help of professionals to guide them in their process of integration was shared by all of the teachers I spoke to in the bridging school. They were proud of the work they were doing, which, they believed, was crucial not just for the young people's futures but also for the future of Swiss society at large. They saw their efforts to "integrate" the young refugees as a significant step toward more harmonious forms of cohabitation between migrants and Swiss citizens. The teachers repeatedly voiced the opinion that if the cantonal authorities failed to invest in such integration measures, they risked the development of parallel societies (*Paralellgesellschaften*) that would undermine Swiss social, cultural, and moral norms. As a result, they were less concerned with academic training than with resocializing the refugee students so that they would fit into Swiss society (also see Hilt 2017, 591).

The "integration work" the teachers were performing on their students resembles the dynamics Jaffe-Walter (2016, 91) observed in her research on the interactions between teachers and Muslim migrant youth in Danish schools. She found that teachers often engaged in "culture work" rather than focusing on academic work. Like the teachers in the Swiss integration classes, the Danish teachers did so because they believed assimilation to be a necessary precondition for academic success. In a similar vein, the teachers in the integration classes tended to get caught up in small behavioral details, thereby shifting the emphasis from academic to cultural questions. This becomes apparent in the following brief interaction that occurred one morning when I joined Samuel's class. As I was looking for a free chair, Mrs. Lange, the German teacher, told me to take the seat right in front of her. After I sat down, Samuel entered the classroom, looking confused to see me sitting in his usual spot. "Oh, this is my seat," he said. "But I give it to you as a present," he added, grinning. The teacher was not happy with Samuel's behavior. "That's not very polite, telling her that this is your spot," she scolded him. Noticing Samuel's embarrassment, I hastened to jump to his defense. "But he just told me that I can have it," I said. Mrs. Lange gave Samuel a warning look. "You better be nice to others," she said. "Here in Switzerland people are very polite." By emphasizing politeness as a particular Swiss trait, the teacher insinuated that its supposed absence in Samuel was a cultural shortcoming. She went on for another ten minutes to elaborate on the ways "the" Swiss displayed their politeness, pointing out the importance of the "magic words" *thank you* and rehearsing moments when they needed to be used. The hidden message this exercise delivered to the students was clear. The teacher's belief that they had to be taught even the most basic traits of politeness—a banal and everyday set of values that could be assumed to be shared by most other people in the world— revealed to them their cultural inferiority. It also signaled "Swissness" to be the ultimate measure of all things. Even though Mrs. Lange was a much-loved teacher who showed a great deal of enthusiasm for her job, she continuously engaged in a project of cultural resocialization. Like her colleagues, she believed integration to be her main educational mandate. Despite the liberal, humanistic approach toward migrants she believed the pedagogy of integration to advocate, the interactions in the classroom showed it to be steeped in ideas of cultural supremacy and expectations of assimilation.

In putting the spotlight on the ways the teachers in the bridging school used the seemingly inclusionary notion of integration as a means of implementing exclusionary practices, I do not intend to belittle their work. It is important to keep in mind that the teachers, like the young people this book focuses on, are not one-dimensional human beings. They are complex individuals with different biographies, bringing various ideas, convictions, and motivations into the classroom. Because of the low reputation of the bridging schools in the Swiss education system, the teachers—not unlike their students—were in a marginalized position compared to their colleagues from secondary schools. In the classrooms they were confronted with a heterogeneous group of students, many of whom were involved in challenging legal battles to secure their right to stay. The teachers' scope of work thus covered many areas and required a great degree of social versatility. Furthermore, it is important to note that in an era marked by neoliberal reforming zeal, teachers themselves are increasingly subject to measures of accountability and control. In a school landscape where competitive individualism, early selection, and standardized testing are held high, teachers often have little scope to advocate for the inclusion of students labeled as second and third tier (Slee 2011, 144).

Jaffe-Walter's (2016, 77) suggestion that researchers attempting to expose the ways racialized ideas are enacted in school settings should not reduce their analysis to the normative evaluation of individual teachers is therefore crucial. At the same time, it is also important not to misconstrue teachers as passive agents or mere onlookers to politicized debates on integration and immigration. Teachers actively "adopt, resist, adapt discourses as they negotiate their own identities and the cultural complexities of their students" (Jaffe-Walter 2016, 77).

Rather than singling out the behavior of specific teachers, I chose to zoom in on the teachers' interactions with their refugee students to make visible social imaginaries of belonging and nonbelonging that reflect Swiss society. The strength of ethnographic research in classrooms is precisely that it allows scholars to tease out the ways racialized discourses are negotiated between different actors at a local, everyday level (Jaffe-Walter 2016, 77). This attention to social details is particularly important in multicultural education settings, as critical questions related to race and discrimination are often not part of accepted discourse in schools. Yet, even if these topics are silenced or banned from classroom discussions, this does not mean that the underlying problems have disappeared. In her study of engagements with questions of race and multiculturalism in two middle schools in Utah, Angelina Castagno (2008, 321) found that teachers hardly ever referred to race during their lessons. Instead, they used code words, such as "language minority students," or "refugee students." Educators used these words as a less dangerous way of speaking about race. In the classes where I conducted research, *integration* turned into such a code word. It allowed teachers to reproduce generalizations about the refugee students' supposed cultural and educational deficiencies while maintaining the sense that their "integration work" was not based on racialized stereotypes but on their students' special needs. The educators' conviction that they were "helping" and "caring" for their students' integration by promoting assimilationist ideas corresponds with the strategies of "race evasion" (Jupp and Lensmire 2016) that scholars of education have repeatedly described in multicultural school settings, where humanist ideals come to be used as a means of covering up questions of racialization and marginalization (Gillborn 2005; Applebaum 2010; Matias 2016). The "integration work" the teachers were performing thus turned out to be yet another variation of inclusive exclusion: seemingly inclusionary pedagogical measures aimed to form bridges into Swiss society proved to fortify the young people's position as problem cases and outsiders in need of professional remedy.

To gain a more nuanced understanding of the ways this logic of inclusive exclusion came to permeate the interactions between teachers and students in the integration classes, it is necessary to sketch a genealogy of the notion of integration in Switzerland. Against the backdrop of the role of integration discourses in

Swiss social and political life, the small, seemingly minuscule everyday classroom exchanges through which the teachers communicated their refugee students' cultural inferiority lose their isolated character. Rather than scapegoating the teachers' views, it embeds them in a wider, self-perpetuating system of Swiss (white) exceptionalism and supremacy.

FOSTER AND DEMAND

Since the early 1990s, integration has turned into a powerful concept in Switzerland, making its way into virtually every corner of society, from government bodies to institutions and social life at large. Anthropologist Hans-Rudolf Wicker (2009, 23) describes the notion of integration as so powerful that it has turned into a *Leitidee* (central idea) governing Swiss approaches to immigration ever since it entered the public discursive arena. Like other scholars, he links the forceful way the notion of integration entered public debates to the long-term rejection of policies of multiculturalism in Switzerland (D'Amato 2010; Dahinden, Duemmler, and Moret 2014). The social currents underlying this rejection are complex and directly linked to the country's multiethnic makeup.

Throughout its history as a nation-state, clichéd self-representations of Switzerland as a harmonious and peaceful neutral country of ethnic and linguistic diversity have played an important role in the creation and maintenance of a unified Swiss national identity. These narratives allowed the German, French, Italian, and Romansh ethnic and linguistic groups to overcome historically ingrained relationships of distrust. The specific Swiss type of "multiculturalism" this created is very fragile. It is not based on the idea of intercultural encounter and dialogue but on the autonomy of each of the four linguistic groups to determine the rules and regulations for the respective territories they inhabit. While this prevents conflicts between the various groups, it also prevents the creation of cultural overlaps, leading to a detached form of multicultural cohabitation. Given this fragile national equilibrium, it is probably not surprising that efforts to maintain the idea of a Swiss "we" have always been based on the shared suspicion toward the "other." This "other" is most explicitly embodied in the figure of the *Ausländer*, the foreigner, or literally the "out-of-this-land person," threatening the country's complex stability. The myth of the small Swiss nation fighting against the threat of *Überfremdung* (over-foreignization) has thus been part and parcel of Swiss identity politics since its birth as a nation-state in 1848 (Kury 2003; Niederberger 2004). This went hand in hand with cultural supremacist imaginaries of Switzerland as an exceptional place—an island of stability, wealth, and peace that is above the conflict and corruption reigning in the rest of the world.

While multiculturalism turned into a dominant paradigm for the inclusion and participation of migrants in many other European countries from the 1970s onward, in Switzerland it was predominantly used to refer to the country's four established national linguistic groups. Despite the multicultural setup of the population, Swiss people fervently rejected the notion of multiculturalism and, in fact, the very idea of being a country of immigration. As a result, Switzerland developed restrictive naturalization practices, leaving many migrants who had been living in the country for generations without access to citizenship (Salis Gross 2004, 152). Migrants were only welcome as transitory guests, not to be included in the social fabric of Swiss society. Until the 1990s, the denial of the presence of migrants permeated federal politics to the point that Gianni D'Amato (2010) argues that Switzerland needed to be characterized as a multicultural country without multicultural policies.

Although the paradigm of multiculturalism never found acceptance in Switzerland, the notion of integration entered the public discursive arena with great force. In the 1990s, it made its way from debates in social work circles to the political sphere, where it turned into a key principle of cantonal and national immigration policies. Initially, the notion of integration promised a move away from the exclusionary principles that had dominated Swiss immigration debates for so long. Its emphasis on tolerance, equality, and participation seemed to herald a new, more open approach to migrants (Piñeiro 2015, 20). Policymakers from all parties promoted integration as the cornerstone for a socially sustainable immigration policy, acknowledging the importance of actively facilitating migrants' inclusion in Swiss society. The integration craze of the 1990s initiated a flurry of activities. National programs and cantonal integration initiatives sprang up overnight, giving migrants access to resources such as language classes and facilitating intercultural dialogues. In a revised version of the immigration law in 1999, the Swiss state added an article on integration, and in September 2000, the government released the first detailed regulation on the integration of foreigners.

Although the principle of integration has been written into Swiss law, the notion was never clearly defined, leaving it open to many different interpretations. In his history of the integration debate in Switzerland, Esteban Piñeiro (2015, 25) argues that despite its societal significance, the notion of integration is so ill defined that it could be described as "empty." Integration is a notion of such vagueness that it can cover various—often completely opposing—principles, motivations, and desires. As a result, politicians from all spectrums make use of the notion of integration without diminishing its power and effectiveness. Social scientists have noted that it is precisely *because* of its fuzziness that integration has managed to evolve into such a powerful social imaginary across Europe, carrying with it specific ideas of the nation, society, and the boundaries between self and other (Anthias 2013; Rytter 2019). When the notion of integration entered Swiss public debates in the 1990s, it signaled an openness toward cultural difference and the sociopolitical participation of migrants in society. Around the turn of the millennium, however, these interpretations started to shift. With the rise of the populist far-right Swiss People's Party (SVP) in the early 2000s, the country was gripped by a repressive turn that has not left integration discourses ever since (D'Amato 2012, 89). The assumption that migrants were eager to integrate into Swiss society if only they would be provided access to certain resources came to be overtrumped by voices doubting migrants' good-natured intentions and calling for more coercive measures. Migrants' right to integration (*Integrationsrecht*) increasingly turned into a duty to integrate (*Integrationspflicht*) (Piñeiro 2015, 20). The revised version of the law on the integration of foreigners that came into effect in 2018 exemplifies this shift. Foreign nationals living in Switzerland now have to agree to an integration contract (*Intergrationsvertrag*); otherwise they risk sanctions. Eduard Gnesa, head of the Swiss Federal Agency for Migration at the time of the law's overhaul, was convinced that Swiss people needed to "regain the courage to set boundaries and enforce sanctions" (cited in Vonarburg 2018).[4] His emphasis on the idea that Swiss people needed to "regain courage" captures the ideological shift in Swiss integration debates. The sense of openness toward cultural plurality that marked earlier approaches to integration has disappeared. It is now laughed at as a negligent act of naivete that needs to be corrected through clearly demarcated acts of boundary drawing.

The main pillar of the integration contract is assimilation: migrants are seen as guests who are in no position to make claims but who should socially and culturally adjust to the practices of the society hosting them. While there is still a degree of acceptance of the fact that migrants should receive access to resources facilitating their integration, these resources are no longer open to all migrants. Contemporary Swiss discourses on integration create a clear delineation between desirable migrants deserving access to integration measures and undesirable migrants not worthy of these expenses (Piñeiro 2015, 21). On these scales of un/deservingness, individuals from EU member states with skills that are in demand on the job market and with sufficient social, economic, and symbolic capital are seen as the most desirable migrants, while individuals with few educational skills and from countries that are perceived to be culturally too distant from Switzerland are seen as undesirable (also see Wicker 2003, 33; Skenderovic and D'Amato 2008, 168). It is important to note that the shape of this undeserving cultural other is not stable. While the figure of the welfare-scrounging African asylum seeker or the dangerous Muslim intruder are the most forceful personifications of unwanted otherness, the latest wave of anti-EU sentiments and the toughening of integration requirements for EU migrants in Switzerland has shown that these sentiments can easily spill over to other groups. As Ghassan Hage (2017, 7) notes, the power of racialized figures is precisely that they continuously morph into new shapes. In doing so, they gain the "capacity to target a variety of people, sometimes many at the same time."

The frequently repeated mantra "foster and demand" (*fördern und fordern*) perfectly captures the ways the logic of inclusive exclusion has come to permeate Swiss approaches to integration: while the Swiss state fosters the conditions for migrants' inclusion in society (*fördern*), it only does so on the basis of a set of requirements migrants are demanded to fulfill (*fordern*) (Piñeiro, Bopp, and Kreis 2009). At first glance, the language of integration seems to insinuate an open, more human approach to migrants. But underneath this surface lurks a powerful racialized subtext charged with fantasies of cultural supremacy and deeply rooted anxieties about loss of power. It mirrors similar developments across Europe, where integration policies have turned into key building blocks of interior frontiers. Cultural pluralism is now seen as an urgent societal problem rather than an enrichment, leading to practices that have been described as "paranoic integrationism" (Karakayali 2009) or "repressive liberalism" (Joppke 2007). Mikkel Rytter (2019, 685) characterizes the popular use of the notion of integration as dystopic. It promises migrants future inclusion in society but simultaneously invokes fear that failed integration processes could provoke upheaval and the fragmentation of society. "Without stating this explicitly, integration talk is always pre-emptive and a means to avoid latent catastrophes" (685).

The dystopic fears playing into current integration debates reveal deeply entrenched patterns of racialization. They bespeak the prevalence of a "paranoid nationalism" (Hage 2003) on the side of (white) majority populations who fear losing their positions of privilege and power. They translate into hierarchies of "good" and "bad" types of cultural diversity (Anthias 2013). Based on the assumption of a homogenous cultural "we" holding the indigenous right to determine the inner workings of the nation-state, integration talk prescribes migrants the duty to fully absorb into the given sociocultural setup. This duty to blend in is coupled with an onus on migrants to quietly accept their subordination. "Good," well-integrated migrants do not just become culturally invisible. They also accept their relegation to the lowest position on the societal ladder without protesting against this marginalized role.

The creation of the integration classes for unaccompanied refugee youth needs to be read against the backdrop of these societal dynamics. Their existence signals two antithetical moves. On the one hand, the cantonal authorities' willingness to facilitate the integration of this particular group of asylum seekers confirms their classification as "good" migrants deserving access to public education resources that will foster their inclusion in society. On the other hand, the decision to teach the young people in segregated, specialized classes signals the conditionality of this inclusion. It confers on the teachers the task of making sure their refugee students understand and stick to the integration contract. In this sociopolitical climate, teachers turn into frontline workers of the integration regime. Not only are they expected to prepare their students to take on their allocated roles in Swiss society, but they are also expected to monitor and control their integration efforts.

The interactions in the integration classes showed how strongly the refugee youths' educational opportunities depended on the teachers' assessment of their "integration" progress. Even though they had received access to education resources other asylum seekers could only dream of, the unaccompanied minors' status of deservingness was not cast in stone. It required them to continuously display their integration efforts or risk being marked as unthankful troublemakers who did not deserve the gift of integration they had received. Yet as I sat in on the lessons, it became evident that the process of integration the teachers were aiming at was a one-way street. While it required the full submersion of the young people into Swiss society, it did not require Swiss people to show any flexibility in accommodating the ideas or habits migrants or refugees had brought along. This asymmetrical integration process was based on particular ideas of host-guest relations. In his research in Denmark, Mikkel Rytter (2019, 687–88) also found this host-guest equilibrium to play a crucial role in integration debates. It is best captured in the saying "When in Rome, do as the Romans do." According to this logic, refugee guests who do not obey the rules and who disrespect their hosts should leave (687). Yet the problem with this model of integration is that even if refugees do their best to accept the wishes of their "hosts" and blend in, that does not preclude the constant emergence of new "interior fences" (Gullestad 2002): "Actual integration seems to be impossible because there are always new fences to climb and new stones to roll up the mountain" (Rytter 2019, 688).

This tendency to keep erecting new fences shows itself in Samuel's struggles in the classroom. It reveals the ways the logic of inclusive exclusion permeates spaces of everyday life, turning measures intended to foster young people's participation in society into yet another set of cornerstones in the expansion of interior frontiers.

THE SISYPHEAN TASK OF INTEGRATION

Samuel's effort to stylize himself as a poster child for integration shows how quickly the young people came to learn and *inhabit* the attitudes they were expected to display in order to pass the test of un/deservingness. As I accompanied him into the classroom, I observed his fervent attempts to gain his teachers' approval. He was entirely submersed in the lessons, eager not to miss a single point the teachers were making. He displayed his active cooperation by continually asking the teachers for clarifications and making sure he was quick to raise his hand if they posed a question. In tests he was determined to finish first, and when the teachers split the class into different levels, Samuel accepted nothing but being allocated to the advanced group. Furthermore, he had already mastered the task of securing a couple of *Schnupperlehren* and was entirely committed to the challenge of finding an apprenticeship in a trade. He had buried his dream of going to college because, to reuse Samuel's own words, *in Switzerland they really like you when you work.*

In displaying his willingness to give his all to become an honest, hardworking, well-integrated person, Samuel strove to satisfy the benchmarks of deservingness circulating in public discourse. In public debates, the deserving commonly appear as individuals of good moral character who have come into a situation of neediness through external circumstances that are no fault of their own. The status of deservingness is measured by individuals' attitudes, such as the level of gratitude, compliance, and docility they display. Another crucial criterion is the degree of reciprocity or future payback the individuals' advancement through public resources promises (Meanwell and Swando 2013, 498). By stylizing himself as a poster child for integration, Samuel attempted to tick all these boxes. In emphasizing his willingness to learn and assimilate, he tried to demonstrate both his gratitude for having received access to the public good of education and the promise that this investment would pay off. He did everything in his power to avoid being assigned the opposite role as a lazy and immoral fake refugee who did not deserve the help and protection of the Swiss state. Samuel's struggle for deservingness was not restricted to his educational opportunities. Pressured by right-wing parties, the Swiss government had just started to tighten its stance toward Eritrean asylum seekers. Samuel's eagerness to perform as the poster child for integration has to be read against the backdrop of the wave of rejections of asylum applications engulfing the Eritrean community in Switzerland and the anxiety this caused in young people with ongoing asylum procedures.

Although Samuel did so much to prove the seriousness of his integration efforts, the teachers did not react the way he had hoped. Even though Mr. Müller and Mrs. Lange frequently complained about the lack of enthusiasm students displayed in their search for a trial apprenticeship, they did not welcome Samuel's proactive approach. When I started fieldwork in Samuel's class, he was absent for several weeks because he had organized *Schnupperlehren* in various businesses. Mr. Müller repeatedly diminished this success by scolding him for missing so many classes. When Samuel returned to school and enthusiastically reported that the boss of a carpentry company had agreed to take him on for a full four-year apprenticeship (EFZ), the teacher reacted with disbelief. At the radio group gathering that week, Samuel told us that the teacher had refused to believe him, portraying him as a liar. When Samuel insisted that he was telling the truth, the teacher had said that for people without a secure immigration status, obtaining a full apprenticeship was almost impossible because businesses did not want to take the risk of training somebody who might have to leave the country again. In front of the entire class, Mr. Müller had asked Samuel what his immigration status was. He had made him admit that he had a status *N*, meaning that he was still an asylum seeker without any guarantee that he would be able to settle down in Switzerland permanently. This question upset Samuel deeply. "He has no right to ask me this," he said, fighting off tears. The fact that he had to reveal in front of all his classmates that he only had an N status and that he might have to leave the country again felt like an insult to him. It pained him so much that he even considered quitting school altogether. It took the intervention of Mr. Ronald, Samuel's elderly Swiss friend, to convince the teacher that the apprenticeship offer was not just wishful thinking.

The teachers' negative reaction to Samuel's attempts to tick off all the boxes of integration they themselves were continuously promoting surprised me. During the lessons I sat in on, I observed that they responded to his efforts with irritation. They were annoyed about his eagerness to participate and ask questions, repeatedly putting him down or scolding him for disrupting the class atmosphere. When I talked about this with Mr. Müller and Mrs. Lange during a coffee break, they argued that their attempts to hold him back were in Samuel's own best interest. They interpreted his eagerness to succeed and start an apprenticeship not as integration efforts but as an unwillingness to properly settle down. "I am not sure what to think about the whole thing," Mr. Müller said, referring to the apprenticeship offer. "I know he really wants this, but it's so rushed." He explained that he was worried that Samuel was rushing into everything without taking the time to properly arrive in Switzerland, learn German, and understand the Swiss system. Even the fact that Samuel had learned German in record time was used against him. The teacher was convinced that as he had invested all his intellectual energy into that task, he did not have space left to take in anything new at the moment. Mr. Müller took offense at Samuel's success in securing an apprenticeship so quickly, which allowed him to skip important stages of the integration ladder. "He has no understanding for the steps that have to come in between," the teacher said. "That he has to learn the language first, that he needs to understand this new culture and the education system. He has no idea what an apprenticeship actually means."

The teachers' negative reaction to Samuel's efforts to fulfill the benchmarks of integration reveals the exclusionary undercurrents of the seemingly positive, benevolent pedagogy of integration. It shows the ultimate state of integration the refugee students were encouraged to work toward to be a Sisyphean task. As Rytter (2019, 681) poignantly puts it, "they have to keep trying, but enough is never enough." In Samuel's case, the teachers held his success against him, interpreting it as an unwillingness to go through the process of integration properly. They used a language of care to justify their tough stance on him, arguing that it was in his own "best interest" to slow him down, as he himself was not able to judge the long-term consequences of his decisions. Driven by this conviction, Mr. Müller intervened in the negotiations with the carpentry company that was willing to accept Samuel as an apprentice. He told the boss that he believed Samuel was not ready for a full, four-year apprenticeship (EFZ). As a consequence of this estimation, the company scaled down its offer to a short-term EBA apprenticeship. Although Samuel was glad that he had secured any form of apprenticeship at all, it meant that he was channeled toward the lower-qualified end of the job market. Here, the ambiguous potential of treating unaccompanied minors as vulnerable victims shows again. While the narrative of the hyper-vulnerability of the unaccompanied minor had enabled Samuel's special access to education, it then came to haunt him as the idea of acting in his best interest was used to justify his educational segregation.

The teachers' active attempts at scaling down Samuel's educational ambitions on the basis of an argument of care mirrors common patterns of racialization. In the Swiss context, scholars of education have coined the term "aspiration cooling" (*Aspirationsabkühlung*) to capture these dynamics (Imdorf 2005; Haeberlin, Imdorf, and Kronig 2005). It describes the ways teachers gradually cool down the hopes of marginalized students by planting in them the idea that because of their insufficient academic performance, they cannot achieve their ambitions. To keep up the facade of equal opportunities, teachers subsequently offer alternative pathways, which, in the Swiss context, almost exclusively take on the shape of lower-qualified apprenticeships. In their research on a Swedish post–obligatory education program for youth labeled as at risk, Marianne Dovemark and Dennis Beach (2016, 179) also observed that teachers routinely cut down on their students' academic incentives. Students showing a great degree of motivation to enter secondary schooling were told to slow their pace. As in Samuel's case, the teachers were suspicious of this enthusiasm, fearing that the students did not have the capacity to keep up with it in the longer run. While the teachers justify their acts of aspiration cooling through a narrative of care, this care is not driven by an incentive of fostering their students' abilities. It is driven by the incentive of preparing them for a life at the margins of society.

In his landmark book *Learning to Labour*, Paul Willis (1977) shows the social dynamics through which male students from working-class backgrounds attending a British secondary school were channeled into low-wage labor positions. Building on his work, Dovemark and Beach (2016, 187) argue that students from migrant backgrounds in post–obligatory education projects like the bridging schools are no longer prepared for a life as laborers. Instead, teachers prepare them for a life of impermanence on the margins of the labor market and, I would add, society at large. Dovemark and Beach note that the creation of separate educational tracks for marginalized student groups signals a politics of precaritization. Instead of focusing on the young people's abilities and training them for inclusion in mainstream public education, their education is marked by a "process of abandonment of a genuinely educational contract" (Dovemark and Beach 2016, 175). The young people attending such programs become "educationally neglected, hidden, overlooked, dismissed, pitied and quite literally de-valued" (175).

EXPOSING INTERIOR FRONTIERS

Even though Samuel's teachers attempted to scale down his ambitions, he did not passively submit to these acts of subordination. His urge to understand and expose the inner workings of interior frontiers also showed in the classroom. After the argument in which Mr. Müller accused him of being a liar, Samuel lost confidence in his teachers. He started to dissect their behavior and make comments that frustrated their attempts at keeping questions of race and marginalization outside the classroom. Through small acts of resistance, he signaled his refusal to obey the expectation that the students in the integration classes should be thankful for the "gift" of integration. In doing so, Samuel exposed the unequal social mechanisms of the integration regime. To avoid risking his future in Switzerland, he had to voice his critique in skillful ways. This becomes apparent in the following incident that occurred not long after the clash between Samuel and Mr. Müller. Shortly before the morning break, the teacher wrote "life/I am alive" (*Leben/ich bin lebendig*) on the blackboard. To demonstrate the different ways the word *life* can be used, he wrote down the sentence "I love life" and asked students to come to the blackboard and add other sentences containing the word. In his usual manner, Samuel was one of the first to volunteer. He went to the blackboard and wrote "I hate life." It caused a strong reaction in the other students, who were overcome by a collective laughing fit, releasing suppressed reflections on their lives in Switzerland and the countless hurdles they had to deal with on a daily basis while being forced to keep up a positive facade. Samuel's action was a clear message to the teacher. The reversal of the positive language of love allowed him to bring into the open the experiences of marginalization he and his classmates were struggling with on a daily basis. Without explicitly naming it, he expressed his frustration with the teachers' attempts at diminishing his educational ambitions. It also allowed him to vent his anger about the asylum system and his anxieties about living in a legal limbo. On yet another level, the sentence communicated Samuel's refusal to slavishly submit himself to the role of the ever-thankful guest who did not have the right to critique the form of welcome his hosts deemed appropriate. Cleverly disguised as an act of compliance with Mr. Müller's call for the students to come forward with their own sentences, it allowed him to expose some of the inner workings of the interior frontiers they were up against without overstepping his role as the poster child for integration.

For the remaining six months he spent in Mr. Müller's class, Samuel continued to perform this double role with astonishing creativity and perseverance. He repeatedly upset the carefully cultivated silence surrounding issues of race and discrimination in the classroom by asking seemingly naive questions that forced the teachers into discussions of inequality and discrimination or by caricaturing the host-guest equilibrium underwriting the integration classes. Because he was one of the best students in the class and had already secured a short-term apprenticeship, the teachers lacked the moral means to rebuke him for this behavior. Samuel's acts of *compliant resistance* display the creative and well-thought-through measures the young people had to resort to in order to express critique and opposition against the integration regime they had been thrown into. In a social environment marked by a fragile hierarchy of host-guest relations, acts of resistance do not always show in the most obvious, loudest, or most aggressive ways. Samuel's story shows that to avoid endangering their future projects, refugee youth need to tailor their expressions of opposition in concordance with the logic of inclusive exclusion. Paradoxically, overt performances of compliance can enable refugees to question their unequal treatment and cause cracks in the makeup of interior frontiers.

For Samuel, the results of this double role were ambiguous. On the one hand, his plan of securing his future in Switzerland by performing the poster child for integration panned out. The fact that he had secured an apprenticeship, had internalized a convincing narrative about his political persecution in Eritrea, and was able to communicate in German greatly advanced his chances in the second asylum hearing. He was the only participant from the radio group to receive full refugee status. Unlike the temporary protection status most other youth received, it gave Samuel the legal right to remain in Switzerland permanently. It also gave him access to social welfare, refugee assistance services, a better apartment, and a work permit. On another level, the strategy of satisfying all the expectations of deservingness came at a great cost, as it required Samuel first to give up on his dream of completing a university degree and then to scale down his ambition for a full EFZ apprenticeship. At the moment of writing, he has successfully completed his two-year apprenticeship and has found work in a carpentry company. Even though this has enabled Samuel to gain a steady income and make his way into the Swiss labor market, he is not content with where it has left him on a larger scale. True to his critical nature, he often questions the steps he was required to take to secure his future in Switzerland and is frustrated about the dreams he was forced to let go of.

Just as I was completing this chapter, a text message from Samuel once again acted as a reminder that despite the downward spiral of un/deservingness migrants and refugees are subject to in contemporary integration regimes, we should never underestimate their urge for existential freedom and self-worth. "Annika, you know what I want to tell you?" his message began. "I have to tell you something important." Alarmed that he might be in a difficult situation, I responded that he could reach me at any time. "Well, I think it is a good message," he continued. "I am writing my own book." In the subsequent conversation, it turned out that Samuel had spent the past six months writing down his life story in German and needed my help with copyediting it. As I started reading his book, I was impressed to find an advanced manuscript of over a hundred pages. The story he tells in the book attempts to make visible to a Swiss audience the many struggles he has faced, from the troubling experiences marking his journey to Europe to the racist and exclusionary treatment he received in Switzerland. I see Samuel's book as the ultimate refusal to remain silent about the structural violence inflicted upon refugees trying to build a future in Europe. It is at once a touching story about a young man's struggles for self-worth in a world interspersed with inequalities and a unique document of social critique against the persistence of interior frontiers. This story, however, is not mine to tell.

NOTES

1. I first discussed some of the ethnographic vignettes presented here in a blog post for *Allegra Laboratory* as part of a thematic week on "Displacement and New Sociabilities" I curated together with Heike Drotbohm in August 2018: http://allegralaboratory.net/on-being-made-feel-out-of-place-displacement/.

2. In 2016 the Swiss Secretariat for Migration reported that 63% of the asylum seekers categorized as unaccompanied minors were between sixteen and seventeen years old (SEM 2016).

3. In Switzerland it is common practice that aspiring judges become members of a political party. Judges have to make their party membership public.

4. The original in German reads as follows: "Wir müssen wieder den Mut haben, Grenzen zu setzen und Sanktionen zu vollziehen."

FOUR

—ɯ—

THE UNLUCKY MANY

HIERARCHIES OF LUCK

On a cold February afternoon in 2016, Thierno, Abdi, and I made our way to the church community house. That week most of the participants of the radio group were preoccupied with trial apprenticeships, so it was only the three of us. Seventeen-year-old Thierno from Guinea was unusually talkative that day. The absence of the clique of headstrong Eritreans who tended to set the tone for discussions allowed for new voices and themes to surface. Although he had been a member of the radio project from the beginning, Thierno usually preferred to stay on the sidelines of discussions or comment on them with a removed sense of irony. This afternoon, however, he was visibly eager to share what was on his mind. As we entered the community house, he sighed. "*La vie est dure,*" he said in French, the language he had grown up with in Guinea—life is hard. I asked Thierno whether he did not believe that life was sometimes hard and sometimes easy. "Yes, but for me it is almost always hard," he answered. Throughout the conversation evolving from this exchange, the mounting sense of anxiety that gripped Thierno became palpable. He was going to turn eighteen in a couple of months and had not yet received a decision on his asylum application. The supervisors in the home for unaccompanied minors had told him that he would have to move out of his room soon and that he needed to find a Swiss person willing to take him into their private house or would risk being transferred to one of the overcrowded accommodations for adult asylum seekers. However, finding somebody willing to offer him a room for the low monthly rent allowance that the migration office allocated to asylum seekers felt like an impossible task. On top of these worries, he was struggling to focus on school and had not been successful in sourcing an

113

apprenticeship. What weighed most heavily on Thierno's mind was the fact that his asylum procedure had taken much longer than that of most of the others in the radio group. While the predominantly Eritrean youth in the group had received their decision letters within six months to a year of arriving in Switzerland, he had been waiting for more than two years. Listening to Thierno's list of worries, Abdi shook his head. He had only arrived four months earlier and was waiting for his asylum hearing. Like Thierno, he was anxious about the outcome. "We have to wait," Abdi said resignedly. "There's nothing we can do. Switzerland is this: waiting and punctuality." There was a moment of silence. "You see, it is difficult," Thierno said, giving me a testing look. "This life gives me so much stress."

In an attempt to cheer him up, Abdi said that he was convinced that everything would end up fine for him. "Inshallah, may you get a visa *B*," Abdi said, hinting at the holy grail of permits. Given the low chances of being among the lucky ones to receive full refugee status, Abdi's suggestion that he would receive a permit *B* made Thierno grin. "*B*?" he asked unbelievingly. I threw in the idea that so far most of the young people in our radio group or in the integration classes had not received a permit *B* but that they had at least been granted humanitarian protection permits. While this humanitarian protection status, described as "permit *F*" (*Ausweis F*), had to be renewed annually and gave less access to social welfare and education resources than a permit *B*, it offered a minimum degree of stability and protection from deportation. But Thierno did not agree with my suggestion that he might get a permit *F*. "*F*-politics (*F-Politik*) is just for Eritreans," he responded. "For all the others it is different." I asked what kind of permit all the others got. "Maybe *F*, maybe nothing at all," Thierno responded. I asked what happened to people who got "nothing at all." "Their life is fucked," Thierno said decidedly.

The conversation with Thierno and Abdi exposed a grave imbalance in the radio group's social makeup. It was an imbalance that also permeated the integration classes, homes for unaccompanied minors, and peer groups—in short, all the key social sites where my fieldwork took place. This dissymmetry was directly linked to the scales of un/deservingness marking the Swiss asylum landscape. While the radio project had consolidated around a more or less stable group of young people who knew and trusted one another, their chances of being granted asylum and hence being able to anticipate future trajectories in Switzerland varied widely. These chances depended on the young people's nationalities and whether they happened to belong to a "lucky" group of asylum seekers whom the Swiss authorities deemed worthy of protection at that moment. For the three radio group participants from countries other than Eritrea, the chance that they would receive asylum and the permission to stay in Switzerland was everything but certain. Yusuf and Abdi were from the Somali minority in Ethiopia and Thierno from Guinea—countries the Swiss authorities regarded to be safe and democratically ordered. They sometimes talked about the bad luck of being from a country that was "on the list." This much-feared list was the "safe countries of origins list" composed by the European Union, which identifies countries considered to be safe to return failed asylum seekers to. As a result of this list, people applying for asylum from countries that are on it are categorized as motivated by economic incentives and subject to accelerated detention and deportation procedures.

The conversation with Thierno and Abdi that February afternoon revealed the arbitrariness of the scales of un/deservingness. In the absence of the "lucky ones" in the group—their Eritrean friends for whom life seemed to be so much easier than for them—Abdi and Thierno were able to articulate the deep sense of uncertainty facing people whose future projects and sense of social worth are determined by something as random as a list. That they chose to speak of their worries in this particular constellation, while keeping them hidden from the other participants, reveals that hierarchies of un/deservingness manage to eat their way into social relationships. As much as the young people trusted and looked out for one another, the feeling of being one of the unlucky ones could not be shared. Through my conversations with Thierno, Abdi, and Yusuf, I came to see that the fear of being rejected—the sinking feeling that the hopes and dreams that had propelled them on their dangerous journeys to Switzerland were about to collapse—did not just make the anticipation of a future in Switzerland impossible. This feeling of disallowance, of being somehow less worthy than others, crept into young people's bodies and minds, thereby shaping the ways they were oriented toward the world. In doing so, it also entered the social fabric of the radio group, creating a divide between those deemed the lucky ones and those out of luck.

In the pages that follow, I inquire into the deeply felt pain and shamefulness of being among the masses of asylum seekers in Europe currently categorized as undesirables. To do so I need to take a look beyond this book's predominant focus on Eritrean refugee youth—who at the time of my research largely received humanitarian protection status—and shed light on the story of Thierno, who stood little chance of being granted asylum or humanitarian protection. By making this detour, I can pay attention to the ways young people marked as undeserving deal with feelings of rejection, indifference, and abandonment. Despite the special treatment—including care, access to education, and supervision—Switzerland affords unaccompanied underage asylum seekers, young people like Thierno often experience these child-friendly, inclusionary measures as nothing more than a very brief reprieve from a life of precarity and marginalization. This raises the question of what role education projects can play in such a context. Giving certain refugee youth the chance to work toward a future while simultaneously signaling the impossibility of these futures bestows education projects such as the integration classes with a sense of cruelty. Representative of the tales of many "unlucky"

African refugee youth I encountered throughout my fieldwork, Thierno's story sheds light on the ways political acts of cruelty seep into education settings. It brings to the fore the structural violence inflicted on youth in education environments that are marked by the logic of inclusive exclusion—how school settings, which are supposed to form a pathway to inclusion in society, relegate migrant youth to the bottom of the societal ladder, making young people like him feel inadequate, diminished, and abandoned.

Yet Thierno's story also reveals that as disruptive as such cruel acts might be to an individual's sense of existential equilibrium, they never manage to fully determine that individual's ways of being and acting in the world. In social environments marked by the logic of inclusive exclusion, open acts of opposition or resistance might not be within the realm of possibility. However, people develop their own responses to the symbolic and structural violence inflicted on them, articulating alternative ethical assessments about their worthiness as human beings.

THE ASYLUM LOTTERY

On a wintery Tuesday afternoon, about an hour into our weekly radio gathering, there was a knock on the door. Thierno entered the room, loud music beats resounding through his large headphones. He had received them as a thank-you for volunteering in the kitchen of a holiday camp for disabled children the previous summer. They had turned into his most precious belonging, leading to countless jokes in the radio group about the inseparability of Thierno and his "girlfriend," the set of headphones. As he walked around the table shaking everybody's hands, he slowly took them off. "How are you today?" I asked. "Half-half," Thierno replied in his usual laconic way. "What does that mean?" I asked. "I am half well and half not," he explained. "What would have to happen so that you can get rid of the unhappy half?" I asked. This question made Thierno laugh. "I need lots of luck," he answered. "Like winning the lotto." Listening to our exchange, Meron threw in: "But she's asking you about something that can happen, not about something that will never happen." Thierno smiled his agreement. That was exactly the point he had been trying to make: to win the lottery, one needed an immense, cosmic proportion of luck. He desperately needed such an improbable lucky strike. Without it being spelled out explicitly, it was clear to everybody in the room that the "lottery" Thierno was hoping to win referred to his pending asylum application.

At that point we did not know much about his reasons for leaving Guinea. While Thierno had been the radio project's first participant from way back when Thomas had founded it, he hardly talked about his personal history. From the snippets he had shared with the group, we knew that he had grown up in Conakry, the capital city of Guinea, and that he was from the ethnic group of the Fulani. We also knew that he had been the only child of a poor family and that his father had died shortly before he left the country at the age of fourteen. Our knowledge about Thierno's biography was limited to these few vague details. At one of the first radio group gatherings in the summer of 2015, when Jamila and I had tried to find out more about his upbringing, Thierno had asked us not to inquire after his family. He had explained that he could not speak of his parents, particularly not of his mother as he did not know if she was still alive. Talking about his past, he said, made him feel bad inside, leaving him sleepless at night. "I cannot stop and look back," Thierno explained. "I come to the radio group because it helps me forget."

Thierno was one of only two Guinean youth living in the home for unaccompanied minors. While the other young people never spoke about it in front of him, in the quiet they whispered about his low chances of receiving asylum. In public discourse, West African asylum seekers appeared as the most common representation of the figure of the opportunistic, economically driven migrant trying to cheat his or her way into Switzerland. The ethnic and political turmoil marking many West African countries was not considered to be serious enough to justify people's decision to seek protection in Europe. Instead of being recognized as fleeing from political persecution, asylum seekers from countries such as Guinea, Nigeria, or Gambia were suspected to be *Wirtschaftsflüchtlinge*—economic refugees who left their countries in search of better economic opportunities elsewhere. Swiss migration authorities have introduced fast-track procedures to deal with the cases of asylum seekers from such countries, allowing them to speed up the legal and return procedures. Of the nine hundred Guineans who applied for asylum in Switzerland in 2016, not one single person was granted refugee protection, and only 2 percent received a humanitarian protection visa (Amnesty 2017). On top of hearing these narratives of the undeservingness of West African refugees, most of the young people had either witnessed or heard the tragic story of a boy from Guinea who had been living in the home for unaccompanied minors for several years. Soon after his eighteenth birthday he had received a rejection letter and was summoned to leave Switzerland. Terrified of a forcible return to Guinea and lacking the funds to escape Switzerland, the young man had seen no way out. He had committed suicide by throwing himself off Bern's most iconic lookout. Even though the social workers tried to keep a lid on this story, it kept circulating in the home for unaccompanied minors, turning into an example of the Swiss authorities' relentless stance on Guinean asylum seekers.

Despite ample evidence of rejected, detained, or deported Guineans in Switzerland, Thierno remained stoically positive and hoped for his asylum application to be the exception to the rule. He spent day and night listening to music to distract himself from "bad thoughts." The headphones he had received as a gift did not just allow him to block out the sounds of the surrounding world. They enabled him to retreat into his own protective shell and block out the threatening future scenarios looming at the horizon. This act of blocking out included the avoidance of conversations about the status of his asylum case, personal history, and emotional state. It was as if the mere thought of a negative outcome of the asylum procedure could make it become true. This "magical" thinking was not just visible in Thierno's engagement with the asylum system. None of the young people I encountered throughout my fieldwork ever used the words *rejection, negative outcome*, or *deportation notice*. They avoided openly speaking of friends or acquaintances whose asylum applications had been denied. On the rare occasions they did talk about such individuals, they described them as having had "bad luck." The young people were convinced that the question of whether an asylum seeker received full refugee protection (permit *B*), humanitarian protection (permit *F*), or a rejection notice was largely determined by luck and that this luck came and went in waves: if one month everybody had received a permit *B*, they saw it as a natural law that this lucky wave would be followed by an unlucky one. When they discussed the chances of their asylum cases among one another, they tried to figure out which cycle they belonged to, hoping that they would not be part of a negative one.

Thierno desperately hoped that he would be part of a lucky wave. To avoid bringing bad luck on himself, he did everything in his power to achieve the opposite—to block out the possibility of anything negative, thereby hoping to attract good luck to come his way. When he spoke about the difficult position the asylum system had forced him into, he usually did so by referring to the fact that everything in life happened according to God's will and that he could not do anything against it. All there was left for him to do, he suggested, was to hope that God's plan for his life included a stroke of luck. "Inshallah things will turn out well for me in the future," he would often say. In the meanwhile, he added, he needed to continue being patient and "search for a life" (*ein Leben suchen*).

CHASING LUCK

Thierno's almost fatalistic insistence on waiting for luck to come his way resembles the dynamics observed by scholars studying the migratory movements of people from West Africa (Rouch 1956; Bredeloup 2013; Bachelet 2019). They show that contemporary mobility trajectories of West African youth toward Europe are linked to a history of movements of young men and women who leave behind their families and villages to search for luck. The "luck" they are looking for is connected to the acquisition of desired modern capitalist goods and lifestyles. However, it is also linked to an urge to do something out of the ordinary, to leave behind the monotony of daily life and become the author of their own destinies (Bredeloup 2013, 174). While these journeys initially took West African youth to surrounding cities or countries, increasingly the search for luck has brought many of them to Europe. Susanna Fioratta (2015), who studied the migratory pathways of young Fulani men from Guinea, found that they described their motivations to leave as "going seek." Similarly, the West African migrants Sebastien Bachelet (2019) encountered during his fieldwork in Morocco described their journeys as "looking for a life." When Thierno spoke about the need to "search for a life" and "wait for luck," he thus used notions commonly applied in Anglophone and Francophone West Africa to describe the existential kinetics underlying the migratory trajectories of young people.

In popular narratives circulating across Muslim West Africa, luck is not described as a random event but is linked to the destiny God allocates to individuals before they are born. According to these accounts, the luck a person will encounter throughout life is established by God when the embryo is formed in the mother's womb. The course of a person's luck is therefore predetermined and cannot be altered. When Thierno said that he had to wait for the kind of future God had spelled out for him and hope that God would help him find his luck, he referred to these Muslim cosmologies. Tracing the role of conceptions of luck in young Gambian men's migrant trajectories, Paolo Gaibazzi (2015, 228) points out that while God throws migrants into a destiny that is not of their making, they are expected to play an active role in "scouting out the routes to what has been allotted to them in this world." So even though people do not know their fate, they are expected to actively search for the luck God has predetermined for them. Young West African migrants' quest for luck does not therefore mean that they fatalistically ascribe outcomes that are out of their control to destiny. Rather, the invocations of "luck" and "searching" need to be looked at as practices through which they actively engage with uncertainty and precarity (Gaibazzi 2015, 228). Migrants' search for luck includes an "openness to the unexpected, an attitude of receptiveness and serendipity vis-à-vis the possibility, even the ineluctability, of unpredictable twists and turns in their lives" (228).

In a similar vein, Thierno's description of his asylum application as a form of luck and his refusal to let the possibility of a negative outcome enter his thoughts and vocabulary should not be misinterpreted as signs of fatalism or capitulation to forces that were out of his control. His insistence that he needed to keep waiting for luck to come his way can be read against the backdrop of an extended history of young Fulani men from Guinea venturing out into the world to search for their luck. In a country where ethnically based human rights violations happen on a regular basis (Amnesty 2017) and real food prizes are among the highest in the world (Knierzinger, Engeler, and Ammann 2016, 1–2), young people grow up amid an environment of uncertainty. In that environment, the search for luck provides them with a framework to actively deal with the indeterminacy of life (Gaibazzi 2015, 239). On yet another level, the continuous search for ways of improving uncertain livelihoods is folded into the social fabric of Fulani communities. The Fulani (or Peul) of Guinea trace their ancestries back to hundreds of years of nomadic pastoralism across West Africa (Stenning 1959; Dupire 1962). The migratory movements of young Fulani men and women thus do not happen in a temporal void. They are intimately linked to a history of mobility and the need to continue searching for ways of ensuring livelihoods.

While historically embedded conceptualizations of the uncertainty of existence explain some of the ways young people deal with the processes of subjectification they face in the rigid Swiss asylum landscape, they do not tell the entire story. For Thierno's attempts to block out the negative future scenarios looming at the horizon did not mean that these scenarios were not present. Scholars writing about West African migrants' historical and contemporary quests for luck have emphasized time and again that for most individuals these quests do not lead to the desired outcome (e.g., Lucht 2012; Fioratta 2015). Despite enduring grave struggles, only a minority of the young migrants manage to return as lucky heroes, and the forceful return of failed migrants often equals a fall from grace (Bredeloup 2013, 179). Thierno's joking reference to the extra-earthly proportion of luck he needed to win the asylum lottery suggests that as much as he was hoping for God's help, he was acutely aware that he might end up among the unlucky many who would never win the lottery.

As I accompanied Thierno to school and he slowly started to let me in on his life, I came to see what this awareness does to young people—how it silently, persistently enters their lifeworlds. I came to observe how the feeling of being the unlucky one literally sinks into bodies, creating an anxious state of anticipation for the final, most decisive act of exclusion—the condemnation of one as an undeserving, deportable alien subject. Thierno's experiences in the integration class made me grasp that refugee youths' educational, legal, and existential struggles do not occur in separate spheres. They go hand in hand, reinforcing the forcefulness of the blows youths have to endure.

SCHOOL PROBLEMS

When I started to accompany the young people into the bridging school, Thierno attended the beginner's integration class headed by Mr. Müller. Unlike Samuel, who had such a strong presence in the class, Thierno did not show much enthusiasm for the classroom activities. In interactive tasks, when other students vied with one another for the teacher's attention and approval, he usually remained quiet, observing the happenings with an absent-minded look. Once when I was sitting next to him during a weekly dictation test, I realized that he was struggling to follow. He often drifted off, stressed to catch up with the others. The task of turning the sentences the German teacher Mrs. Lange read out into written words was so hard on him that this fifteen-minute exercise left him exhausted. At the radio gathering Thierno showed me the corrected text. Resignedly, he said that his dictations always returned the same way—with the teacher's red corrections dominating the page, making his own handwriting disappear.

Learning German did not come easy to Thierno. He often complained about the malice of the Swiss asylum bureaucrats who had allocated him to a German-speaking canton even though he spoke French fluently. Although the neighboring French-speaking canton was only a twenty-minute train ride away, he had to be schooled within the boundaries of the canton of Bern. Thierno could not understand why the authorities forced him to learn a completely new language rather than allowing him to live in one of the French-speaking cantons, where he would have had a much easier time following the lessons. But his complaints went unheeded. After their registration and first screening, the Swiss State Secretariat for Migration distributes newly arrived asylum seekers to different cantons according to predetermined statistical patterns. Personal circumstances or preferences are not taken into account, and asylum seekers are obliged to remain in the canton they have been allocated to until they receive a decision on their case. This leads to absurd situations such as Thierno's, where people who speak French fluently are allocated to a German-speaking canton. There is no way for them to contest this distribution policy. Whenever Thierno raised the topic, teachers, social workers, and legal guardians generally responded that he should be thankful that he was allowed to attend school at all.

Besides the language issue, Thierno was struggling to read and write. Unlike most of the Eritrean students in the integration class, he had only received basic schooling. His parents had often lacked the money to buy the schoolbooks. Without these books, he was not allowed to attend school, and so he had sometimes missed weeks of schooling until his parents had been able to raise the funds. On top of these difficulties, the public school in his impoverished neighborhood in Conakry had often been subject to shutdowns because of power cuts or political unrest. On a regular basis, the government failed to pay for the teachers' wages, leading to strikes and days or even weeks of school closure. Taken together, these complications had led to an erratic educational trajectory. While Thierno was not illiterate, he was not confident in reading and writing.

It did not take long for me to grasp that in the unspoken classroom hierarchy of "good" and "bad" students, Thierno was located at the bottom. He was not a problem student in the sense that he disturbed the lessons, but he was slow, and the teachers often had to attend to him to explain things once again. During a coffee break, the German teacher Mrs. Lange said that she felt sorry for Thierno because he was such a nice young man but had so much bad luck. Although he had already spent a year in the beginners' class, she and Mr. Müller had not seen enough progress to promote him to the advanced group. He therefore had to repeat the year with the slower learners in the beginners' class while most of his classmates had moved on to the next level. Mrs. Lange said that this had been a great setback for Thierno, as he felt that he was stagnating while everybody else was moving on. "But he just isn't that far yet," she explained. "What use is it putting him there [the advanced group] if he's not far enough yet?"

As I sat in on the integration class, I observed how strongly Thierno had come to internalize this feeling of not being far or good enough. This feeling of inferiority did not just mark his interactions in the classroom. The sense of deficiency, of somehow being an impediment to others, crept into his body and mind, affecting his orientation toward the world. On days when I attended her lessons, Mrs. Lange sometimes asked me to sit next to Thierno to help him out. As we worked together, I came to see that he was not incapable of solving the tasks; rather, he constantly held himself back. The feeling of "I cannot" was so overpowering that he had entirely lost trust in himself. Even though he often knew the answers to questions the teacher posed to the class, he did not want to risk exposing himself by raising his hand. While Thierno struggled with reading and writing tasks, he excelled in geopolitical, historical, or societal questions. In our one-on-one sessions, he often made brilliant observations about the wider implications of the texts the teachers made them read. His ability to turn boring and moralistic German language exercises into political parodies of the students' status as unwanted foreigners in Switzerland often had the other radio group participants in stitches. Yet when I tried to encourage Thierno to make his knowledge more visible in the classroom, he immediately retreated back into his shell. Even during the lunch breaks at school, he preferred to stay by himself, usually searching out a quiet corner to listen to music. He did not seem to believe that what he had to say was of any value to the world.

Thierno's "I cannot" attitude resembles the dynamics highlighted by many educational scholars working with students from poor and racial minority backgrounds (Willis 1977; Darby and Rury 2018). In his ethnographic research with students in Germany who did not manage to make the jump to secondary schooling (*Hauptschüler*), Stefan Wellgraf (2012) describes how the young people came to take in, embody, and perform the sense of stigma attached to educational demotion. He argues that public discourses complaining about "problem students," teachers' deficit-centered attitudes, and disparaging remarks by peers or family members contribute to a distinct social practice of devaluation. Students develop their own ways of grappling with this sense of inferiority. Some might use school failure as a form of resistance against dominant white, male, and middle-class ideology, even if this means that they reproduce their status of subordination (Anagnostopoulos 2006, 8). Others, like Thierno, come to internalize the sense of being problematic or less worthy, leading to detachment, low self-esteem, and indifference. Throughout the months I spent at school with him, however, I came to see that this embodied sense of inferiority was not solely linked to his educational deficits. It was intertwined with the anticipation of receiving a rejection notice and the violence of being judged to be less worthy than others. His struggle for legal recognition leaked into the classroom setting, making it impossible to separate his school problems from the legal ones.

ANTICIPATING MISFORTUNE

It took almost a year of knowing Thierno and meeting him regularly before he started to open up. For months he observed my activities with the radio group, every now and then taking me aside to find out more about my background and the intentions of my research. With his dry sense of humor, he would test me out, thereby exposing the power imbalances underlying the relationship between the refugee youth and myself as a white, middle-class academic with an EU passport. "If only I had lots of money," Thierno said one afternoon during a radio gathering. "But I am very poor." "Life in Switzerland is expensive," I responded. "Not for you, you are rich," Thierno said. "Am I rich?" I asked. "Well, you can go on a holiday to New York, so you must have money," he countered, hinting at the fact that I had told the group that I was planning to fly to the United States to attend a conference. "I can never go on a holiday, I cannot even afford to go to Paris," he added.

Thierno only came to trust me after he was sure that I was not connected to the social workers, teachers, or immigration authorities and that he agreed with the aims of my research project. An afternoon in April 2016 was a decisive moment in our relationship. As we arrived at the church community house, Thierno told me that he was happy that he had met me. "When Thomas first introduced you to us he said that this girl could help us with some things, but I was worried because you couldn't speak French and I didn't know how to talk to you," he said. I responded that I had never had the feeling he could not speak to me, that he had learned German quickly. "Oh, but the first time I met you I didn't know how to talk to you," he said. "But now it is very good, I can come here, and we can be friends and you can help me to understand things." After this conversation, Thierno started to actively seek me out to help him understand things he was struggling to cope with.

One of Thierno's most pressing problems was his move into the age of majority and the pending decision on his asylum case. As his eighteenth birthday came
nearer, he opened up to me about the grave anxieties that were raging inside him.
While he had tried to keep them contained for a long time by exercising patience
and restraint, he was now gripped by nagging doubts that this longanimity might
not lead him anywhere, that he might still end up out of luck. With increasing
frequency, he talked about these doubts. During a radio group gathering, Thierno
approached to tell me that he was afraid Switzerland was not the right country for
him. When I asked him to explain why, he said, "Here they help some people, but
not the others." His statement showed that he had started to lose faith in winning
the asylum lottery. Thierno told me that he was almost sure that he would receive a
negative decision on his asylum application. "I look around me, none of the others
from Guinea are allowed to stay," he said. With a sigh he added, "People like me are
only allowed to stay until we are eighteen, then we are told to leave." On another
occasion he told me that he was very stressed about his asylum case, that he did
not know where to go if he received a rejection letter. "Where can I go?" he asked
me. Referring to the high rejection rate of Guinean asylum seekers, he noted, "We
didn't come here as tourists, we cannot go back home as if it were nothing."

Besides these verbal expressions of anxiety, the existential sense of nausea and
crisis also showed in nonverbal, bodily ways. Thierno suffered from sporadic,
medically inexplicable back pains and insomnia. As a consequence of these sleeping problems and pains, he was almost always tired. His absent-mindedness and
inability to focus in class were linked to this general state of exhaustion. Sometimes Thierno tried to explain what these bodily symptoms did to him, but he
was struggling to find the right words. "My brain is dead today," he would say,
or "sleep is broken." He often complained about headaches or flu-like symptoms
that made it impossible for him to go to school. The frequent absences further
intensified his difficulties in following the lessons, feeding into a vicious cycle of
illness and learning difficulties.

The teachers interpreted Thierno's physical problems and exhaustion as signs
of psychological stress. They did not specify where this stress came from. They
ascribed it to a general sense of vulnerability and disorientation caused by the
experience of displacement. In a conversation I had with Mr. Müller, he argued
that Thierno was so restless and stressed because he was the only Guinean among
predominantly Eritrean unaccompanied minors. He believed that the absence of
others he could talk to in a familiar language made him feel stressed and out of
place. Mr. Müller said that the decision to make him repeat the beginners' level
had been motivated by the need to take some of this stress off his mind and let him
find his own pace of learning. The teachers' interpretation of Thierno's struggles
shows how difficult it was for the young people to have their experiences of marginalization heard and recognized by others. The pedagogue did not grasp the

forceful entanglement of Thierno's legal, educational, and existential struggles, attributing his anxiety and depression to a general sense of disorientation as a refugee. Rather than ascribing them to the condition of displacement, however, I believe that they need to be seen as bodily manifestations of the structural violence inflicted upon refugee youth by an asylum system that pushes them to the edge of society.

Throughout the last decades, the logic of innocent until proven guilty has been reversed for individuals seeking refuge across Europe: until they can prove the contrary, asylum seekers are treated as economic migrants attempting to take advantage of their hosts' generosity. This general atmosphere of suspicion has legitimized the use of more severe criteria for the recognition of refugee status and the restriction of social rights. It has legitimized the introduction of fast-track procedures for people from countries considered to be safe. The slow but steady erosion of the asylum system has made for the production of a mass of "unlucky" deportable or illegalized migrants across Europe. These undesirable alien subjects are stigmatized through allegations of opportunism and undeservingness and pushed so far outside the polis that any outcry of protest becomes inaudible (Fassin 2005, 379–80; De Genova 2013, 1181).

In the current sociopolitical climate in Europe, asylum seekers do not have to await the decision on their asylum cases to feel the effects of these intense processes of exclusion. In the somber and overcrowded facilities where they are forced to spend their days waiting for the outcome of their asylum cases, they quickly learn that they are not supposed to be hopeful. Ghassan Hage (2003) has pointed out that wealthy neoliberal societies jealously guard the allocation of hope, leading to an unequal distribution of recognition of one's social worth as a human being. Building on these thoughts, Nauja Kleist and Stef Jansen (2016, 383) note that while people often choose to leave their countries as a means of escaping hopeless situations, refugee-receiving states engage in their own politics of hope. Refugee policies are marked by distinct messages "of the *absence* of societal hopes for/to (would-be) immigrants" whom they try to hold at bay through restrictive regimes of mobility (383). Many politicians use these messages of hopelessness toward refugees to create a sense of hope in their own citizens who are confronted with growing inequality and downward social mobility. This sends asylum seekers such as Thierno the message that they should not raise their hopes of ever becoming an equal part of society.

Thierno's description of the asylum procedure as a "lottery" and his insistence that the Swiss only like to help some while casting out the others show that such processes of boundary drawing manage to shape people's demeanors. Having been subject to years of waiting—a tactic frequently described as a means of disciplining unwanted "others" (Bourdieu 2000, 228; Auyero 2012)—Thierno had slowly lost hope in his ability to counter and overturn bad luck. Instead, he had come to anticipate the possibility of a future as *sans papier*, an illegalized alien living at the margins of European societies. The anticipation of such a future was not uncommon among the refugee youth I met. Even though its ramifications were so threatening that the young people kept themselves from dwelling on this possibility, that premonition was always present. It might help explain why so many unaccompanied minors across Europe disengage from bureaucratic processes and disappear without a trace (Terre des Hommes 2009; Council of Europe 2014). To them, the option of living at the margins of society as undocumented migrants is preferable to the possibility of being deported to a country they often have little connection to (Allsopp and Chase 2019). For young people like Thierno, the eighteenth birthday often becomes equivalent to a move into illegality.

With his eighteenth birthday coming closer, Thierno was increasingly anticipating such a future. This anticipation should not be thought of as a passive act of waiting for the inevitable. Rebecca Bryant (2016, 27) points out that anticipation is about more than expecting something to happen. In anticipation, we prepare ourselves for a resolution by means that include the body and encompass our entire sense of being-in-the-world. When we anticipate something, "our bodies ready themselves in anticipation of it happening" (Bryant 2016, 27). I have come to see Thierno's sleeping disorder and physical pains as signs of the ways he readied himself in anticipation of the immanent verdict of undeservingness. This anticipation of misfortune displays the complex ways humans experience and *know* the world. To paraphrase Arthur Kleinman (1997, 326), it calls attention to the fact that experience needs to be located "both within and without the boundary of the body-self, crossing back and forth as if the boundary were permeable." Thierno's anticipation of misfortune shows the permeability of these boundaries. While he was not able to formulate with academic precision the conditions of his suffering, he tacitly knew that the system he had been thrown into was determined to keep him from leading a meaningful and dignified social life in Switzerland. Madeleine Reeves (2019, 21) poignantly describes the ways institutional processes of subjectification determining migrants' worthiness as citizens come to penetrate their bodies—how individuals come to know "'here', in the hairs on the back of one's neck, that one is being singled out." Similarly, Didier Fassin (2011b, 294) speaks of a "creeping inscription of inequality within bodies" that is the effect of structural violence. He points out that structural violence is more difficult to grasp than political violence, as its relation to the state is less obvious. Yet the traces it leaves on the body are often more profound.

The wanton division of asylum seekers into deserving and undeserving individuals and the extended periods of waiting for the verdict need to be seen as forms of structural violence. What makes these acts even more cruel is that they are often dressed in a language of care that allows young people like Thierno to partially grasp the lives they are hoping for. While his status as an unaccompanied minor enabled him to go to school where he was expected to prepare for a future in Switzerland, he was simultaneously made aware that this future was likely to never materialize. The logic of inclusive exclusion marking the treatment of asylum seekers as simultaneous "citizens-in-the-waiting" and "deportees-in-the-waiting" (Haas 2017, 93) produces novel forms of suffering. Bridget Haas (2017, 88) points out that these ambiguous dynamics can create a sense of existential limbo in which life itself is experienced as stalled or immobilized. Prolonged waiting can be experienced as another form of violence, which often surpasses the suffering that propelled people to leave their home countries. Thierno also came to describe the asylum system as a form of cruelty. As he anticipated the misfortune the asylum procedure could bring upon him, he started to question his decision to apply for asylum. "If I had known what asylum means I would have never gone down that route," he said. "I did not know that it would destroy me like this." When I asked what he would have done instead, he explained that he would have preferred living as an undocumented migrant. Even though he knew that *sans papiers* did not have an easy life, he believed that it was better than the suffering the asylum procedure had exposed him to. Some months later, when the topic came up again, he said, "Before I came to Switzerland I did not know that they give us so much trouble because of asylum." Considering it for a moment, he added, "If I had all the information about this country beforehand, I would not have come here. But I did not choose. That's why I always say, 'I did not come here by myself, it is as if somebody has thrown me into this country.'"

Thierno's statement that he felt as if he had been thrown into Switzerland without his own cooperation captures the ways the asylum regime eats into people's sense of personhood, making them feel like spineless objects who are thrown around at the will of opaque forces. Caught in the maelstrom of this system, he was tossed back and forth between the desperate hope for a little bit of luck and the anxious anticipation of an imminent catastrophe. The suffering this caused in him did not just manage to suck out all his energy, leaving him exhausted and unable to focus. It also destroyed his ability to anticipate and work toward a better future. It replaced the hopeful expectations of progress many of the youth attached to education with a hopeless attitude of "I cannot."

I CANNOT

Thierno's educational struggles were not solely linked to the internalization of his classification as a weak "problem" student. They were also manifestations of the structural violence he was exposed to in the Swiss asylum system—of the creeping feeling that his life was not considered worthy of protection and care but was treated as disposable. In the classroom setting, this feeling of "less" translated into a conviction of *being* less, of somehow being less capable, important, or knowledgeable than others. It made him lose faith in himself and led him to utter "I cannot" before attempting to find solutions. When looked at from a critical phenomenological perspective, Thierno's "I cannot" attitude gives deep insights into the experience of being a body out of place—more specifically a male, West African, Muslim body—in institutions that are politically and habitually oriented toward white, middle-class Swissness. It allows glimpses of the opaque power of interior frontiers, how they do not just come to determine who or what is to be regarded as external to the polity but manage to make people *feel* other.

Thierno often talked about the awareness of being a Black person amid a society organized around whiteness. When the radio group met at the official meeting point in the train station of Bern, he called to tell me that he was waiting somewhere else. Terrified of the police officers who regularly patrolled the station, he did not like to be seen in the presence of a group of African youth. Walking past the kindergarten that was located close to the home for unaccompanied minors, he pointed out that the children were staring at him in horror. "They are afraid because I am Black," Thierno said. Noticing the shocked expression on my face, he added, "In the beginning it hurt me, but I am used to it now. I try to walk past them so that they don't see me." When discussing his interactions with the Swiss students in the bridging school, Thierno said that he had learned not to bother them. He explained that he had the natural inclination to talk to people, curious to find out something about their lives. But every time he had tried to initiate a conversation with the Swiss students, they had reacted awkwardly or ignored him. After a while he had learned to accept that "the Swiss" were not interested in him. "They don't want to know about me, and I don't make them talk anymore," Thierno said. Becoming "integrated," he explained, meant learning not to take these things personally but to understand them as part of normality.

In attempting to decode Thierno's internalization of inferiority and its relationship to his educational struggles, I find Franz Fanon's (1986) and Sara Ahmed's (2007) thoughts on the relationship between race and the body helpful. Analyzing the ways Black people adjust their repertoire of bodily habits in the presence of white people, Fanon (1986, 111) urges us to consider the "historic racial" schema underlying embodied actions and experiences. He argues that the composition of the self as a body that is located in a spatial and temporal world is not based just on habits but on implicit knowledge of its historicity (Fanon 1986, 111–12). He believes that corporeal schemas are shaped by histories of colonialism and exploitation and that Black people cannot inhabit a white world untouched by the countless tales, stories, and histories that relegate them to the lowest end of civilization. Responding to Fanon's thoughts, Sara Ahmed (2007, 153–54) notes that his work allows us to shed light on the phenomenological ways bodies remember histories of domination, even when they seem to be forgotten. She notes that such histories "surface on the body, or even shape how bodies surface" (154). Thus, Fanon's work enables us to move beyond phenomenology's unspoken focus on being-in-the-world as oriented toward whiteness. While classical phenomenology is all about motility, about the successful body that is able to extend itself in space and act on the world, Fanon's phenomenology of the Black body captures "the bodily and social experience of restriction, uncertainty and blockage, or perhaps even in terms of the despair of the utterance 'I cannot'" (Ahmed 2007, 161). Whereas white bodies extend into social and institutional spaces that have already taken on their shape, Black bodies learn to inhabit a negative—an experience Ahmed describes as "to be not" (160). They learn to fade into the background and become invisible.

When Thierno spoke of the need to make himself disappear in front of small children to avoid shocking them with his presence or argued that he had to learn to accept his treatment as an outsider as part of a new normality, he hinted at the lived experience of inhabiting a negative. If we are to understand the educational struggles of refugee youth amid a system that is driven by the logic of inclusive exclusion, it is crucial that we make this experience of *to be not* a part of our analysis. While the realization of the existence of interior frontiers made some of the young people I worked with leap into action and develop strategies to foil or dissolve them, in others, like Thierno, it caused a feeling of powerlessness and defeat. Thierno's pains and illnesses prove that this experience of negation cannot be reduced to the discursive level. They show how societal discourses manage to inscribe themselves in the bodies of individuals and get woven into the fabric of everyday social interactions (Das 1995, 22). The feeling of negation puts pressure on the body and creates a constant feeling of anxiety, thereby restricting people's ability to act on the world. As I attended school with Thierno, I came to see the grave consequences these restrictions can have on young people's educational opportunities. Whenever I tried to encourage him to trust in his abilities and participate in tasks the teachers had given, he would shrug resignedly and say, "This is too high for me." His mantra of things being "too high" for him did not just suggest that he did not trust in his own capabilities. It suggested that he had come to internalize his positioning at the lowest end of the social ladder—that he believed he was too small, subordinate, or "low" to be able to fully participate in school, and by extension in society at large.

Thierno's default attitude of "I cannot" needs to be understood in the context of the diminishing effects the asylum regime had on him. The experience of self-negation this regime manages to instill in individuals cannot be understood apart from historic-racial schema determining the ways Black bodies are to behave, move, feel, and disappear in the presence of white people. But his "I cannot" attitude also reflects the school's role in reproducing rather than critiquing these racialized politics of belonging. Given the absence of a postcolonial critique in Swiss pedagogy and the blanket refusal to deal with questions of racialization, the teachers were not equipped to grasp or respond to Thierno's struggles. Helpless about the despair the asylum regime caused in some of their students, they reacted by creating a code of silence around the issue.

When I asked Mr. Müller and Mrs. Lange whether they believed that there was a connection between Thierno's school problems and the asylum procedure, they agreed that the long wait for a decision was debilitating. But when I confronted them with the hopelessness of his asylum case given the low recognition rate of Guinean refugees, I was surprised to learn that they knew nothing about his legal struggles. The teachers' reaction made it obvious not just that they lacked the knowledge about his particular case but that they were not interested in learning more about the ways asylum politics determined their students' lives. Even though the pedagogues insisted on the importance of segregated classes to cater to the needs of this especially vulnerable group of refugees, they did not inquire into the nature of this vulnerability. Whenever I brought up the topic, it became apparent that they often did not know whether particular students had already received an immigration status or were still in the midst of the asylum procedure. They actively tried to unknow these things, as they followed the principle that the school was a space of respite where everybody was treated the same. While the teachers had received special training and understood the various steps in the asylum procedure, they consciously bracketed off the explosive issue of Swiss refugee policy. They agreed that the asylum system formed a source of stress in their students' lives. However, they felt that their hands were tied and that the best way of helping was by creating a positive atmosphere and daily routine that distracted the young people from their worries. The teachers tried to support their students as best they could in achieving their educational potentials, but they did not regard the details of their asylum cases as part of their educational mandate.

As a result of this silence surrounding their legal struggles, the students felt that they were not allowed to talk or voice critique about the violence inflicted on them by the asylum regime. The teachers actively encouraged them to remain positive while banning negative thoughts and ideas. They based their decision to disallow debates about the contentious issue of Swiss immigration policy on humanist ideas of caring for their students' well-being. This caring attitude, however well-intended, had the side effect of covering the most pressing questions determining the young people's futures with a blanket of silence.

The educational literature is rife with examples of practices of silencing students' questions about race and inequality. Ethnographic research in schools shows that white teachers are often put off by minority students' critiques of racial discrimination, as they experience such critiques as expressions of blame that are directed at them personally (Castagno 2008, 319). The shushing of conversations about the dehumanizing practices of immigration authorities sends refugee students the message that they are not relevant or that they divert from topics that are of "real" relevance (324). In the context of the integration classes I attended, the pressure on students to display a positive can-do attitude even as they faced desperate legal battles led some of them to switch off and disengage. Knowing that they were not allowed to openly speak of the dehumanizing treatment they were subject to, they internalized their struggles, leading to a sense of hopelessness and inferiority.

In her research on the increased presence of unaccompanied minors in US classrooms, Theresa Catalano (2017) found that young people internalized the stigma of inferiority attached to their status as youth with an unclarified legal status. She describes the process through which refugee youth are turned into "problem students" through the metaphor of the "circle of silence" (cf. Jefferies 2014). Like the teachers in the Swiss integration classes, the pedagogues Catalano encountered often did not understand the young people's complex backgrounds and tended to naturalize their marginalized status by ignoring the problems and fears they faced. The enforced silence around their status further alienated the refugee youth from school. It was detrimental to their participation in the classroom, which in turn justified their continued education in segregated and lower-tiered classes for English language learners.

Similar to the dynamics described by Catalano, in the Swiss integration classes students like Thierno—young people who were especially vulnerable as they were located at the bottom of the Swiss asylum hierarchy—got sucked into a circle of silence. The teachers expected them to display a positive attitude and keep focusing on their educational ambitions, making them apply for apprenticeships as if they would be able to remain in Switzerland and complete them. They did not take into account the impossibility of this task or understand the cruelty of asking the young people to participate in this make-believe educational show while they felt that their existence was on the line. Even though the teachers privately displayed pity for the "bad luck" of people like Thierno, they had no way of dealing with it other than pretending that it was nonexistent. As a result, the "unlucky" students did not just feel that their struggles for legal and social recognition were nonexistent. They felt as if their social existence, their presence as breathing, thinking, feeling human beings, was made to disappear. Rather than using the integration classes as spaces of hope and respite, they came to experience them as "zones of social abandonment" (Biehl 2005)—as spaces of last resort before they would be written off by the immigration authorities. Instead of

strengthening their students' sense of dignity and self-worth, the classes repro-
duced the hierarchies of un/deservingness marking the Swiss refugee regime. In
doing so, they prepared young people like Thierno to accept their allocated place
as societal outcasts and undesired illegal aliens who could not claim the right of
a dignified social existence.

The production of such educational zones of abandonment is not a new phenomenon in Switzerland. In their research at the turn of the millennium, Winfried Kronig, Urs Haeberlin, and Michael Eckhart compared data collected by
the Swiss federal agency for statistics within a nineteen-year time span, starting
from the 1980s. The data displayed a significant increase in the transmission of
migrant children to "alternative" or segregated types of schooling (Kronig, Haeberlin, and Eckhart 2000, 16–17). They found that the majority of the migrant
children were transferred to schools specialized in the education of children with
disabilities and learning impairments (*Sonderschulen*). The authors argue that the
decrease in separate classes for disabled children from the 1990s onward, which
was driven by the rapid spread of the paradigm of inclusion, was compensated
for by the increase of special schooling for migrant children (13). It shows that the
practice of exclusionary measures masquerading as inclusion has been present in
the schooling of migrant and refugee youth for decades. While official education
policies in the canton of Bern constantly use a language of inclusion, recom-
mending steps that allow marginalized groups to become part of mainstream
education programs, the creation of segregated spaces such as the integration
classes proves that these narratives of inclusion stand in stark contrast to distinct
practices of exclusion (Svaton 2017). Thierno's story shows that the dynamics in
the integration class did not fuel his educational ambitions or appetite for learning. The conditions of this schooling made him retreat and believe himself to be
somehow less than others. The rejection and diminishment he experienced in the
Swiss asylum system were mirrored in the education system, where the teachers'
indifference to his hopeless situation left him to feel abandoned and ignored.
Thierno's story shows how easily schools are turned into tools of immigration
control—not by legal means but by making young people like Thierno feel inadequate, diminished, and alienated.

THE STORIES BEHIND SILENCES

Anthropologists might cringe at my account of the ways the teachers in the integration classes silenced the voices of refugee students, making them perform
a make-believe show of positivity amid a situation of despair. However, I believe
that it would be too easy to condemn the teachers' behavior without critically
examining the modes of silencing marking our own engagements with refugees.

Anthropological accounts of displaced people are often tangled up in their own paradoxes of voice and silence. Similar to the silencing enacted by the teachers, the shushing of some experiences of structural violence in scholarly texts on displacement is not based on malintent. It often originates in a liberal, humanistic impulse to "do good" (Fisher 1997) and act against systems of domination and oppression.

There is a tendency in ethnographic accounts of refugee communities to search for alternative stories able to counter the dehumanizing strategies of immigration regimes. One key concern of the last decades of refugee studies has therefore been to make the voices of refugees audible. By making those voices and individual stories heard, anthropologists attempt to move beyond popular media narratives that tend to portray displaced people as anonymous, voiceless, and ahistorical masses (Malkki 1996) or "floods" of bodies (Anderson 2017). An implicit expectation emanating from this engagement with refugees' "voices" is that ethnographic accounts based on refugee stories will be able to uncover their agency. Rather than depicting refugees as passive victims, the logic goes, a focus on refugees' stories can direct attention to the "weapons of the weak" (Scott 1985) they deploy to foil, circumvent, or resist restrictive immigration regimes, thereby turning their migratory movements into subversive political acts (Monsutti 2018; De Genova 2017). While I sympathize with the political intentions of this argument, and although much of my own work has been propelled by it, an unintended side effect of the "voice" paradigm is that ethnographic accounts of refugees are often replete with agentive border crossers who defy systems of oppression, but do not seem to have much space for the experiences of people like Thierno—refugees whose capability of acting on the world has been diminished to the point that they cannot and will not tell their stories. If such experiences appear, they are usually phrased in psychological terms that ascribe the silence and suffering refugees might display to the effects of trauma. However, I believe that it would be dangerous to pathologize the experiences of Thierno and the unlucky many whom the cruelty of interior frontiers renders speechless. Reducing their experiences to bodily symptoms runs the risk of bypassing the complex political stories these bodies have to tell, thereby feeding into a circle of silence not dissimilar to the one created in the integration classes.

Heath Cabot (2019, 268) suggests that the anthropological obsession with the agency of refugees might have more to say about the hopes for resistance emanating from Western, liberal academics than about refugees' actual lived experiences. She notes that this has grave consequences for the anthropological production of knowledge on refugees: "When border crossers are not radical in the appropriate way, do not cooperate with anthropologists' political projects, or turn out to be unlikeable according to anthropologists' own norms, such moments are hard to reconcile with anthropological tendencies towards domestication and capture" (Cabot 2019: 268).

In the current political climate, in which parties gain political currency by spreading moral panic about asylum seekers and in which refugees are time and again reminded of the disposability of their lives, is it not also the task of anthropologists to ethnographically make sense of the ways such acts of structural violence manage to seep into individuals' lives, creating a sense of hopelessness and despair? I do not intend to argue that refugees are devoid of agency—many stories presented in this book so far have proven the opposite. But I believe that there is an urgent need for anthropologists to develop ethnographic tools able to examine the *voiceless* traces violent acts of boundary drawing leave behind in individuals. We need to be able to lay open the existential struggles for being that underly outcries such as Thierno's "I cannot" and to find the means to tell the stories behind silences.

Thierno's "I cannot" did not just relate to his educational capabilities. It also related to his existential struggle for being—a struggle that cut down on his ability to tell his story and have his voice heard. When he told me and Jamila that he did not want to talk about his life in Guinea, he did not simply choose to disengage. As I got to know Thierno better, I realized that he lacked the vocabulary to turn the experiences of violence and social abandonment that made up his life into a coherent story. Whenever he tried to talk about his experiences, his voice refused him after a few sentences. One afternoon he took me aside during a radio gathering and started to talk about his journey to Europe. He said that his arrival in Switzerland had been very difficult for him because he was only sixteen years old and very sick. I asked him what had happened, why he had felt so unwell. Thierno made a dismissive gesture with his hand. "Oh, I was very, very stressed after all I had been through," he said. He wanted to add something but stopped himself from saying it. He paused for a moment before he spoke: "And I had not eaten for weeks." I asked how this had happened. He sighed. There was a heaviness in the air, the unspeakability of his migratory experience hanging in the room. "What can I say. Here in Switzerland people have enough to eat but where I came from it's not like that," he said. "During my journey there was a man who gave me a piece of bread, so I ate it with some water." He stopped in the middle of the sentence. The memories of this time drove tears into his eyes. "I cannot talk about this, I really cannot," he said, giving me an apologetic look.

Thierno's inability to finish his story is just one of many moments when his voice gave up on him and he was forced to remain silent. In these half-told story snippets, some contours of his childhood in Conakry became visible. Without getting to know the details, I learned that his father died suddenly and that his mother had never reappeared from a trip to her home village, leaving him at the mercy of his father's second wife, who refused him food. In rushed, incomplete sequences, he told me about his father's friend who helped him to leave the country and about the agonizing uncertainty of not knowing what had happened to his mother. Sometimes he was convinced that his father's second wife had used her family connections to the district police boss to have her imprisoned and gain the sole right to inherit his father's modest house and kiosk in Conakry. At other times he worried that she had fallen victim to the 2015 Ebola outbreak in Guinea and died. Every now and then he even uttered the unthinkable: that his mother had decided to abandon him. None of these unfinished story fragments ever came to a conclusion, and they could not be pieced together into a coherent biographical narrative. They tended to start off in the middle of nowhere, in a temporal void that had no before or after. As suddenly as such story snippets appeared, they disappeared again, making it hard to grasp their intention or meaning.

As erratic and fragmented as these half-told story snippets appear to be, I believe that they should not be ignored or written off as inconclusive. They reveal something essential about the ways people who do not possess the social, emotional, or political capital to turn their experiences into a coherent story line make sense of the tumultuous world they find themselves thrown into. In the context of her work with victims of the Bhopal disaster in India, Veena Das (1995, 22) argues that for people whose lives are marked by violent events, it becomes extremely difficult to formulate the conditions for their suffering. She notes that rather than trying to establish a meaning in suffering, we need to pay attention to the victims' own understandings of the world, which are often accidental, chaotic, and contingent in nature. What Das (1995, 23) attempts to ethnographically capture in her work, then, is what she describes as the "truth of the victim." This truth is "not made up of the abstract iniquities of a system but of the daily suffering, the daily humiliation, and the everyday experience of being humiliated" (23).

Das's analysis allows one to move the focus away from the idea of meaning making as a universally applicable tool for understanding and relating to the world. Her work suggests that meaning making is a concept that often does not fit for the desperately poor and marginalized, who are mainly preoccupied with the sheer exigency of surviving (Kleinman 1997, 318). Thierno's fragmented attempts to explain and make sense of his life should therefore not be interpreted as miscommunications. It is exactly in their shocked breathlessness and inability to come to the point that they give crucial insights into the ways people who cannot tell their stories *do* tell their stories. Not overlooking or silencing such accounts requires efforts on the side of the ethnographer. It requires us not to expect people to distill their experiences solely in the form of narratives but to sharpen our perception to other forms of communication, such as gestures, silences, or half-spoken sentences.

I WILL SHOW YOU WHAT IT IS LIKE IN MY COUNTRY

As Thierno and I grew closer, I started to be able to hear and decode some of the stories behind his silences. The afternoon when he broke off his attempt at telling me his migration story, it became clear to me that Thierno's silence was not absolute, that he did try to tell me about his life. The story he wanted to tell me, however, was not a straightforward biographical account.

In disjointed fragments Thierno started to talk about the struggles of his ethnic group, the Fulani. From a third-person perspective, in the tone of an independent journalist observer, he explained to me that even though the Fulani form one of the largest ethnic groups in the multiethnic makeup of Guinea, they are subject to discrimination and persecution. Thierno said that because the Fulani were particularly active in the opposition movement, government forces regularly raided Fulani houses in the middle of the night, trying to find young men suspected of participating in protests. Human rights reports about Guinea confirm Thierno's point. They show that the current president, Alpha Condé, a Mandinka, violently crushes oppositional protests on a regular basis (Amnesty 2018; Human Rights Watch 2019a). At no point in the telling did Thierno place himself as an actor in this story. Yet it was not difficult to imagine that he had been one of these young Fulani men rounded up by the police. In a detached voice, he continued to tell me how he followed the protests via the YouTube channels of Fulani activists. He said that the week before he had found a video showing how soldiers caught a young Fulani man whom they accused of being part of the opposition. They put truck wheels around his body and lit them, burning him alive. Thierno shook his head. "Just imagine this life," he said. "How can they make me go back to that?"

For a split second, Thierno's "how can they make me go back to that" positioned him as an actor in the story. It moved the account from an abstract, removed level into a here and now that was marked by the cruelty of an unresponsive asylum regime. As the afternoon continued, I realized that it was this cruelty he was trying to give an account of. Rather than framing his critique in words, however, Thierno used visual means. He started to show me video after video depicting the violent suppression of riots in Conakry, the lynching of young men by plainclothes police officers, and the burning and looting of houses. Whenever I left for a moment to attend to the other youth, he immediately called me back again, asking me to have a look at yet another video. Observing the shocked look on my face while watching the scenes of mayhem, Thierno was satisfied with my reaction. "I will show you what it is like in my country," he said. As we were watching a scene depicting three policemen with machine guns running toward a house and kicking the furniture belonging to a little food stall into pieces, Thierno stopped the video. "This is like in a movie, right?" he asked. "Yes, but a very bad movie," I responded. "You see?" he said. "That's what life in Guinea is like: it's like a movie, but for us this is reality."

Thierno's attempt to *show me what it is like* in Guinea was not just an attempt to give me insight into the violence and suffering he himself had been subject to. It was also a way of telling me about the inhumanity of the Swiss authorities who were ready to send him back into such a world. He might have lacked the words to explain in detail the politicized role of youth in Guinean society—a practice dating back to the 1950s, when youth organizations formed a driving force in the struggle for independence, and to the resulting socialist state, where young people were seen as core drivers of the revolution (Engeler 2016, 70–72). And he might not have been able to voice the complexity of the socioeconomic and political problems following the breakdown of the socialist government, which fanned the flames of ethnic conflict in Guinea. But the videos of hounded, beaten, and shot Fulani youth did not need any words. In showing these images to me, he made me see with my own eyes the life he had escaped by coming to Switzerland. These images were not just intended to give me glimpses into the reality of Guinean youth. Importantly, they were intended to show me the arbitrariness of the scales of un/deservingness, to illustrate that there was no plausible reason why somebody who had escaped the repressive political regime in Eritrea was considered worthier of protection than young people fleeing the violence in Conakry's streets.

Anthropologists need to carefully consider whether their desire to capture individual stories is actually in refugees' interest or whether refugees should have the right to remain opaque or silent (Cabot 2019, 270; Besteman 2014; Khosravi 2020). The layers of story behind Thierno's refusal to tell his own story show that the ability to render one's experiences into a plot is not self-explanatory. For people whose status as subject is reduced to mere objectivity, the request that they make sense of their experiences can be an impossible task. Michael Jackson (2002, 45) points out that people reduced to such a position often feel that they no longer exist "in any active social relationship to others, but solely in the passive relationship to himself or herself." Pushed to the margins of the public realm, they are turned into objects of compassion, abuse, attack, care, or concern, into figures "whose words and actions have no place in the life of the collectivity" (45).

Thierno had been made to feel this way when he had summoned all his strength to tell his story at the asylum hearing. He ended the afternoon of watching YouTube videos by returning to the asylum system, attempting to explain the injury it had caused him. While turning off the computer, he told me that during his asylum hearing, he had acted against his instinct by telling the committee everything about himself, even about experiences he felt incapable of putting into words. But his story had fallen on resistant ears. While he had opened his heart to this panel of strangers, they had remained unmoved. Struggling to explain the violence of this experience of negation, Thierno pulled up his T-shirt and pointed at three large scars on his back. They were testament to the suffering he had been exposed to as a child in Guinea. Yet, while these bodily marks so clearly spoke of his painful past, the asylum authorities had refused to see them during his asylum hearing. The chairman had stated that he would only consider evidence that was presented within the framework of the oral interview or as part of an official medical examination. This refusal to properly listen to his story had left Thierno so violated that he had stepped in front of the chairman and lifted his T-shirt. "I pushed them into his eyes," Thierno said, pointing to his scars. "He had to see them."

The increased mistrust and suspicion marking the asylum system leads to the silencing of refugees' stories. Their own accounts of the persecutions they endured or the journeys they undertook to save their lives are routinely discredited (Fassin 2011b, 285). Their voices become replaced by the dry and empty accounts of professionals, such as the lawyers or legal advisers who help refugees prepare particular narratives or the doctors and psychiatrists who deliver medical evidence of the physical and psychological torture refugees have endured. As Thierno's experience of his asylum hearing shows, in a general atmosphere of suspicion, medical certificates are often given more weight than refugees' own accounts. Fassin (2011b, 287) likens the role of the state in asylum applications to the biblical figure of Thomas, "the skeptical apostle, who could only believe after having touched the open sores of Jesus." Yet Thierno's dramatic act of pushing his scars into the eyes of the irresponsive asylum officer shows that even physical evidence does not manage to dissolve the many layers of violence permeating the asylum system. Fassin (2011b, 289) notes that as refugees lose their moral credit, physical evidence does not suffice: "The search for truth by the state supposes a minimal level of trust not only toward applicants but also toward asylum as such."

Even though Thierno had worked so hard to convince the asylum committee of his trustworthiness, their indifference made him feel that he had been unable to do so. This complacence toward his story had not just left him hurt and defeated. It had rendered him speechless. Hannah Arendt (1944) has argued that the worst thing about being a pariah is not the maltreatment by the state. The greatest injury society can and does inflict is to make the pariah "doubt the reality and validity of his own existence, to reduce him in his own eyes to the status of nonentity" (Arendt 1944, 114, cited in Jackson 2002, 50–51). That afternoon when Thierno told me that he had pushed his scars into the chairman's eyes without receiving a noticeable reaction, I came to grasp the layers of violence behind his silence. His words showed the great existential harm the telling of a story can do to people, particularly if it passes unheeded. They made me realize that to better understand Thierno's "I cannot" attitude, I needed to take seriously this experience of negation and start listening to the things he could not do or say. Rather than expecting him to tell a coherent story—thereby repeating the cruelty of the asylum regime—or accepting his silence as a given, which would have added to the silencing he faced at school, I needed to become attentive to the ways he made his silence speak. I came to see Thierno's "I cannot" as more than a sign of defeat. It hinted at a complex everyday ethics—the "fragile conditions under which vulnerable populations such as refugees or poor migrants are compelled to make their everyday life" (Das 2012, 135).

BANALITY OF EVIL

Thierno's urge to show me what it was like in his country and his statement that he had pushed his scars into the asylum officers' eyes reveal something profound about ethics—not as a set of rules or norms but in terms of people's everyday struggles for a dignified existence. The question of how individuals develop and articulate such an everyday ethics becomes even more pressing for people such as Thierno, people who have been beaten to the ground and whose lives are marked by a pervading sense of social abandonment. While ethics is often approached from the perspective of normative societal rules or life-changing, transcendental moments, Veena Das suggests that we need to consider it as a crucial dimension of everyday life. Das (2012, 134) notes that ethics and morality should be thought of as "threads woven into the weave of life rather than notions that stand out and call attention to themselves through dramatic enactments and heroic struggles of good versus evil." Such a perspective on ethics allows one to grasp the "minutest of gestures" (135) through which people express their regard or disregard for the world they have been thrown into. It allows refugee scholars to resist the temptation of hearing only spectacular stories of resistance, instead making room for the "small acts that allow life to be knitted together pair by pair" (139).

In relation to research with unaccompanied refugee youth, such a reading of ethics moves beyond equating agency with resistance. It allows us to locate agency in the small, easily overlooked gestures through which youth who are defeated by the structural violence of the asylum system attempt to knit together their lives again. Consider Thierno's act of pulling up his T-shirt to show me his scars, or his unfinished story fragments. They speak of his efforts to question and actively work against the negation of his worthiness as a human being. It was in such moments that he was able to leave behind the "I cannot" frame of mind and articulate critical ethical assessments of the violence inflicted upon him by Swiss society. While Thierno could not base his ethical assessments on sweeping statements about the moral sanctity of human rights, or on the questioning of normative legal frameworks of asylum, he was able to lay bare the fragile social ground these rights were based on.

I keep returning to Thierno's question of *how can they make me go back to that*. In its simple facticity, it manages to expose the sinister nature of interior frontiers and the ruinous lives they foster (Stoler 2018, 9). The hierarchies of worth his question hints at are not the result of dramatic, extraordinary acts of evil. Thierno's question unveils the banality of evil—how violent acts of boundary making are anchored and acted out in the course of daily life (Arendt [1963] 2006; Das 2012, 143). This cruelty showed in the asylum officers' irresponsiveness to his story. It surfaced in the teachers' refusal to know about his legal struggles and in the general atmosphere of suspicion toward asylum seekers. It appeared in the Swiss students' unapproachable behavior and in Thierno's urge to make himself invisible. In relation to the integration classes, this cruelty manifested itself in the pretense of a happy future the teachers forced the students to perform, day in, day out, even though many of them knew that they were likely to never gain access to these futures. Some of them, including Thierno, were all too aware that the minute they reached the legal age of eighteen, they would join the ranks of the unlucky many inhabiting the margins of European societies. In an attempt to explain how difficult it becomes to imagine a future in such highly precarious circumstances, he once explained to me, "People like me never have the time to learn how to swim. We get thrown into the ocean, and if we want to survive we cannot but swim, otherwise we will drown immediately."

His statement perfectly illustrates the painful ways the logic of inclusive exclusion pervades unaccompanied refugee youths' everyday lives. As Thierno points out, people like him have to be extremely agentive and resourceful to "learn how to swim" in a deeply hostile environment. While he attempts to get a sounding from the world around him, this world constantly spits back mixed signals, ranging from his right to become a part of society to the need to control, expel, and banish him. Thierno's struggle to keep his head above the water amid the maelstrom he found himself thrown into reveals the darkness underlying the logic of inclusive exclusion. While driven by a morally charged compulsion to help those deemed especially deserving, this deservingness is built on such unstable grounds that it vanishes as quickly as it appears, leaving behind a trace of despair and ruination.

THIERNO IS KAPUT—IS HE?

In July 2016 I received a phone call from Thierno. "How are you?" I asked. "Bad," he responded. "Very bad." He asked me to meet him the next day so that we could talk. As I tried to figure out where and when to meet, he interrupted me. "*Thierno ist kaputt,*" he said. Thierno is broken. The blunt certainty with which he spoke this sentence caught me off guard. I made a weak attempt to calm him down: "I am sure you are not broken," I said. "Oh yes, he is kaput," Thierno responded. "He is kaput-kaput."

When I hung up the phone, my hands were shaking. An intense feeling of nausea went through my body. Although my year of participating in the young people's everyday lives had taught me to remain calm in the face of the repeated provocations the Swiss asylum regime spat at them, Thierno's third-person account about his brokenness hit something deep inside me. Is this what interior frontiers ultimately aim to achieve? I asked myself. Shattered, defeated, *kaput* lives? Is it not just the jealous protection of an "us" against unwanted intruders but the deep and lasting damage to these undesirables? Is it this brokenness the builders of interior frontiers are after?

The next afternoon, as we sat down in the back of his favorite café in Bern, Thierno struggled to tell me what was wrong. Knowing that words often evaded him, I started to talk about mundane things. I asked Thierno if he had already received notice from the teachers which class he would be assigned to after the summer break. He frowned and shook his head. "I won't go to school anymore," he said. "It's over. I am kaput." I asked what had happened. "Oh," Thierno responded, "it is very, very bad." He paused for a moment; then he told me that he had received "a very bad answer," mumbling that "it's all over for me now," that "this is the end." I asked whether he had received a negative decision on his asylum case. On hearing the word *negative*, Thierno gave me a shocked, desperate look—as if my speaking of the word made the full severity of the reality come to life. "Yes, negative, it's a negative," he answered, swallowing his tears. He explained that the decision letter claimed that Guinea was a safe and democratically ordered country and that he did not have well-founded reasons to seek protection in Switzerland. Repeating the authorities' reasoning angered Thierno. "They only look at the country, not at me, at the person," he said. Throughout the afternoon, he kept on returning to his experience of the asylum hearing, saying that the worst thing in all of this was that the officers assigned to his case had never listened to what he had to say. "I told them everything, absolutely everything that happened to me, but they didn't listen to me," he noted. The pain of not having his story acknowledged weighed the heaviest on Thierno's mind. It made him feel not just rejected but disowned by the Swiss.

When we met again a few days later to decipher the decision letter, the cruelty of the logic of inclusive exclusion became painfully apparent. In the letter the migration authorities held the education Thierno had received in Switzerland against him. As the "healthy, intelligent, well-educated young man" he had turned into thanks to the educational opportunities he had been able to access over the past three years, the letter argued, he had no reason to worry about his future prospects in Guinea, despite the recurrent outbreaks of violence against the Fulani minority that had compelled him to flee the country in the first place. While the authorities admitted that their attempts to locate Thierno's mother or any other family member had failed, they had come to the conclusion that he was old enough to fend for himself. Besides sending such a deeply insulting message of disregard, the migration authorities made Thierno feel the gravity of this formal act of exclusion by making him attend a return consultation within days of receiving the rejection letter. They threatened that if he did not show up for this appointment, he would immediately be regarded as an undocumented immigrant and subject to detention. Because he was no longer classified as a child, he had also lost access to free legal counseling. This meant that Thierno was now left to fend for himself in an illegible legal and bureaucratic system. The legal aid assigned to his case when he was still classified a child was not ready to write an appeal for him—firstly because he was no longer responsible for his case, and secondly because the chances of an appeal by a Guinean asylum seeker making it to the Federal Administrative Court for a reopening of his case were very slim. In the weeks, months, and years that followed, I became heavily involved in Thierno's struggles for a dignified existence.

Conducting ethnographic research with unaccompanied refugee youth—as with any other vulnerable human being—can and should never be reduced to a straightforward technical research relationship. When people who have been pushed to the margins of society decide to open up to researchers, even though they have every reason to doubt that revealing their struggles to us will be beneficial to them, we need to honor and appreciate the ethical commitment this creates. The idea of ethics I am aiming at cannot be standardized through agreements or verified by university committees. It is an intersubjective understanding of ethics growing out of people's everyday engagements with one another. This understanding of ethics is close to what Jackson (2013, 11) describes when he argues that questions of ethics need to be approached from the fundamental idea that our existence is always interwoven with others. The ethical can therefore not be reduced to norms, rules, or regulations. It appears at the interstices of human relationships in the "mundane struggles to decide between competing imperatives or deal with impasses, unbearable situations, moral dilemmas, and double binds" (11). The afternoon in April when Thierno told me that he regarded me as his friend who could help him understand things, I felt that we had entered into a relationship that required me to be more than receptive to his worries. It required me to become an active participant, not just in terms of my research but in our relationship and, by extension, his life.

When Thierno stated that he was broken, I could not stand back and passively analyze the social and existential ruination the asylum regime creates in people.

I felt compelled to do what I could to assist him in piecing himself together again. I sought advice on his legal options and raised the funds to pay for legal aid to formulate an appeal letter. When Thierno received notice that his appeal had surprisingly made its way past the screening stage and was going to be looked at again in the Federal Administrative Court, I convened with Swiss colleagues to plot strategies to enhance his chances. An asylum law expert advised us that even though Thierno's chances of receiving asylum remained slim, he needed to keep displaying his "integration efforts," as they heightened his chances to be granted a hardship permit (*Härtefallgesuch*)—a permit he would be eligible to apply for after five years in Switzerland. These permits are granted on a discretionary basis by the cantonal authorities to people facing extraordinary hardships. While some cantons virtually never grant such permits, Bern was known to be more lenient in its practice. The lawyer explained that even though Thierno was still two years short of the five-year deadline, working toward this type of permit was his best option. In the hope that the decision on his appeal would be delayed, he needed to make sure that he fulfilled the most crucial criteria for the hardship permit: the applicant's degree of "integration" in Swiss society. The most effective way for him to prove this would be by participating in the labor market, for example by doing an apprenticeship.

And so I found myself getting caught up in the inescapable pull of the logic of inclusive exclusion, as I talked insistently to Thierno about not quitting school but continuing to work toward his future, knowing full well that this future was everything but certain. We laughed and cried together about the awfully absurd situations this created. Only a few weeks after the shock of the rejection letter, we found ourselves in my university office, writing a hopeful, happy letter of motivation for an apprenticeship, even though Thierno felt that his life was falling apart. Having squeezed out a reasonable letter, I asked whether he wanted to add something or whether we had forgotten anything important. Thierno looked at me in ironic amazement. "Maybe add that I'm kaput," he said. "Maybe tell them that I have lots of stress and that it is destroying me." Thierno's sarcastic comment captured the madness of the situation so well that it released something in both of us. It made us laugh uncontrollably, fantasizing about an ever-growing list of amendments to the text that would have changed it from a letter of motivation into a testimony of destruction.

We were not alone in the struggle to fend off a deportation. Friends, family members, and colleagues joined in, and Thierno established links to refugee law activists willing to look over his legal case. A work colleague talked to his friend who headed an old people's home in Bern. She was compelled to help Thierno and take the risk of offering him a short-term apprenticeship (EBA) as a cook, despite his unstable immigration status and low school performance. An elderly Guinean man who had been living in Switzerland for over a decade took Thierno under his wing. He introduced him to Binta, a young Fulani woman from Conakry. Like Thierno, she had come to Europe as an unaccompanied minor, and she had traveled to France, where she had received political asylum. Rather than causing Binta to write Thierno off as a loser, the shared experience of displacement and her readiness to understand his desperate situation created an immediate bond between them. Even though they lived in different countries and Thierno was not allowed to leave Switzerland, they started a relationship. Bit by bit, Thierno managed to gather himself and cautiously recreate a sense of stability and hope. He accredited this mainly to the apprenticeship. "When I went to school I almost lost myself for a while," Thierno said, reflecting on his time in the integration class. "But now I have a sense of perspective because besides school I am doing an apprenticeship." The daily routine of work in the kitchen and the feeling of being a valued part of a team weakened the anxiety about his future. Even though Thierno had never envisaged himself as a cook and the apprenticeship was a product of necessity rather than choice, he came to identify with the profession. On good days he even dared to dream of opening his own restaurant.

Despite my critical stance toward the logic of inclusive exclusion pervading the integration classes, Thierno's experiences show that education remains a crucial catalyst for a social, emotional, and existential sense of mobility. Through the daily routine of learning and working toward something, he was able to stabilize the shaky grounds he was standing on and reach for new horizons of possibility. Working in the kitchen helped him stay sane and patch together some of his brokenness. However, we need to be careful not to romanticize the role of education as a form of healing. While education has assisted Thierno in regaining a sense of balance, it never managed to block out the dark future scenarios continuing to loom over the horizon. In September 2019, Thierno's first child was born in Paris, but because of his unresolved visa status, he was not able to leave Switzerland and live with Binta and his son. As Binta is on a temporary residence visa in France, she could not move to Switzerland either. This situation created a great amount of anxiety in Thierno, as he desperately waited for his asylum case to be resolved so that he could travel while simultaneously fearing its outcome. "Every time there is a letter in the letter box I am very stressed," he explained one afternoon as we were talking about his long wait for the decision on his asylum case. "My heart goes boom, boom, boom, and I don't want to know what news I will get this time."

Amid all these doubts, one thing became abundantly clear to Thierno. No matter the verdict of the Swiss immigration authorities, he did not want to return to Guinea. "I'm not going to let them send me back," he said as we were talking about his pending asylum case. Discussing the options he would have if he received another rejection letter, Thierno explained that he could not go to one of the neighboring countries and apply for asylum again. Because of the Dublin Convention, they would recognize that his fingerprint was already registered in Switzerland and return him straight into the arms of the Swiss immigration authorities, who would then be able to deport him. Talking about the cruelty of this trap, Thierno started to laugh. "You know what?" he said. "I could just cut off all my fingers and drown them at the bottom of the ocean." Thinking about it for a moment, he added, "I'm sure they would start looking for my fingers all over Europe. They would send divers to the bottom of the ocean to find them."

Thierno was correct to be worried. In 2020 his appeal was rejected, and he was summoned to leave the country. Before the Swiss authorities had a chance to detain him, he made his way to France to live with Binta and his son. Forced to abandon his apprenticeship and holding no permit to work or remain in France legally, Thierno found his situation highly precarious. Always on the alert for police controls and unable to find cash-in-hand jobs in the midst of the turmoil of the global COVID-19 pandemic, they depend on Binta's meager welfare payments. Yet despite the difficulty of life as a *sans papier*, Thierno insists that the certainty of uncertainty is better for him than the continuous waiting he was exposed to in Switzerland. At least in France he feels a bit more at home with the language and is embedded in a community of other Guineans. As I am writing, his battle for legal recognition has entered another round. With the help of refugee rights activists, he is looking for ways to legalize his status in France. As to my inquiries about his legal status, Thierno laughed. "You know me, Annika," he said. "I always have hope."

ETHNOGRAPHIC AFTERNOTE

As I move the ethnographic focus from the radio group to my second research site in Zürich, I believe it important to provide some concluding remarks on how I exited this particular field site. Research with marginalized groups of young people poses crucial ethical questions not just in terms of gaining access and establishing trustful relationships but also in terms of the ways researchers leave the field again. In the context of my research in Bern, this process was subtle and gradual. There was no clearly defined ending of the radio group or my research. In the autumn of 2016, the church community ended their contract with the child welfare organization, meaning that we lost our meeting space. For a while we kept catching up on a semiregular basis—at times in my apartment, at times in parks, in coffee shops, or in the young people's shared houses. Slowly these meetings became less frequent. The youth who had started apprenticeships had a full-time work week and did not have the energy for our regular gatherings. Other young people were preoccupied with bigger problems, such as their struggles at school, worries over their asylum procedures, or the effects of turning eighteen. While I kept in touch with all of the youths, at some point the importance of the group meetings dwindled away, until finally they came to a halt.

The tales of the four young people I focused on in the past chapters are only a selection of the gripping, touching, and thought-provoking life stories I came across during my collaboration with the radio group. While I found it immensely difficult to leave these stories out, I decided to keep the focus on youths I had been able to accompany to school, which allowed me to also give insights into their interactions with the teachers. It pains me that this choice means that some of the youths I worked with are not represented in the book. Their stories would have also made important points about refugee youths' struggle for social recognition and their attempts to defy the power of interior frontiers. This includes the story of Ella, a highly intelligent and self-determined young Eritrean woman. She was one of the most outspoken members of the radio group, and many of the youth turned to her for advice. When she was sixteen years old, she decided to leave Sudan, the place where she had been living with her mother and younger sister under extremely precarious conditions for over a decade. Tired of the daily abuse she had faced as an undocumented refugee working in constantly changing illegal jobs, she had left Sudan unannounced to pursue her educational dreams in Europe. If I had written a chapter about her, it would have been about the complex interplay of self-determination and social obligation that marked her experience of Switzerland. It would have been about the ways Ella's hopes for higher education and self-fulfillment increasingly came into conflict with the responsibility she felt to remain a good, deserving daughter and sister toward the loved ones she had left behind. It would have shown the gendered nature of these expectations and the impact the impossibility of living up to them had on Ella's ability to focus on her education.

Another amazing story that remains to be told is that of Lula, a young Eritrean woman who was the most sporadic member of the radio group. Like Ella, she had left her family in Eritrea when she was sixteen years old, determined to achieve a better education in Europe. Her story would tell of her disappointment about the educational opportunities she was denied access to in Switzerland and of the unknown strengths she developed in response. It would tell about the spring of 2016, when Lula suddenly disappeared, and about the news that started to surface about the incredible journey she had embarked on to gain access to the education she believed she deserved. After boarding a plane to Mexico, she made her way to the Mexico-US border, joining a group of young people from Central America who planned to cross the desert to go to the United States. After she had successfully crossed the border, she traveled through the entire country to make her way to Canada. Once again, she managed to cross the border and lodge an asylum application with the Canadian authorities. In 2018, when I heard of Lula again, she had not just received full refugee protection; she had also completed secondary schooling and was about to enroll at a Canadian university.

The book of untold stories would include another disappearance—the escape of Yusuf, who left Switzerland after his asylum application was rejected. Like Abdi, he was from the Somali minority in Ethiopia and had grown up in bitter poverty. Like Abdi, he had left the country to escape the violent ethnic conflict he had been socialized into, which he had increasingly grown tired of. And like Abdi, he had come to Switzerland hoping to make up for the schooling he had missed by training to become a computer specialist. Yusuf's story would be another testament to the creative and agentive determination the young people displayed in their struggle for education and a better future. After Yusuf received a negative decision on his asylum application, he called me to say goodbye, announcing that he was not going to sit around waiting for the Swiss to return him to Ethiopia. The next day he made his way to Germany. With the help of legal activists, he managed to lodge an appeal about the validity of the age-determination tests the Swiss authorities had performed on him, leading them to conclude that he was eighteen years old. The German authorities proved Yusuf right, arguing that he was only sixteen years old. As he was now regarded as underage and unaccompanied, he did not fall under the Dublin Convention. This meant that the authorities were not permitted to return him to Switzerland and that he was able to start a new asylum application in Germany. The ending of Yusuf's odyssey allows me to finish this brief excursion on a happy note. As I am writing, he is still living in Germany, where he managed to complete secondary schooling. At the moment Yusuf is attending a polytechnic specialized in IT. He is certain that this will enable him to fulfill his long-cherished dream of becoming a software specialist.

FIVE

—ɱ—

THE INTEGRATION PILOT

THE HOME FOR THE "INEDUCABLE"

In August 2015, I started research at my second field site, an education institution on the outskirts of Zürich. For a year I spent one full day per week there, spending time with eight unaccompanied Eritrean refugee youth who were attending an education program called the "integration pilot." I joined the boys in the training workshops, tagging along as they went about their work assignments. The institution offered training and closely supervised apprenticeships in seven trades: carpentry, metalwork, janitorial services, recycling, cooking, gardening, and housekeeping. During the year I conducted research there, the young men went through a cycle of work placements in each of these trades. The idea was that this would give them insights into the different work fields and help them decide which to choose for a two-year apprenticeship (EBA). I had also gained permission from the institution's head teacher to sit in on the boys' daily German lessons. Besides these educational activities, I participated in the shared lunch breaks, took part in meetings with the social pedagogues, and attended sports activities and excursions.

The beginning of my fieldwork coincided with the arrival of Abel, Kibrum, Haileb, Fikur, Kidane, Robel, Aaron, and Yonas, the eight Eritrean boys aged between fifteen and seventeen who were selected to participate in the pilot project. This was the first time the institution was offering its educational services to refugee youth. It was well-known across the canton for its expertise in education concepts targeted at young men from difficult backgrounds. The home's focus was on the rehabilitation of young offenders. The youth typically enrolled in the program were assigned there by the youth protection services in lieu of a prison sentence. The eight Eritreans did not fit into this profile. They had neither committed a crime nor been in trouble with the police. The only element uniting the two groups of youth living and working in the home was their interrupted schooling.

Because of the rhythms of life in an institutional setting, my fieldwork in Zürich was characterized by very different dynamics than my research in Bern. While I had met many of the young people in Bern in an institution, we had quickly moved beyond the walls of the home for unaccompanied minors. The creation of a social space that was determined by the young people themselves rather than by a set of rules and expectations imposed on them allowed the forging of relationships that were based on trust and a sense of mutual understanding. The creation of such a space allowed for personal experiences, alternative narratives, and critical questionings to become shareable. In my research in Zürich, there was no escaping the institutional boundaries, and that led to a radically different ethnographic angle. The eight young men were surrounded by a team of social pedagogues, work instructors, psychologists, teachers, and legal guardians, and their everyday paths were almost entirely channeled by the institution. From the 6:00 a.m. wake-up call to the five minutes set aside for brushing their teeth in the presence of a social pedagogue who checked their dental and bodily hygiene, the coffee breaks, the noon lunch routine, the apartment cleaning schedule, the hours set aside for supervised study or relaxation, and the time when they were supposed to turn off the lights, the boys' every move within the home followed a predetermined schedule. While hanging out and doing everyday things together had come naturally with the young people in Bern, in Zürich it was much more difficult for the youth to create pockets of autonomy.

The institution in Zürich was driven by a pedagogy of discipline. The core idea underlying its education program was that the young men attending it needed social, educational, and behavioral correction. This emphasis on correction is reflected in the word that was colloquially used to describe the institution: *Heim für Schwererziehbare*—a home for the ineducable. It was a place of last resort for young people who could not be reached with standard education measures. The pedagogues would frequently use the label *ineducable* to talk about the difficulty of channeling young men with a history of violence and family breakup into the right pathway. This sense of hopelessness showed in the program's high fluctuation rate. Only a small number of the young offenders enrolled there remained in the home long enough to complete their apprenticeships. Most of them stayed for a short while before they got into trouble again and were transferred to either youth prison or another rehabilitation program. The eight Eritreans were therefore thrown into a highly volatile environment. While they had joined the integration pilot in the hope of a better future, the other students had not come to the institution of their own free will. For many of them it was just another stopover on a long journey between educational and correctional facilities.

There was something deeply troubling about the social fabric of the institution. Outwardly, this was hard to grasp. The shared apartments and communal areas were located in beautifully renovated historic buildings, the workshops were equipped with top-notch machinery, the institution had sufficient funding to ensure one-on-one therapy sessions, and pedagogically trained work instructors guided the youths. But despite these outward signs of a healthy educational institution, its inner workings were not driven by a pedagogy of inclusion, hopefulness, or emancipation. My research revealed the contours of a space of educational abandonment—a space where youth marked as failures, dangers, or unruly young men were being "warehoused" (Slee 2011, 149) in the most unobtrusive way, until they were ready to be shipped off again. That the eight unaccompanied refugee youths ended up in this institution despite having had no history of criminal offense was no coincidence. As has become clear throughout the book, the creation of spaces of educational exclusion that are hidden behind a veneer of inclusion has a long historical trajectory in the Swiss education landscape. While clearly racialized, these spaces do not just affect unaccompanied refugee youth. The various groups the home for young offenders catered to hints at a much deeper rift within the Swiss education system that channels young people marked as problem cases into segregated and lower-tiered forms of schooling.

In the final chapter of the book, I turn my focus on the zones of educational abandonment the logic of inclusive exclusion brings about. I inquire into their social texture and explore how far the educational exclusion of unaccompanied refugee youth corresponds with wider sociopolitical dynamics that lead to the creation of new educational underclasses. Having spelled out the various ways the logic of inclusive exclusion enters and permeates refugee youths' lives, in this chapter I trace the micro and macro dynamics whereby the idea of fostering refugee youths' inclusion in society through an institution designed for the exclusion of the "ineducable" becomes perfectly acceptable. I do so by zooming in on the everyday hopes, ideas, and expectations underwriting the integration pilot. The social pedagogues' and refugee youths' different perceptions of the project expose the damaging power of the logic of inclusive exclusion. This logic does more than affect the education of marginalized individuals. In fortifying divisions between a cozy, uncomplicated "us" of shared values and a troubled, unruly, nonintegrable "them," it reaches into the heart of interior frontiers. The stories of the eight young men attending the integration pilot show that the experience of being cornered into such an educational dead end does not just come at the expense of upward social mobility in the realms of Swiss society. It impinges on the young people's most intimate hopes for forward movement in the realms of their own lives.

THE OTHER SIDE OF THE ROAD

By September 2015 all of the eight young Eritreans selected to participate in the integration pilot had arrived. They had moved into three shared apartments in a building next to the busy road that formed an unspoken boundary between two distinct social spheres in the microcosm of the institution: while the youth classified as "dissocial" (*dissozial*) lived in tightly supervised shared apartments in the main building complex, the refugee kids were placed in a house on the opposite side of the road. The house had been empty for many years, but social pedagogues who had been around long enough remembered a time when it had accommodated young offenders who had proven themselves trustworthy enough to be placed in less strictly monitored living arrangements. However, they noted that this was back in the days when the institution still received "easy" cases—youth who had briefly lost their path and just needed some help to get back on track. Nowadays the cantonal child protection authorities refused to spend money on expensive preventive measures, and so the youth assigned to institutions like this were all "hard-core" cases—the most aggressive, dangerous, and damaged young people, for whom help was usually already too late.

The official statistics showed a steady decline in criminal offenses committed by youth in Zürich between 2012 and 2014 (Kantonspolizei Zürich 2014, 5). However, the social pedagogues argued that this did not mean that fewer young people were going astray. The decline was mainly attributed to the fact that the authorities were less likely to classify young people as delinquent. This had two positive side effects for the cantonal government. It made the crime rates look better and justified cost-cutting measures in the area of youth development. In the home this led to a noticeable decline in the number of youths the authorities allocated to the rehabilitation program. In an interview, Mr. Brugger, the director of the home, said that besides the decline in young offenders, he had observed a general trend of sending troubled youth to short-term programs that only offered daytime supervision rather than to more expensive institutions that also offered supervised housing, apprenticeship trainings, and in-house schooling. He noted that youth welfare agencies often used the principle of inclusion to justify their decision, arguing that young people's prolonged stay in separate educational streams was not desirable. Mr. Brugger was not convinced of the sincerity of that argument. "The problem is that nobody knows whether it is really that much better to treat them [the youths] as outpatients rather than inpatients, or if they [the cantonal authorities] are only doing it for economic reasons," he said. Mr. Brugger emphasized that he was not against the principle of inclusion per se. He was in his midsixties and had spent his entire career dedicated to the education of youth in difficult situations, almost two decades of it as the head of the home for young offenders. He passionately believed in the importance of giving marginalized youth a chance to complete their education, yet he was not sure that inclusive education concepts were the right way to get there. "Nowadays we have to integrate everybody, the normal ones and the very conspicuous ones," he said. "But in the end of the day we are not doing them [the latter] a favor, because they remain outsiders and finally, they will end up in a place like this again." The bottom line of all these developments was that the institution received fewer young people and that those who arrived had typically already been through a number of measures before the authorities agreed to finance their stay in the home.

In 2015, when the cantonal department for youth and career counseling called upon education institutions in Zürich to help accommodating the great number of unaccompanied minors waiting to be schooled, Mr. Brugger saw this as an opportunity to do something with the available education structures, which had few resources left. Together with Sebastian, the head of the pedagogical program, he developed the integration pilot, and after some lobbying, he successfully gained funding for it. Ironically, the refugee crisis thus formed a lucky coincidence for the institution. The director liked to frame his decision to initiate the project for unaccompanied minors in terms of the need to respond to the refugee crisis and the overburdened education system. The social pedagogues were less diplomatic about the motives. They were up-front about the fact that the decision was based on the institution's financial crisis rather than a humanitarian urge to help needy children. One work instructor even joked that the refugee youth "saved our asses." This ironic observation was not too far from the truth. The three-year pilot project with the unaccompanied minors helped the institution weather a financial dry patch. Midway through the project, the youth crime rates started to pick up again (Kantonspolizei Zürich 2017), and by the end of it, the home was back to its former occupancy rates.

The institution had a long history of dealing with troubled youth. It was established in the nineteenth century as a charitable foundation, initially as a home for impoverished girls. In 1945 the foundation turned its focus to the education and resocialization of delinquent young men, and this has remained its area of expertise ever since. The pilot project with unaccompanied refugee youth was the first such experiment in the institution. In cooperation with Daniel, one of the three legal guardians for unaccompanied minors in the canton of Zürich, they selected eight Eritrean youth to participate in the program. At the time Daniel was responsible for the well-being and legal guidance of over one hundred unaccompanied refugee youths, most of whom were past the obligatory schooling cutoff age. As there was no cantonal education strategy for them, he saw the integration pilot as a rare opportunity to give some of the youth access to apprenticeships. There were no clear selection criteria for the pilot project, except that the youth needed to have successfully completed the asylum procedure and learned enough German to communicate on a basic level. "Of course, we made sure that we didn't take the antisocial ones," Mr. Brugger explained, when I asked him how they had chosen the eight Eritreans from the hundreds of unaccompanied refugee youths in Zürich eager to gain access to education. "We said that if we are doing this and the state spends so much money on them, we have to ensure that the ones we pick are going to be successful and financially independent afterwards." His statement reveals the ways the project intersected with frameworks of un/deservingness from the get-go. Given the heated debates about the un/deservingness of refugees' access to public resources, the institution needed to make sure that they only chose youth who fulfilled the benchmarks of deservingness. They needed to be individuals of good moral character who had been judged to be genuine refugees, who had proven their willingness to "integrate" (or assimilate), and who had shown the capacity to join the workforce. In the words of neoliberal discourses about cost effectiveness and self-sufficiency, education needed to be an investment that would pay off.

Scholars have demonstrated the ways ideas of un/deservingness intersect with the neoliberal transformation of welfare states (Oorschot 2000; Haney 2003) and the moral economies of immigration regimes (Watters 2007; Dhaliwal and Forkert 2016), leading to the moralization of distribution and forms of "welfare chauvinism" (Jørgensen and Thomsen 2016). Yet so far very little research has looked into the ways these dynamics affect the funding of education programs for refugees. In their analysis of school finance reform in the United States, Emily Meanwell and Julie Swando (2013, 504) found that public narratives about marginalized children's deservingness played a crucial role in the funding of education projects. As in the funding claims of the integration pilot, some children were depicted as less deserving of educational resources than others: "In particular, children who were considered troublemakers, who had been violent, or who were assumed to not put an appropriate amount of effort into their education were sometimes portrayed as less deserving of educational resources. In this way, claims that all children are deserving were countered by the argument that some children were not *as* deserving" (Meanwell and Swando 2013, 506).

As in the dynamics described by Meanwell and Swando, my conversation with Mr. Brugger shows the funding of education projects for marginalized youth to be inextricably connected to moral delineations of un/deservingness. This does not just concern the education of unaccompanied refugee youth. The directors' struggle to justify the costs of educating youth categorized as "dissocial" shows that the question of whose education deserves to be advanced is part of much wider societal debates about the distribution of shared resources. In times of neo-liberal spending cuts, access to scarce common resources is highly competitive. In the run for these goods, migrants and refugees are often the first ones to lose out. This was shown in Wim van Oorschot's (2006) comprehensive analysis of deservingness perceptions in European welfare states. He speaks of a "deserving-ness culture" that is shared across Europe. It is driven by the hierarchization of poverty that ranks elderly people as most deserving, followed by sick and disabled people. While unemployed people are seen as less deserving, migrants are situated at the very bottom of this hierarchy.

The initiators of the integration pilot needed to carefully consider the kinds of refugee youth they were targeting in order to convince the funding bodies that they were not wasting public money on the wrong individuals. That they only accepted refugee youth who had completed the asylum procedure was not a co-incidence. It was linked to the insistence by the Swiss government that education needed to be treated as an integration measure and that such valuable resources should only go to individuals who had received permission to stay. It was also no coincidence that only refugee youth classified as unaccompanied minors quali-fied for the project. At the height of the wave of compassion surrounding the refu-gee crisis, the exceptional vulnerability of these child figures worked to justify the funding of programs such as the integration pilot. It was much harder to justify projects for the education of refugee youth who had arrived in Switzerland with their parents or of young people who were over the age of eighteen.

Driven by these underlying ideas and dynamics, the legal guardian helped the project initiators select eight young men who had struck him as particularly bright and motivated. Abel and Kibrum, for example, had come to Daniel's atten-tion as they had repeatedly called him, begging for his help in finding a way for them to go to school. Some of the other youths had caught his attention through their cooperativeness in taking over little chores in the home for unaccompanied minors or their good German language skills. The idea was that the eight young men who were selected for the project should benefit from the established educa-tion structures in the institution, which would guide them through apprentice-ships and get them used to a working routine. Ultimately the project should lead to the successful completion of a short-term apprenticeship and the ability to live self-reliantly and gain financial independence from the state. Throughout this process the Eritrean youth should be kept apart from the "trouble kids" as much as possible, mainly by separating their living arrangements; the communal areas where they had breakfast, lunch, and dinner; and their lessons in the internal school. Despite this separation, the pedagogues fostered interactions between the two groups in the workshops, mainly in the hope that the refugee youths' enthusiasm would exert a positive influence on the other youths.

The division between the youths living at the two sides of the road brought about uneven relationships. The young offenders were continually told to follow the refugee youths' example. This added another spin on the theme of un/deservingness, as the majority of the youths classified as "dissocial" were first- or second-generation migrants and thus fed into dominant narratives of "good" and "bad" migrant youth. At the same time, the eight Eritreans were continually reminded that if they were not diligent enough, they could easily end up with the kids on the opposite side of the road. While Mr. Brugger was adamant that the unaccompanied refugee youths should not be integrated into social structures of delinquency, most of the rules designed to monitor the resocialization process of troubled youths also applied to the refugee kids. This included random inspections of the apartments, the prohibition of unpermitted guests, the duty to hand in keys and mobile phones when at work, the social pedagogues' control over weekly allowances, adherence to a strict daily schedule, the duty to check in and out when leaving the premises, and compliance with the night curfew. The strict routines show how quickly categorizations of deservingness become blurred and shift into other, less desirable attributes, such as potential delinquency, loss of the right path, or distrust. While the young Eritreans occupied the highest position on the home's internal scale of un/deservingness, this position was everything but stable.

The idea of inclusion promoted in the home was thus marked by many ambiguities. On the one hand, the integration pilot was meant to enhance unaccompanied refugee youths' inclusion in Swiss society. On the other hand, it did so through an institution designed to cater to educational outcasts. Even within this irregular educational program, the refugee youths were treated as exceptional cases in need of separate education. The exclusionary idea of inclusion the integration pilot was based on might appear to be paradoxical. The social pedagogues working in the project, the director and pedagogue who designed it, the legal guardians who supported it, and the authorities who funded it, however, did not perceive the idea of enhancing inclusion through exclusion to be irreconcilable. That they did not says a lot about the inner workings of the logic of inclusive exclusion and the ways it has come to permeate education landscapes, leading to the normalization of zones of educational abandonment.

INCLUSION THROUGH EXCLUSION

As in many other parts of the world, the notion of inclusion has made a triumphal march through the public discursive sphere in Switzerland. In the so-called Curriculum 21 (*Lehrplan 21*), a major educational overhaul aimed at harmonizing elementary school curricula across the twenty-one German-speaking Swiss cantons, the principle of inclusion plays a crucial role. It recommends the creation of heterogeneous classrooms, where rich and poor, abled and disabled children, as well as children from all national backgrounds, are taught together (D-EDK 2016). Mirroring this aspiration, the education board of the Canton of Zürich officially recommends that "newly arrived children and youth, including refugees, have to be supported so that they are able to gain access to all levels of regular education as fast as possible" (Bildungsdirektion Kanton Zürich 2017, 6, my translation). This shift toward inclusionary education policies is not new. It is the outcome of debates from the 1980s, when scholars and practitioners rallied against the educational segregation of disabled children. They were eager to create alternative understandings of school failure and move beyond the emphasis on defect, expert diagnosis, and remediation marking the education of children with disabilities (Slee 2011, 110). Their suggestions for an inclusive education reform were picked up and promoted by a number of international bodies, such as UNESCO, UNICEF, and OECD. These combined efforts culminated in the Salamanca Statement and Framework for Action on Special Needs Education in 1994. The statement urged governments around the world to develop new educational frameworks that take into account the diversity of students and their specific needs. It also suggested that all students should have access to regular schools and that schools must be equipped to accommodate the inclusion of heterogeneous groups of youth.

While the impetus for the statement had come from debates in the field of disability education, it did not treat educational segregation as an isolated problem affecting this particular group of children only: "The guiding principle that informs this framework is that schools should accommodate all children regardless of their physical, intellectual, social, emotional, linguistic or other conditions. This should include disabled and gifted children, street and working children, children from remote or nomadic populations, children from linguistic, ethnic or cultural minorities and children from other disadvantaged or marginalized areas and groups" (UNESCO 1994, 6).

The Salamanca Statement opened the door to the formulation of a much wider critique of the complicity of schools in the reproduction of marginalization and inequality. It formed a breakthrough moment for the principle of inclusion in education policies across the world, initiating a range of reforms. These international discourses also made their way to Switzerland and into education concepts aimed at migrant children. From the 1970s, the conference of cantonal education directors (*Konferenz der kantonalen Erziehungsdirektoren*, or EDK) started to formulate policies for the inclusion of migrants in state education programs. In its recommendations the EDK emphasized that schools should develop measures to enable migrant children's participation in mainstream public schooling and that school success should not be made overly dependent on language proficiency (Kronig, Haeberlin, and Eckhart 2000, 11–12). Over the years, these recommendations have been repeatedly adapted and extended, emphasizing the importance of migrant youths' inclusion in mainstream schooling. In its response to a parliamentary inquiry into the rightfulness of the separate schooling of migrant children in 1999, the Swiss Federal Council was clear that this was a discriminatory practice that left migrant children at a disadvantage. The government put on the record that "the formation of separate classes is irreconcilable with the education and integration task of the school" (EDI 1999, my translation).

Given this long-standing commitment to inclusive education principles, the question arises how it can be that two decades later refugee youth are still taught in separate educational tracks. How is it possible that segregated education institutions such as the home for young offenders continue to exist? Why are migrant youth much more likely to end up in such places than Swiss nationals are? And how can the aim to create participation and equality go hand in hand with the compulsion to separate? These contradictory impulses reveal the ambiguous shapes the paradigm of inclusion has taken on since entering the policy arena in the 1980s. As inconsistent and questionable as these impulses might seem, they feed into a much wider landscape of contradictions characterizing the education of marginalized youth. Over time, this contradictoriness has taken on a logic of its own and become normalized to the point that the principles of inclusion and exclusion no longer appear to contradict each other.

Roger Slee (2011, 117) points out that as groundbreaking as the Salamanca Statement was, it almost immediately led to the introduction of cascade models, which subverted and evaded the principle of inclusion. He links this development to the effect of neoliberal school reforms and the new pressures they have put on schools and teachers. Such reforms have also had an impact on Switzerland, a country with a long tradition of economic liberalism. Swiss education policies have long promoted the idea of individualized responsibility and the need to educate young people to become flexible and adaptable citizens (Schwiter 2013). Students are to be molded into resilient and productive citizens who do not rely on state support. The flip side of these developments is the disqualification of those who fail to conform to these expectations. Slee (2011, 121) argues that in an age of neoliberal school reforms, narrow understandings of standardization have compromised the educational imagination to such a degree that children who do not conform to the picture of the ideal, individualized student are perceived as threats. Disabled and disruptive children, or—as in the case of refugee youth— young people who deviate from normalized educational trajectories, are seen as additional burdens on schools. As pointed out before, this leads to an impulse to protect successful, "normal" students from contagion by "problem" students who risk bringing down the standard for everyone. Despite schools' often genuine interest in fostering inclusive learning environments, the fear of negative rankings incentivizes the outsourcing of students believed to be too slow, compromised, or troubled to keep up with the standard (Crea et al. 2018, 253). It has led to the creation of special tracks for a growing number of students who are labeled as second and third tier, thereby undermining attempts to create genuinely inclusive education environments (Slee 2011, 144). In Switzerland, political promises of inclusive education concepts have largely remained rhetoric. Scholars have repeatedly voiced critiques of the unwillingness of cantonal authorities to commit to the creation of inclusive education environments and of their countless attempts to justify the continued exclusion of disabled children, "trouble" students from low socioeconomic backgrounds, or migrant youth. It has led to the stubborn persistence of *Sonderschulen* (separate schools for disabled children), separate educational tracks, and multitiered selection processes sieving out academically minded students from those designated for the lower-skilled job market (Achermann 2017; Hofstetter 2017; Oester and Lems 2017). As the education projects for unaccompanied minors that are detailed in this book show, these alternative provisions are often not labeled as irregular or "special" forms of schooling. But even though they carry agreeable-sounding titles such as "integration pilot" or "integration classes," in practice they reproduce spaces of segregation. Once students are sidelined and marked as problem cases, it becomes difficult, if not impossible, for them to make the jump back into mainstream schooling.

The logic of inclusive exclusion does not take on one single shape or form. At times it appears in explicit ways, as in the home for young offenders, where youth marked as "problematic" are permanently excluded and kept apart from regular schooling. More often, however, the logic of inclusive exclusion shows in much more subtle ways—for example through separate tracks within mainstream schools or, as in the case of the bridging schools, through the relabeling of irregular forms of schooling to give them the pretense of leading toward mainstream education. What makes the exclusionary nature of these forms of schooling so hard to grasp is that they do not openly propagate the segregation of students with access needs but operate under the smoke screen of inclusive education policy (Slee 2011, 144). The schooling of disabled children in separate classes is justified by the argument that this is for their own good as they would struggle and be marked as outsiders if they were included in a mainstream setting. Segregated education institutions for "troubled" youth are justified by the students' emotional and psychological vulnerability and their need for specialized care. The educational isolation of refugee and migrant youth is backed up by the argument of providing a protected space for them to arrive and catch up on their educational deficits. Despite its broad emancipatory ambitions, the paradigm

of inclusion has thus not succeeded in dissolving discriminatory educational practices. Instead, such practices were often simply "transformed into more sophisti-
cated, less offensive, and at least superficially inclusive forms" (Baumann 2004, 11).

The logic of inclusive exclusion legitimates the creation of zones of educational abandonment, places such as the home for young offenders, where young
people marked as problem cases are made to disappear from the radar—without,
however, doing so in an obvious way. In relation to the education of low-income
African American and Latino youths in the United States, Tyson E. Lewis (2010,
34) describes forms of education that hide away young people who have been
written off as problem cases as "necroschooling." It is a kind of schooling "that
is more concerned with abandonment than with social investment, protection,
etc." In signaling to certain youths that they cannot be trusted to participate as
valued members of society, in giving up on them and anticipating their futures
in low-wage labor jobs or prison rather than empowering them to achieve more,
such schooling exposes them to a form of social death.

Despite its powerful effects, the abandonment that is the outcome of inclusive exclusion does not occur in obvious, explicit ways. Often these mechanisms
operate below the surface of perceptibility, in ways that do not filter down to
people's consciousness. The "local moral economies" (Willen 2015, 72) marking
social interactions in the home for young offenders makes graspable the hidden,
often unconscious ways the logic of inclusive exclusion inserts itself into everyday
life. Sarah Willen (2015) coined the term "local moral economy" to capture how
the un/deservingness of refugees is negotiated and made sense of on an everyday,
local basis. She stresses that moral economies should not be thought of as homogenous normative frameworks but as vernacular frameworks of reference, which are
constituted by historically and culturally specific constellations of affect, value,
memory, and expectation. Willen notes that within the intimate realms of local
moral economies, "individuals and human communities struggle with fundamental questions of 'what's at stake' and 'what really matters' either in a single moment
or as they proceed through life's scenes and stages" (Willen 2015, 72; cf. Kleinman
2006). As I turn to the local moral frameworks of reference underwriting the integration pilot, I explore the question of *what really matters* to the young people
involved in it and how this corresponds or clashes with the social pedagogues'
ideas of what is at stake in the project. In keeping my focus on the refugee youth, I
want to make visible the social traces the logic of inclusive exclusion leaves behind
in individuals and the ways it affects their orientation to the world.

HOPES AND THEIR TRAJECTORIES

In the first two months of my fieldwork in Zürich, I had many conversations with
the eight young Eritreans about the expectations they had for the institution and

about the hopes they held for their futures. While they had different stories and trajectories, each of them had joined the integration pilot in the hope of making up for the years of education they had lost. Having spent months, often even years, in refugee camps and child protection institutions, they saw their participation in the project as an opportunity to finally start working on their futures.

I soon realized that many of the young men were entangled in long-lasting relationships of care. Besides protection, trust, and support, these relationships were held together by shared histories of hope. Seventeen-year-old Fikur and Kidane had grown up in the same village close to the capital city of Asmara. They had gone to school together and spent their afternoons playing soccer with other village youths. It was at the soccer pitch that they had first heard about the possibility of leaving for Europe. Other young people had told them about brothers, sisters, or cousins who had left the country to escape the year in the Sawa military training camp and complete their education elsewhere. Fikur and Kidane had traveled independently, but ever since meeting each other again in Switzerland, they had become inseparable. They had shared a room in the home for unaccompanied minors, and when Fikur learned that he was selected for the integration pilot, he had insisted that he would not go without his friend Kidane. Sixteen-year-old Robel, Aaron, and Abel had met in an Ethiopian refugee camp and spent several years there. When they left their families in Eritrea, Aaron was only ten years old and Abel and Robel were twelve. In the camp the younger children had relied on one another's social and emotional support as they were largely left to look after themselves.

In a harsh environment such as the Ethiopian refugee camps, the forging of relationships of care with other young people was essential. The social weight of such friendships was symbolized in the handmade tattoos I kept noticing on the upper arms of young Eritreans I met throughout my fieldwork. They depicted the initials of their closest friends, usually same-aged boys and girls they had met in Ethiopian refugee camps or on their journeys to Europe and who had become their most important companions and surrogate families. When I asked Robel about his tattoo, he stroked it affectively, telling me that it stood for his three closest friends, two boys and a girl he had met in Ethiopia. They had looked after one another in the camp, and even though they were living in different countries across Europe now, they remained the most important people in his life. I asked whether it had not hurt to scribe the letters into his skin without proper tools. "Oh, it hurts a lot," Robel responded. "But that's Ethiopia. Everything hurts there." Reflecting on their time in Ethiopia, Abel, Aaron, and Robel said that besides the daily struggle for food and survival, they had felt that their lives were stalling. The school inside the camp did not lead them anywhere, and they did not have permission to go to local schools. While each of them set off at different times and had their own means of paying for the journey—some through their families, others by working along the way—the hope for education played a major role for all of them in their decision to follow the thousands of Eritrean youths heading for Europe.

In the young men's accounts, the lack of access to education often featured as a troubling condition of enforced stasis, causing them to feel sick, empty, and hopeless. They told me about the endless hours they had spent in Ethiopian refugee camps, not knowing what to do. "We couldn't do anything all day," Kibrum said, reflecting on his time in the camp. "All we did was sleep, and when there was food, eat." Haileb and Fikur said that they had developed sleeping disorders during the two years they had spent in the home for unaccompanied minors in Zürich. They were convinced that the fact that they had not been allowed to go to school had caused this sickness. Similarly, Kibrum and Abel said that they had fallen into depression after they realized they would not be able to go to school in Switzerland. They had arrived in the home for unaccompanied minors around the same time and supported each other like brothers ever since. "Nobody listened to us," Kibrum said, referring to the countless attempts they had made to enroll at a school. When they understood that neither the social workers nor their legal guardian were able to help them, the two friends had fallen into a deep sadness. This sadness, they explained, had been so powerful that it made it hard for them to perform essential daily routines, such as getting out of bed, eating, or socializing.

The social paralysis the humanitarian regime (be it in Ethiopian or Swiss refugee camps) forced them into was not what the young men had had in mind when they left Eritrea. Abel's decision to leave was largely driven by the hope for educational advancement. When he was eleven years old, his world was turned upside down. His mother was admitted to the hospital after a complicated birth, and when his father asked for extended leave of absence from national service duties to be with her and the children, the request was turned against him. The authorities accused him of intended desertion, and he was led away by the military police in the middle of the night to be incarcerated in an unknown place. These events led Abel's mother to take him out of school—partially because she feared for his safety and partially because she needed his help at home. As a result of his father's arrest, Abel had been forced to stay at home all day, unable to do anything to improve his family's situation or at least work toward a better future. The lack of future opportunity was one of the main reasons he had decided to leave. The other seven young men had similar reasons. While each of them had different stories, they had all left the country to escape the forced recruitment into the Eritrean national army. The impossibility of upward social mobility and, most importantly, of freedom of movement were key factors propelling them to leave. They felt that in Eritrea they could not move in any direction, that they were held back by a system that paralyzed their futures. Alcinda Honwana (2012) describes this sense of paralysis as "waithood," a condition shared by many young people attempting to get by in African postcolonial societies, which are marked by political instability, unemployment, and failed neoliberal structural adjustment programs. These uncertainties have created a generational trap for young people, making it impossible for them to move beyond the social category of youth and attain the perquisites of adulthood. The militarization of the Eritrean state exposes young people to a general atmosphere of uncertainty, distrust, and lack of future prospects. Drawing on research in Eritrean schools, Jennifer Riggan (2013) found that students and teachers constructed emigration as a national duty, as a sacrifice they needed to make for the greater good. Similarly, Magnus Treiber (2018, 60) notes that the absence of opportunity has led to a situation in which Eritrean youth "feel guilty for staying, and for being a burden to their family, when they should instead be trying their luck migrating towards a better future."

The eight young Eritreans had hoped that the journey to Europe would allow them to move onward and upward, not just economically but also socially and, perhaps even more importantly, existentially. They considered education to be the driving force that would allow them to achieve this kind of forward movement, and as they could not gain access to it in Eritrea or Ethiopia, they went in search of it elsewhere. When I asked Abel what had propelled him to leave the refugee camp and embark on the dangerous journey to Europe, he responded that it had been the idea of getting an education. The content of these educational aspirations remained rather vague, partially perhaps because he had no idea how the education systems in other countries actually worked and, as Abel put it, because he was on a journey where "you do not know whether you will still be alive the next day." But one idea about the future kept him going: "What I always thought about was that when I arrive, I will first get to go to a good school and after that I will look for work." The idea of "a good school" kept reappearing in the young men's accounts. It had also been the main reason Haileb had decided not to remain in Italy after his voyage across the Mediterranean. Even though he had been sick and weakened from the passage, which he had spent in the cheapest and worst spot of the boat—underneath the floorboards right next to the engine—he mustered all his energy to evade the police controls and make his way to Switzerland. "Somebody told me 'in Switzerland you can go to school and it is not so far away from Italy,'" Haileb said, recounting a crucial moment in his journey. "That's what I heard and that's why I came over here."

Just as the young men's migratory paths followed a web of relationally constituted trajectories, so did their hopes of education as a vehicle for forward movement. These hopes can be traced back to Eritrea's long struggle for independence and the important role ideas of youth and progress came to occupy in this context.

Eritrea's thirty-year war with Ethiopia was never just about gaining indepen-dence. It was driven by hope for a social revolution that would encompass the entire society. Education and youth played a major role in these plans. Schooling was seen as a key tool for creating a modern, enlightened, and just society, and youth were regarded as the bearers of this revolutionary change (Treiber 2018, 50). Magnus Treiber (2018, 54) points out that in the first decade after independence, Eritrean youth were eager to take part in this new project of nation building, and they saw their personal futures as linked to the future of Eritrea. This changed at the outbreak of the bloody border war with Ethiopia between 1998 and 2000. It caused a collective feeling of disenchantment and initiated an authoritarian shift in Eritrean leadership, the dismantling of the higher education system, and the merging of education with the military regime (56). These shifts and the resulting lack of prospects have initiated a youth exodus from Eritrea.

When attempting to understand this exodus, one cannot look only at the po-litical oppression in Eritrea, even though it undoubtedly plays a crucial role in people's decisions to flee. As emphasized throughout the book, displacement is never a linear phenomenon; it refuses to be captured one-dimensionally. If we are to better understand the social physics leading an entire generation of young Eritreans to look for their futures elsewhere, we need to take seriously the his-tory of hopes propelling their journeys (cf. Ferguson 1999). To paraphrase Stef Jansen (2014, 79), such "emic histories of yearning for movement" allow us to move beyond deterministic explanatory patterns. They enable us to grasp the existen-tial kinetics underwriting migratory movements (Lems 2019). The eight Eritrean youth living in the home in Zürich did not describe the forces propelling them to migrate solely in economic terms or in terms of the oppressive political situ-ation in Eritrea. Rather, they had been drawn toward migration because of the radical transformation of self and personhood they believed it would offer. In his research with unemployed young men in Ethiopia, Daniel Mains (2007, 669) observed that the decision to migrate was driven by the hope that it would allow them to instantaneously transform themselves into self-fulfilled, adult persons. The best way to enact that transformation was by attaching themselves to the modern, progressive values they believed Western countries to characterize. As with the Eritrean youth in my research, their educational aspirations were linked to particular ideas of progress and modernity. Education was seen as a linear process involving gradual improvements: "As one advances from grade to grade, it is assumed that this movement creates a change within oneself. The educated individual expects to be transformed so that his future will be better than the present" (Mains 2007, 665).

For the young men in Zürich, education formed the strongest progressive force, which, they believed, would propel them forward and finally also upward.

It is important to emphasize that this hope of forward movement through education was not purely driven by a desire for upward social mobility, and therefore by the wish to be included in the capitalist order of things. It also contained the hope for personal transformation, a feeling of inner forward movement. Ghassan Hage (2009) describes this inner kind of forward movement—the sense of moving forward within the realms of one's own lifeworld—as "existential mobility." It captures an imaginary mobility, the feeling that one is "going somewhere." This feeling is by no means banal. Hage (2009, 98) points out that it is precisely the lack of a feeling of going somewhere that underwrites many migratory projects. Migrants frequently engage in physical activity because they are after an inner, existential sense of forward movement: "In a sense, we can say that people migrate because they are looking for a space that constitutes a suitable launching pad for their social and existential self. They are looking for a space and a life where they feel they are going somewhere as opposed to nowhere, or at least, a space where the quality of their 'going-ness' is better than what it is in the space they are leaving behind" (Hage 2009: 98).

Hage's statement perfectly illustrates the existential kinetics underlying the young men's hopes of "movement-through-education" (Lems 2019). Throughout their migratory journeys toward Switzerland, the eight young men had been propelled forward by the hope for education as a launching pad for their existential selves. After they received a good education, they hoped, their going-ness would be better, enabling them to finally take charge of their own lives and futures. In doing so, they would not only fulfill their own aspirations; they would also be able to fulfill the hopes of their family members back in Eritrea. The eight young Eritreans often told me that their parents did not expect them to refund the money for their journeys or send remittances back home. But they did expect their sons to use the educational opportunities they received in Switzerland as a means of making something of themselves, of learning a respectable profession and moving toward a better future.

And so the young men had joined the integration pilot driven by the hope of achieving an inner, existential kind of forward movement and an outer, social kind of upward movement. Yet, while they had hoped education to be a vehicle that would allow them to gain control over their own lives and destinies, once they had made their way to Switzerland, what they imagined to be a driving force quickly turned out to be a potential new stumbling block. Thinking back to the hopefulness that had carried him through his excruciating migratory journey, Kibrum laughed about his own naivete. He said that before coming to Switzerland he had been sure he would gain access to the great education system everybody kept talking about. "When I was in Zürich I thought, 'I am here, but where is the good school?'" Kibrum said. "I had heard that there was a good school, but actually it isn't really like that. Until now I have not learned together with the Swiss." As the eight young men settled into the home and integration pilot, they came to the realization that they had been led on an educational sidetrack.

MOOD SWINGS

While the young men's participation in the integration pilot had been driven by particular histories of hopes, the social pedagogues supervising them had joined the project with their own hopes and expectations. When I started my research in the home, they were happy and excited about the young Eritreans' arrival. They told me that they had expected the teenagers to be scarred by their traumatic experiences and by the separation from their parents, which would make it difficult to build relationships with them. They had also worried that it would be hard to communicate with the boys because of their German language deficits. Once the eight participants had arrived, the youth workers were relieved to see that it was not difficult to interact with them. While all four social pedagogues had worked with migrant-background youth before, none of them had experience in working with recently arrived refugees. Their core sources of information about the young Eritreans joining the project were media reports about the situation of refugee children and the terrible journeys they had to endure to get to Switzerland. Deeply touched by these stories, they were eager to provide a social environment that would allow the young men to feel safe and experience a teenage normality.

The supervision team included Marina, a bubbly woman in her midthirties. She was from the French-speaking part of Switzerland and had moved to Zürich after her graduation as a social pedagogue. Having struggled to learn German herself, she hoped that the shared experience of speaking in a foreign language would allow her to form a special connection with the young refugees. The team further comprised George, an introverted and soft-spoken man in his forties who had been working in the institution for over a decade, and Tom, the intern, who was completing his social work degree. The team was headed by Sebastian, a tall and outspoken German with years of experience in youth development work. Together with Mr. Brugger he had designed the pedagogical concept of the integration pilot, an achievement he was proud of. Sebastian was convinced that the project would enable this group of vulnerable young people to advance educationally and emotionally and that they would leave the program as responsible and self-confident young adults who were fit for life in Swiss society. When he spoke of his hopes for the project, he liked to refer to Neuland, a popular Swiss documentary (Thommen 2013). The film depicts everyday life in a reception class for newly arrived migrants in Basel. It follows the ups and downs of the young students in their attempts to secure a future in Switzerland. One afternoon when

I joined Sebastian for a coffee after lunch, he described how he imagined the young men's journey through the integration pilot to follow the storyboard of the film. It started with the moment the boys got out of the car and were introduced to the institution. It went on with their first steps there, showing that the social pedagogues had to teach them basic manners, such as cleaning their teeth and apartments. Spinning the story further, he imagined the camera to capture the boys as they learned in the workshops, signed their apprenticeship contracts, and received their diplomas. When Sebastian came to the ending of the film—the diploma ceremony—he imagined it to be festive and emotional, adding that he was sure the boys would shed some tears. "Just imagine, if we really manage to get all eight of them through their apprenticeships, this will be a great achievement," Sebastian said, concluding his imaginary journey. From my conversations with the social pedagogues, I learned that they saw their work in the integration pilot as an opportunity to take on a meaningful task. As empathetic and open-minded citizens, they were eager to use their expertise to help these parentless children find their way. They hoped that they would achieve a transformation in the young men that was important not just for their individual futures but for the future of Swiss society at large. They understood their roles as social pedagogues as gatekeepers of Swiss society. As if following neoliberal discursive shifts in the education landscape, they saw it as their main task to educate the young men into responsible citizens who would not rely on state support (Chalhi, Koster, and Vermeulen 2018, 851). A crucial part of becoming such a responsible member of society was to be socialized into a Swiss system of values.

All four social pedagogues had previously worked on the other side of the road with the young offenders. Being used to a conflict-laden environment, they were initially perplexed by the unproblematic new working conditions they encountered with the refugee youth. At the same time, they often told me that this behavior was just what they had expected. They saw the boys' eagerness to learn and participate as a confirmation of their belief that the project formed an amazing opportunity for them, a door opener most refugee youth never received. Like the teachers in the bridging school in Bern, they believed that the unaccompanied minors who had come to Switzerland throughout the summer of displacements had severe educational, emotional, cultural, and language deficiencies that were impossible to address through mainstream schooling. They therefore expected the eight young men who were lucky enough to be the "chosen ones" for the education pilot to be grateful for the opportunity.

In the first months of the integration pilot, the eight Eritreans fulfilled the social workers' expectations. They quickly adapted to the daily routine in the institution and showed an interest in the work placements, and the German lessons in the internal school came to fruition. However, as the first cracks appeared, the clashing hopes and motivations underwriting the project came to the fore. At first these cracks were just small fissures, hardly noticeable moments of discontent. The incident described in the introductory chapter, in which Abel stuck the Post-it note to his chest, was the first such fissure. For an instant it caused worry and perplexity among the social pedagogues, leading Marina to call in a special meeting. However, they soon came to the conclusion that the note needed to be read against the backdrop of Abel's experiences of displacement. The social pedagogues reverted to the professional frameworks of conflict mitigation they had learned to deploy in their work with young offenders. They were trained to link "trouble kids'" behavior to classifications of psychological disorder, and they came to read the Post-it note in a similar way, as a sign of traumatization. In their final report about the incident, they even described it in positive terms, as a confirmation that Abel had felt safe enough in the social environment of the home to share his vulnerability.

On the surface everything went back to normal soon after the Post-it incident. But as time went by, more and more fissures started to open. In early October, Kibrum disappeared for a night. When the social pedagogues did their daily checkup just before the evening curfew, he was not in his room, and he did not reappear all night. When he showed up again the next morning, he was drunk and disheveled. When I spoke to him later that day, Kibrum told me that he had been in the neighboring town, drinking to drown his sorrows. He said that after work he had visited Tesfay, his little brother who was staying in a shelter for unaccompanied minors in a town close by. His brother was only thirteen years old and had arrived in Switzerland a few months earlier. When Kibrum wanted to return to the home in the evening, his brother had cried and begged him not to leave him alone. Kibrum felt a deep sense of responsibility for him. It was intensified by the promise he had given to his mother that he would look after him. The social pedagogues knew the importance of Kibrum's brother, as he had repeatedly asked for permission to have Tesfay live with him. But the supervisors and child welfare agencies had denied his request, ironically by arguing that the institution was not a child-friendly environment. Tesfay was only allowed to stay with Kibrum on weekends, and even that was only possible if they followed a complex bureaucratic procedure involving child welfare forms signed by the social pedagogues and handed over to Tesfay's supervisors and legal guardian ahead of time. After Tesfay's emotional breakdown, Kibrum had felt so guilty, angry, and depressed that it had been impossible for him to return to the home. He had met a few friends and got drunk to forget about his situation. Kibrum's disappearance led to a number of disciplinary measures, such as a cutback in his weekly allowance, alcohol checkups, and stricter scrutiny of his movements. As with Abel's Post-it note, however, the social pedagogues did not see Kibrum's behavior as a sign of discontent with his life in the institution but as an expression of the psychological baggage he was carrying because of his experiences of displacement.

More fissures started to appear when the social pedagogues discussed upcoming work placements with the boys. The curriculum for the first year prescribed that they should spend at least one month gaining insights into each of the seven work fields the institution offered. With increasing frequency, the young men voiced their discontent with this measure. When Tom, the intern, informed Aaron that he was assigned to a work placement in the kitchen the following week, he flipped out. "No, I won't go there!" Aaron yelled in a tone of desperation. In the discussion that followed, Tom emphasized that he had no choice, that everybody had to go through all of the work placements, while Aaron insisted that he did not want to waste his time on placements in work fields that did not interest him. He believed that he could make much better use of that time by going to school. In a conversation I had with Aaron and Abel afterward, they told me that they were not interested in completing an apprenticeship in a trade, that they preferred going to school. Similarly, the otherwise agreeable and composed Haileb was vocal about his lack of interest in any of the work fields the institution offered. He dreamed of becoming a car mechanic and had joined the project hoping to fulfill this wish. However, the institution did not offer apprenticeships in mechanics, and whenever he brought up the idea of finding a car workshop willing to take him on, the social pedagogues discouraged him. They said that because of the high level of technical and computer knowledge such an apprenticeship required, it was too demanding for somebody like him, with little foreknowledge in these fields and with German language deficits. Whenever Haileb was assigned to a new work placement, he made his disappointment felt. Unlike Aaron, he did not vent his protest through anger. He made ironic little side remarks, sharp enough that the social pedagogues could not overlook them. In the workshops, he performed the tasks he was given, but he did so mechanically, without displaying any interest in them.

There were also less visible fissures. They became palpable only through a general change of mood among the eight young men. In speaking of a collective mood, I am not referring to ideas, utterances, or critiques that were out in the open. I mean to convey a shared, unspoken, but distinctly noticeable feeling that hung around the eight young men and the spaces they occupied in the educational institution. In trying to conceptually grasp these invisible yet palpable fissures in the social makeup of the integration pilot, I find Sara Ahmed's work helpful. She treats moods as important vehicles for thinking through the sociality of emotions (Ahmed 2015, 15). She describes a mood as an "*affective lens*, affecting how we are affected." As such, moods are directed at the world as a whole. If we are in a particular mood, the whole world appears that way.

In a Heideggerian sense, moods are fundamental existential orientations setting the tone for our being (15). It was in this fundamental, intersubjective
way that the mood of the young men participating in the integration project
changed. The energy and enthusiasm characterizing their first steps through
the institution faded away and were replaced by a sense of heaviness and repressed silence. This change of mood was most palpable during the shared
lunch breaks. In the first few months of the project, the boys had exchanged
jokes and stories about their workday with the supervisors. Little by little these
stories went dry, and the conversations prompted by the social pedagogues
began to feel forced. One rule was that the young men should not converse in
Tigrinya throughout the day, to foster their German language skills. To enforce
this rule during lunchtime, the social pedagogues split the young men into
small groups, with a supervisor or teacher attending to each of the tables. This
rule turned the lunch hour into a sorrowful affair, as it caused the young men
to stop talking to one another whenever the supervisors were around. In the
presence of the social pedagogues, they froze and went silent.

The social pedagogues were puzzled by the change of mood. Initially, they
drew on the trope of refugee trauma to make sense of it. In a conversation I had
with Tom, the intern, he noted that the young men seemed to have psychological
problems. He had read about the sexual violence many unaccompanied minors
experienced on their journeys to Europe. This made him speculate on whether
some of the eight young men could have experienced something similar and
whether the "sadness" he had noticed in them lately could be related to such
experiences. "With all these stories of rape and abuse, we don't really know what
happened to any of them," he said. While the social pedagogues often speculated
about the young men's experiences and feelings, they knew very little about their
lives. To avoid retraumatizing the refugee youth, they refrained from asking them
any questions about their personal histories. This reluctance resembles the dynamics Katrien De Graeve (2017, 82) encountered in her research with guardians
for unaccompanied refugee youth in Belgium. She found that the guardians were
torn between expectations of professionalization and the wish to enter into a personal relationship with the minors. Like the social pedagogues in the integration
pilot, the guardians De Graeve talked to emphasized the importance of keeping a
"healthy distance" from the youth. This distance was a well-intended rule aimed
at emotionally protecting both the social pedagogues and the youth. However,
it meant that besides the social workers' and asylum reports the supervisors had
received from the home for unaccompanied minors, they had no means of grasping the young men's individual stories, hopes, and expectations. Without these
deeper histories of hopes, they also lacked the means to properly make sense of
the bad mood that had seized the project.

AFFECT ALIENS

At first the social pedagogues tried to ignore the bad vibe hanging around the project, describing this moodiness as normal teenage behavior, as a sign that the young men were testing boundaries or processing their past experiences. But as the number of incidents accumulated, they started to doubt their explanatory models. Rather than interpreting the boys' actions through behavioral models or frameworks of trauma, they increasingly deployed a culturalist lens to make sense of them. "They might be traumatized and everything, but this does not excuse their behavior," the German teaching assistant remarked one morning, as she was telling me about Aaron's oppositional attitude in class that day. "With all due respect for their difficulties, but this behavior has nothing to do with it." A few weeks before, the same teacher had described Aaron and the other young men as deeply traumatized, arguing that her responses to their actions in class needed to be carefully considered. Now she blamed them for their unresponsiveness, arguing that she had run out of patience. Similarly, Tom said that he no longer bought into the young men's pretense of vulnerability. He told me how Haileb had come to the office that morning, saying he had trouble breathing and was afraid that he was going to have a heart attack. Even though Haileb's descriptions carried all the indicators of a panic attack, Tom did not believe in it. Instead, he argued that the social pedagogues needed to learn to ignore such incidents as they were just grabs for attention or a means to manipulate them.

With the shift away from medical frameworks, a new explanatory pattern entrenched itself among the pedagogical staff of the integration pilot. They started to put the bad mood taking hold of the project down to the fact that the young men had never learned "Western" manners and that they had to be taught how to behave in a Swiss context. The bad mood was thus a sign that the young men were not attuned to the Swiss way, that they were not in harmony with a shared feeling of Swissness. In a conversation I had with Sebastian and George one afternoon, they brought up the disharmony marking the project. They complained about the boys' lack of enthusiasm for the opportunities they received. "Sometimes it's pretty difficult to keep in mind that this [the boys' lack of enthusiasm] is all culturally driven," Sebastian said. "It's hard to keep being empathetic with them if they are this unthankful."

Sebastian's statement shows that the social pedagogues linked the boys' "bad vibe" to their Eritrean background. They seemed to believe that the boys' allegiance to Eritrean cultural values prevented them from attuning to a Swiss mood. Sara Ahmed (2015, 20) points out that such a "national mood," a sense of being in harmony with a national body of shared beliefs and values, is often treated as an ideal. It turns those who are out of tune into obstacles, into "affect aliens" (14) getting in the way of national attunement. In a similar vein, the social pedagogues started to take issue with the atmosphere surrounding the young men, seeing it as an obstacle to a responsive relation—not just with the supervisors but with the overall Swiss environment. As a result, they required of the eight Eritreans that they work on themselves to overcome this misattunement. They called on them to be more communicative during the lunch and coffee breaks. This request was policed by the social pedagogues, who continually commented on the young men, whom they judged to be too serious, quiet, removed, or phlegmatic. Ahmed (2015, 21) notes that for individuals marked as affect aliens, attunement turns into a form of affective labor. They have to become responsive to the moods of others to learn to be in tune. The social pedagogues' insistence that it was the young men who had to change the mood and not themselves shows that the requirement for attunement is not distributed equally. Ahmed (2015, 22) stresses that collective moods are racialized, as certain bodies are more likely to cause the loss of attunement. She speaks of "diversity work" to describe the efforts migrants have to make to minimize differences and appear to be in tune.

As the social pedagogues could no longer ignore the bad mood permeating the integration pilot, they came to demand that the young people reverse it. They believed that the boys could only do so by actively working to acquire the shared values and beliefs making up a Swiss sense of "we." Like the teachers in the bridging school in Bern, they drew on commonsense ideas of what it means to be Swiss, describing it through attributes such as punctuality, politeness, honesty, and diligence. They explained the bad mood emanating from the young men by the absence of such values. The most important value they believed the youths to lack (and wanted them to acquire) was gratitude. "They always just want and want," Sebastian said in a conversation we had about the boys. He was dismayed by their sense of entitlement, arguing that, evidently, they had to be taught to be more grateful for the educational opportunities they received in the project. As the conversation continued, Sebastian fell back on common public discourses of refugees' un/deservingness by linking the boys' supposed ungratefulness to doubts about the genuineness of their claims to be "true" refugees. "I would not vouch for the truth that all these boys are real refugees," he said. When he noticed my perplexed reaction, he told me a story he knew from hearsay. The essence of it was that most of the Eritrean asylum seekers in Switzerland could have led a decent life in neighboring African countries but that they had decided to come to Europe to gain access to its generous welfare systems. He told me the story to underscore the point that before coming to Switzerland, Eritreans had to travel through several countries categorized as safe and that hence they should have stayed there rather than becoming burdens on the Swiss state. In conversations among the social pedagogues, the young men's ungratefulness increasingly came to be linked to doubts about their genuineness as refugees. They commented on slight differences in skin color, habits, or tone of language to voice their suspicion that some of the young men were Ethiopians pretending to be Eritrean to gain refugee protection and access to welfare money. "Today Aaron was speaking to Yonas, and I could have sworn that they spoke in a different language than Tigrinya," Tom said one afternoon, as I was helping him and the assistant German teacher clean the dishes. He said that he and the other social workers often wondered whether he really was Eritrean. The German teacher agreed. "He is so much darker than the others and his features look different," she said.

In doubting the genuineness of the boys' stories of displacement, the social pedagogues started to mirror the ongoing public backlash against the refugees who had arrived in the summer of displacement. By portraying the eight Eritreans as untrustworthy and unwilling to put in the hard work required to adapt to the Swiss way of doing things, the staff's narratives resembled the countless media reports about asylum seekers faking their age and identity to gain access to precious public goods. On several occasions Sebastian took me aside to complain about the young men's entitlement mentality, which, he noted, was "extraordinary." He suspected that some of them were considering quitting the integration pilot because they knew that if they went back to the home for unaccompanied minors they would receive more weekly allowance. "I know it sounds harsh, but when I see how they behave I think why they don't just go back to where they came from," Sebastian commented bitterly.

In the social pedagogues' discussions, inclusion appeared as a gift, as something the young men had to acquire if they wanted to be part of Swiss society. While they were not against diversity per se, they demanded that the young men show allegiance to a Swiss "we" by giving up on other kinds of allegiances (Ahmed 2015, 24). What was at stake then, was a necessity to deculture and enculture the young men in order to make them adaptable to the Swiss system (Baumann 2004; Abu El-Haj 2010, 256). Gerd Baumann (2004) uses the term "civil enculturation" to capture the ways schools attempt to socialize young people into a set of shared national values. With the establishment of the inclusive paradigm, education institutions can no longer be the bearers of simplistic nationalist messages. However, Baumann (2004, 3) notes that this does not mean that assimilative motives have disappeared. At a time when cultural difference has become a recognized right, the question has turned from "who you are" to "how one does." Similarly, the social pedagogues started to take aim at the ways the young men carried themselves, scrutinizing their attitudes and demanding that they align themselves with a Swiss way of doing things.

Within the local moral economy of the integration pilot, this positioned the young men as applicants to a *community of value* they needed to prove themselves to in order to be included. Bridget Anderson (2015, 2) has coined the term "community of value" to describe the ways its members imagine the national "we" as "composed of people who share common ideals and (exemplary) patterns of behavior expressed through ethnicity, religion, culture or language." In Switzerland, the idea of such a community of value is so deeply entrenched in the national imaginary that there is even a specific term to describe it—the *Willensnation* (nation by will). As Switzerland is not composed of a homogenous ethnic and linguistic group, the nation is commonly imagined to be held together by individuals sharing a political will to live with one another (Inderbitzin 2003). Processes of inclusion, participation, and belonging can therefore not be reduced to legal status. They fundamentally concern the question of how individuals are positioned vis-à-vis a community of value, whether they are admitted to it or kept at a distance. In Switzerland, the openness of the *Willensnation* to accommodate the cultural diversity of the four main ethnolinguistic groups never extended to migrant communities. There is a historical continuity in perceiving migrants and refugees as a threat to the solidarity, respect, and agreement believed to demarcate the established community of value (Gold 2019, 31). As affect aliens, they are suspected to ruin the carefully balanced national atmosphere. Anderson (2015, 4) notes that if we foreground communities of value rather than nation-states, we can cast the spotlight on individuals or groups who are believed to be incapable of living up to moral values and subsequently cast out. Resembling the social pedagogues' portrayals of the Eritrean young men, such individuals are commonly described as figures who lack both values and value. As a result of this lack of value, they endlessly have to prove themselves (5–7). The metaphor of the community of value can help us expose the inner workings of interior frontiers, how they are fueled by opaque powers emanating from the slippage between person and polity. To paraphrase Stoler (2018), it can help us to grasp "what sorts of sensibilities get recruited to produce hardening distinctions between who is 'us' and who is constructed as (irrevocably) 'them.'"

One difficulty of the onus put on the young men to prove themselves worthy of inclusion in the Swiss community of value was that it was not always clearly articulated. Many of the social pedagogues' doubts and discontents never surfaced in front of the young men. They appeared in ways that remained hidden from them, expressed mainly through gossip and chitchat among the staff or through written reports. However, just as the young Eritreans produced a distinct mood, so did the social pedagogues. Even though they did not always voice their criticism of the young men's behavior, it was impossible to ignore the feeling of dissatisfaction that was lingering in the air. Over time, all these small fissures developed into a bigger, more noticeable crack in the social fabric of the project, until finally there was no holding back and the discontent burst out into the open. About two months into the project, these conflicting hopes and expectations came to a head.

One morning, when I checked in at the social pedagogue's office, Sebastian asked me to stay back. He said that he wanted to tell me about a crisis meeting he had called a few days earlier. I asked about the reason for the meeting. "They didn't follow the rules, they constantly had unannounced guests in their apartments, they were awake until two o' clock every night," Sebastian responded. "And then there was the drinking and disappearing. Somehow they behaved like the others." When referring to "the others," he made a gesture to the other side of the road, where the young offenders lived. Sebastian had invited Daniel (the young men's legal guardian), a Tigrinya translator, and Mr. Brugger to join the meeting. In the discussion the boys had been asked to explain their behavior. The young men had complained about having to spend the year doing work placements in job fields that did not interest them. They worried that they were being pressured into traineeships they did not want to do, and they wanted a guarantee from the social pedagogues that they would end up doing apprenticeships in work fields that interested them. Some of the young men also said that they wanted to go to school instead of doing the work placements. For Sebastian, this critique was not reasonable. As he talked about the boys' expectations, he became more and more agitated. "Sometimes it was full on," he said. "They had a very demanding attitude, it was all about getting more and more and more."

Rather than taking the young men's critique of their educational exclusion seriously, Sebastian interpreted it as a confirmation of their moral doubtfulness. In his view, the young refugees were not in a position to make demands about their education. They should be thankful for whatever they received. This was the message the social pedagogues and legal guardian tried to bring home to them in the crisis meeting. With an air of satisfaction, Sebastian told me that Daniel, the legal guardian, had been ashamed of the boys' demanding behavior. He had told them how much it cost to keep each of them in the program and explained that they had been chosen out of a lot of other unaccompanied minors who would be happy to replace them. Daniel had told the young men in no uncertain terms that if they were not up to it, they should quit the project now, but that this would mean they had to go back to the home for unaccompanied minors. He reminded them of how hard it had been to live there and said that even if they did not like the work fields offered in the integration pilot, it would be almost impossible for them to secure an apprenticeship if they were left to find one on their own. Even though it should have been the legal guardian's job to represent the young men's best interests, in the meeting he turned against them and sided with the institution. By telling the eight Eritreans that the only other option was no option, he coerced them into staying in the project.

The crisis meeting brought into the open the resentment the supervisors and other adult guardian figures felt toward the young men's apparent lack of thankfulness for the gift of education they had received. That they described education as a debt the refugee beneficiaries had to repay to their Swiss benefactors through displays of thankfulness corresponds with historically ingrained ideas of deservingness. Throughout the Western history of thought, philosophers and writers have again and again described unthankfulness as the most vicious of all wrongs. In this vein, Hume wrote that "of all crimes that human creatures are capable of committing, the most horrid and unnatural is ingratitude," while Kant described it as "the essence of vileness and wickedness" (Kant quoted in Manela 2015). Having accused the young Eritreans of such wickedness, the social pedagogues used the remaining crisis meeting to set their expectations straight. Sebastian said that their earnest words had shown an immediate effect. Ever since the meeting, the young men had dropped their demanding attitude and went to their work placements without protest.

VARIATIONS OF ABANDONMENT

The interactions between the young people and social pedagogues reveal the irreconcilable hopes, ideas, and expectations underwriting the integration pilot. While the eight Eritreans had joined the project hoping to finally achieve the kind of forward movement they had been looking for, they quickly realized that the institution formed just another blockage that kept them from participating in the "real" world and in "real" society. They did not passively accept their social and educational exclusion. The young men's articulation of demands for more schooling and suitable apprenticeships during the crisis meeting show that they attempted to challenge the curriculum. But their petitions to change the project in ways that would have aligned it with the education they had hoped for failed. Their enthusiasm was brought to a grinding halt by the expectations of the social pedagogues, teachers, guardians, and, by extension, Swiss society at large, who believed that the lower-tiered education they received was just what they deserved.

Now that we have zoomed in on the local moral economy propelling the social pedagogues' actions, the opaque yet powerful mechanisms of exclusion underwriting seemingly inclusive education projects such as the integration pilot come to the fore. These mechanisms function on the basis of morally charged ideas of what is at stake, both in the education of refugee youth and for the future of Swiss society. Cloaked in a language of benevolence and concern, such mechanisms hinder the young people's zest for life, making them feel inadequate, troublesome, ungrateful, bad tempered, or, quite simply, *other*. Faced with the demands of complete affective, social, and political allegiance with an imagined Swiss community of value (the goalposts of which keep shifting), the eight Eritreans were actively made to feel both strange and estranged. It is precisely through such vernacular mechanisms that refugee youth are turned into affect aliens, strangers who need to work on themselves to overcome the supposed misattunement marking their being-in-the-world. This "work" they are required to perform is not based on knowledge the young people could acquire through books or schooling. It is based on the tacit ways people go about things, the ways they walk, talk, express themselves, or interact with others. Asking people to change these structural properties of being is not harmless or noninvasive. If we follow Heidegger's (1995, 68) suggestion that people are affectively grounded in the social world—a groundedness he describes as *Befindlichkeit* (attunement)—a request to change it destabilizes the basic determinants of our being-in-the-world. Heidegger insists that attunements cannot be reduced to the psychological interiority of individuals. They concern the fundamental ways in which we live in the world with others. With Heidegger, Jan Slaby (2010, 103) argues that we should not see attunements as subjective feelings but as "existential orientations" that concern "the entirety of a person's situated existence and thereby also the textures of the situations in which the person finds herself." For the young men, accusations of misattunement formed another crucial building block in the construction of interior frontiers, aimed at keeping refugees from making a claim on the shared affective space of Swissness. But these accusations were geared toward an even more profound sense of nonbelonging. In taking aim with the ways the young people related to the world, they destabilized the basic structures of their ways of being, "the ways in which we *are*" (104).

In the integration pilot, the requirement for a change in attunement occurred on two interrelated levels. The first is the demand that the young men drop their "attitude of entitlement"—an attitude I would rather describe as an acute awareness of their social subordination. The boys' articulation of their own educational demands proves yet again that despite the hegemony of narratives about refugees' undeservingness, they do not passively submit themselves to such disempowering processes. They formulate their own ideas of their worthiness as human beings and the education they believe they deserve. The second level at which the young men were required to change was destined to demolish exactly this will to critique. In requesting that the young men display their eternal thankfulness, the pedagogues turned their utterance of criticism about their continued social and educational segregation into the worst possible sin. On the surface, these pressures seemed to work as intended: after the crisis meeting, the young men stopped questioning the rules or trying to change them. Underneath the surface, however, the critique and disappointed hopes kept bubbling up, edging their way into everyday interactions.

In a conversation I had with Kibrum and Abel about a month after the crisis meeting, they articulated this feeling of discontent. They had been assigned to work in the gardening center—a work field all of the eight young men despised. This dislike for gardening as a profession was a recurring theme throughout my fieldwork in Bern and Zürich. In my conversations with young Eritreans, the figure of the gardener appeared again and again as a strong metaphor for being a loser, of someone who, just like the farmers in their home villages, had to spend their days digging the earth. While in Switzerland the occupation of the gardener is positively connoted, for the young people it was the embodiment of failure. This negative connotation corresponds to occupational patterns observable across East Africa, whereby certain low-status forms of work are stigmatized (Pankhurst 2003; Mains 2007). Engaging in such work equals taking on the social status of an outcast. For the young Eritreans, gardening work represented the kind of future they had tried to escape. In this vein, Kibrum and Abel told me that they had not come to the institution to do "stupid work," like gardening or cooking. "We have been patient long enough," Kibrum said. "Now we don't want to wait anymore. What did we come to this place for? To do dirty work?" He noted that he had come to the project thinking that it would enable him to get a good education, but he had lost faith in it. "My mother believes that I am learning a good profession here," Kibrum said. "I could never tell her that I am doing this kind of work, you know, working in the dirt."

For Abel and Kibrum, the work they had been asked to perform was so unacceptable that they had lost the capability of being composed and patient. When the work trainer told them to collect the leaves in the front yard with their bare hands, they had refused to do it. George, the social pedagogue on duty that morning, had reacted the same way he would have if the young offenders refused to work. He told Abel and Kibrum to do whatever they wanted but said that they would not receive the keys to go back to their apartments and that they could not have their phones back. When I arrived around nine o'clock that morning, I found the two of them sitting on a bench in front of the communal space. They were shivering in the cold without hats or jackets. "This feels like prison," Kibrum said, on the verge of tears. Just as he made this comment, Henry, one of the participants from the rehabilitation program, walked past us. Overhearing our conversation, he laughed. "This *is* a prison," he emphasized. "Haven't you noticed?" "Yes," Kibrum responded. "Why are we treated like prisoners? Why did they put us here? We did nothing wrong, why are we kept like in prison?" Abel, who had remained quiet for most of the time but whose facial expressions disclosed anger and depression, exclaimed, "We are humans, we aren't animals, we are treated like animals here." After a moment of silence, Kibrum said that there was a word for the situation they were in, having to work for others like animals, but that he was struggling to find the correct German word for it. He circumscribed the word: it described the time when the Italians came to Eritrea and occupied it, he said. I asked if he meant the word *colonialism* (*Kolonialisierung*). Yes, Kibrum said excitedly, and he wrote the word down on a small sheet of paper he had in his pocket. "This place is like colonialism," he said.

Abel's and Kibrum's refusal to work in the garden that morning was not just a refusal to perform work they found unacceptable. It was also a refusal to comply with a system that encroached on their innermost sense of dignity. As Kibrum's connection to colonialism and Abel's comparison of their treatment to that of animals show, the young men clearly linked this demand for a dignified existence to racialized histories of exploitation and domination. Their refusal to perform work that, in their eyes, was reserved for people relegated to the outer margins of society can also be read as a refusal to accept their exclusion from the social, educational, and economic progress Swiss citizens seemed to access so effortlessly. Against the backdrop of the histories of hope propelling Abel's and Kibrum's journeys to Europe, their small act of refusal forms "a haunting claim for equal rights of membership in a spectacularly unequal global society" (Ferguson 2002, 565). In some ways, the incident could be interpreted as one tiny glitch in the everyday workings of the integration pilot. By the afternoon, Abel and Kibrum had returned to their work placement in the gardening center, and both of them completed their one-month assignment there without further protest. Despite their inability to overturn the structural inequalities permeating the education institution, however, I believe that it is important to make small, seemingly banal moments of protest such as these a part of social analyses. They show the succinct ways young people are able to identify and critique the exclusionary practices they are subjected to. If we take such everyday utterances of critique seriously, we can begin to grasp the forcefulness with which the logic of inclusive exclusion inserts itself into people's lifeworlds—how it eats into their sense of dignity and unsettles their sense of belonging.

For the young men, the logic of inclusive exclusion translated into a severe curtailment of their capability for forward movement. On an everyday affective basis, this produced one core affectivity: a sense of abandonment. They felt as though nobody cared about them and the hopes they held for the future, that they had been left to fend for themselves in a place that fenced them off from the rest of the world. How deeply this feeling of being abandoned destabilized the boys became apparent the morning when Abel and Kibrum refused to work. Having been locked out of their apartments, they were overcome by the realization that they had nowhere else to go. As they discussed where they would live if they quit the project, they remembered their legal guardian's warning that he would not help them find an apartment. In a competitive housing market like Zürich, where even people with good wages struggle to secure an apartment, Kibrum and Abel knew full well that as refugees with short-term humanitarian visas and a small monthly allowance they stood absolutely no chance of finding a place on their own. All they could hope for, they knew, was to return to the home for unaccompanied minors—the place they had been so glad to escape in the first place. This realization caused a sense of despair in them. They felt that they had been abandoned not just educationally but also on a much deeper-reaching social level. This sense of abandonment became visible in Abel's and Kibrum's repeated utterance that "this is it," that "now we have no house to live in anymore," that if the social pedagogues did not allow them to return to their apartments, they would end up living on the streets. I tried to calm them down by suggesting that I was sure the pedagogues would let them return to their apartments. Suddenly Kibrum directed his anger at me: "Who do you work for? This place, or what?" His question startled me. It captured a core dilemma underwriting my presence as a researcher in an institution like this—a place that drives young people to the abyss of their social existence. As I caught glimpses of that abyss, I was left asking myself how research in such a place was ethically and humanely possible. How could I account for the manifold ways the eight young men were left to feel imprisoned and left behind without reproducing the very structures of abandonment the institution brought forth? Kibrum's question confronted me with the full force of this predicament. Attempting to explain my position, I said that I was not working for the institution. I reminded them of the conversations we had had a few weeks before in which I had explained that I was working for a university and that I was there to understand the situation of unaccompanied minors in Switzerland. "Well, now you can see what it's like," Kibrum said bitterly. "It's shit."

Kibrum's description of their situation as "shit" aptly names the dead end the integration pilot produced. For the young men, the project formed just another variation of the abandonment they had been subject to ever since their arrival in Switzerland. They felt that they had been deserted in yet another place where they were kept out of sight from the rest of the world. The experiential quality of the sense of abandonment I am aiming at showed itself in three ways. Firstly, it was deeply entrenched in the educational institution itself. In a place that was set up to keep unruly kids away from society, the refugee youth joined the ranks of other marginalized youth locked away in separate educational institutions. The institutional abandonment present in the home for young offenders did not play out in the same shockingly cruel way as in João Biehl's (2005) "zones of social abandonment." He coined the term to describe the situation he found in the Brazilian institution where he conducted research, a place where the mentally ill, sick, and impoverished were left to die. These institutions, he suggests, "absorbed those individuals, young and old, who had no ties or resources left to sustain themselves, whose bodies were not worth governing" (244). The zones of social abandonment Biehl aims at are controlled neither by the state nor by welfare or medical institutions. "Here the unwanted were sure to become unknowables, with no human rights and no one accountable to them" (244). Unlike the dynamics described by Biehl, the abandonment the young people experienced in the integration pilot was not marked by the absence of financial resources or intervention by the state. They were subject to a more perfidious kind of abandonment. It happened under the banner of benevolence, inclusion, and the protection of children's rights, in an institution that was properly financed and staffed. Amid all the resources, care, and effort that went into the young men's educational advancement, however, they were quietly led into social and educational dead ends.

Nobody was perceptive to the protests of the young men channeled into these dead ends. This is the second level at which the experiential quality of abandonment becomes graspable. Through affectively charged local moral economies, the young men were pushed into relationships of dependency in which they had no say over their lives, hopes, or futures. As the constant demands for thankfulness and emotional attunement show, the young men were not allowed to control the shape of their futures or the expression of their innermost feelings. Given the social pedagogues' lack of knowledge about their personal histories, the young men were left to feel as if nobody cared about them—as if none of the hopes, experiences, and skills they had brought with them counted. Their protests against this diminishing treatment fell on unhearing ears. Amid bitter public fights over access to public resources, nobody wanted to give audience to refugee youths' demands for equal access to education and opportunities.

This public numbness toward refugee youths' requests for a dignified existence leads to the third experiential outline of abandonment. The creation of zones of educational abandonment such as the integration pilot was only possible because of the normalization of much larger processes of abandonment marking the reception of asylum seekers in Switzerland and, indeed, Europe at large. This showed itself in the short-term humanitarian permits the eight Eritreans had been fobbed off with. These permits left the young men at the mercy of the state for years if not decades on end, with the prospect of a final rejection always looming on the horizon. Even though refugees are continuously exposed to critiques of welfare dependency, the proliferation of such permits produces an increased number of societal no-through roads as they cut down on possibilities for work, education, and mobility. In the context of the education of unaccompanied minors, these no-through roads show in cantonal education boards' refusal to finance the schooling of youth past the obligatory cutoff age if they have not been recognized as refugees in the full sense of the Geneva convention. They also show in such youths' difficulty in securing living arrangements that would allow them to move beyond the human warehousing in asylum centers. Like the education projects for unaccompanied refugee youth, these humanitarian classifications claim to be based on benevolent liberal values of protection and care. In reality, however, they abandon refugees in multiple ways: socially, economically, politically, educationally, emotionally, and more.

How quickly these overall structures of abandonment incite smaller, more intimate forms of desolation can be seen from the actions of Daniel, the legal guardian. When the young men tried to argue for their interests in the crisis meeting, the absence of alternative options led him to abandon his duty to communicate their best interests by siding with the institution. While I do not want to downplay the forcefulness of this act of abandonment, I believe it is important not to be too quick in judging it as sign of professional or personal failure. We need to take into account the impossible situation people working at the interstices of refugee advocacy and welfare organizations find themselves in. In the current sociopolitical climate, people like Daniel continuously have to juggle between restrictive immigration policies, welfare cutbacks, and young people's hopes and interests. With the introduction of neoliberal education policies, such broker figures—often people who would describe themselves as socially responsive and progressive individuals—are forced into a difficult position as the state tries to use them to extend its control into the intimate lives of youth labeled as at-risk (Chalhi, Koster, and Vermeulen 2018). As emancipatory youth education concepts have come under attack for their lack of measurable outcomes, the teachers, social workers, and guardians concerned with marginalized communities are left with little discretionary space in the ways they implement policies (2018). This inability to provide alternative pathways fosters difficult relationships, which are marked by a high degree of mistrust.

Taken together, all these variations of abandonment created a social environment in which the young people could move neither forward nor backward. They were left in a state of stasis, unable to achieve the social and existential mobility they had hoped for. Exacerbating this stalemate was the fact that the young men did not just feel that they had been left behind by a system that did not care about them. They were also grappling with the pain, guilt, and sadness of having abandoned their families and loved ones. Their loneliness was fortified by the fact that they had left Eritrea without saying goodbye to their parents, siblings, friends, or girlfriends and that this drastic step had not paid off in terms of their future expectations in Europe.

SIX

—⚮—

EXISTENTIAL BALANCING ACTS

INTERIOR FRONTIERS AND THEIR HAUNTINGS

"I am not alive. Maybe dead. I am in heaven. Do I still live on this earth?" As this book is drawing to a close, I find myself returning once again to the haunting message marking its beginning. The summer morning when Abel stuck the Post-it note containing these words to his chest, it was still the early days of my fieldwork. I had been to the institution a few times and had only just started to get to know the youth and pedagogues living and working there. I could therefore not resort to the sedimented, experientially grounded knowledge necessary to decode this incident ethnographically. And yet the message stirred up something inside me, making it impossible for me to look past it. It kept resurfacing in my thoughts and bugging me in my dreams, forming a crucial bridge in my process of understanding the ambiguous social texture of the educational spaces I was moving through. In speaking of "understanding," I am not referring to the interior, cognitive processes through which social scientists come to abstract, comprehend, and categorize phenomena. I use it in the interpretive and partici-patory sense with which Heidegger (2001, 143–48) deploys the term *Verstehen*. He argues that human understanding is never a simplistic intellectual process but a functional property of *Dasein*'s existence that cannot be divorced from the potentialities of the environment it grows out of. Understanding is therefore an intersubjective process of approximation rather than the final outcome of internal thought processes. In this existential reading, anthropological under-standing is fundamentally connected to the lifeworlds and places researchers move through, a dialogical process arising from the inner (personal) and outer (social) worlds they inhabit.

It is in this way that the Post-it note instigated a process of understanding in me. In their eerie poetics, Abel's words forced me to develop methodologies that would allow me to make sense of phenomena that did not make themselves noticeable in obvious ways. As the Post-it note shows, they often made their presence felt through what can best be described as hauntings. Woven into the social texture of the home, these hauntings verbalized the unspoken yet clearly palpable ways the young men called attention to their precarious existential struggles. In a social environment that greatly restricted the refugee youths' ability to voice objections to their marginalization, the phenomena I describe as hauntings destabilized the racialized order of things in Swiss society. If only for a split second, they allowed the young men to make visible the grave consequences of the structural violence emanating from the frontiers of belonging. These hauntings also affected my research practice. They forced me to develop ways of *looking* that allowed me to glance beyond the shiny, benevolent surface of the education projects where I was conducting research to grasp the unseeable yet real ways these places nurtured the creation of interior frontiers. They forced me to develop registers of *listening* that allowed me to take note of stories that were scarcely audible, apprehend moments when stories were silenced, and grasp some of the ways silences spoke. They forced me to foster a way of *thinking* that was less dependent on the texts of social life than on its subtexts—to develop my ideas in concordance with the habits, gestures, words, moods, and reactions making up the youths' engagements with the world they had been thrown into.

One haunting inherent in Abel's message speaks of crushed hopes. Throughout the book these hopes have appeared again and again in the form of a longing for education. Education formed an accelerating force in the lifeworlds of the young African men and women who made their way to Europe in the wake of the summer of displacements. While they regarded education as an important means of achieving upward social mobility, there was more to this longing than the hope for economic stability. The personal trajectories of the young people presented in the book show that they also envisaged education as a project of self-making, as a tool through which they would be able to achieve inner change. Driven by distinct histories of hope, youth like Abel endured treacherous journeys to achieve a state of existential mobility, a sense that they were moving forward in the realms of their lifeworlds. This hope of forward-movement-through-education was not entirely individualistic. It was inextricably linked to destinies that were entangled with theirs. The social payoff of the young people's decision to migrate hinged on their educational success. Educational achievement was the main currency through which they could repay the emotional debts owed to the family members they had left, often without their consent. Not being able to achieve the anticipated movement-through-education created an unbridgeable gap in the young people. Abel's Post-it note alludes to this gap. Being denied access to Swiss communities of value while simultaneously having lost touch with communities where they were valued caused an existential chasm in the young people. As Abel's question of "Do I still live on this earth?" shows, it left them wondering where their lives were located and whether they were actually still living in a shared human world.

Throughout the book it has become apparent how much social and emotional work the youth invested into becoming a valued part of Swiss society—or, to put it more accurately, into being included in a shared sense of ordinariness. This wish for inclusion in a sense of ordinariness should not be written off as a desperate act of compliance. It is testament to a deeply human striving to have one's existence acknowledged and valued by others, of achieving a state of equilibrium that allows the creation of a world one co-owns. This equilibrium should not be confused with an ultimate sense of harmony or stability. It involves continuous work—balancing acts Michael Jackson (1998, 19) hints at when he argues that existential equilibriums are "a matter of striking a balance between the countervailing needs between self and other." Existential balancing acts are "an ongoing dialectic in which persons vie and strategize in order to avoid nullification as well as to achieve some sense of governing their own fate" (18). The outcome of these contradictory strivings should not be romanticized. The social work the young people invested into becoming a part of Swiss normality while simultaneously acting against their nullification speaks of the existential aporias these balancing acts can create in people who are pushed to the margins of society. Having their inner sense of equilibrium tipped over again and again in an environment that did not reciprocally respond to their efforts to be heard and seen made some of them lose their footing in the world. As Abel's note shows, it made them question whether they were still alive.

The interactions between the pedagogues and refugee youth in the education projects have shown that these rejections hardly ever appeared in the form of open disaffirmation. It was through small, seemingly banal gestures, habits, or words that the youth were made to feel strange. The subtle modes of conversation and action through which certain people are turned into affect confidantes and others into aliens—the ways some people can enter a room and immediately be subsumed under a prevailing mood, while others stumble and cause the atmosphere to shift—have shown to be everything but innocent. They form the affective cornerstones upon which interior frontiers are built. Abel's note demonstrates that the everyday acts of cruelty the youths were exposed to did not just signal to them their status as applicants or guests to the Swiss polity. The constant questioning of the vernacular apparatuses (such as speech, act, habits) through which they engaged with others worked to unsettle the structural properties of their being-in-the-world. Abel's statement "I am not alive" shows how far interior frontiers can reach into people's lifeworlds, making them feel defeated, alienated, and, quite literally, lifeless. The creeping inscription of such frontiers of belonging also reverberated through Thierno's repeated utterance of "I cannot" and his description of being kaput. It spoke through Meron's question "It's true, they don't want us here, right?" and it echoed through Jamila's desire to tell "normal" stories and her despair over the impossibility of doing so in a language she did not feel at home in. The violence of interior frontiers also spoke through Samuel's statement that regardless of his economic status, in Switzerland he would always remain a "poor" person because nobody cared about his existence there.

The experience of being made to feel out of place confronted the youth with fundamental questions about their future. It made them look for ways to make sense of the traces acts of boundary drawing left on their bodies and souls. Abel's Post-it note is a clear testament to the fact that the young people did not silently accept their subordination. As much as they were pushed back and forth on ever-changing scales of un/deservingness, this did not keep them from articulating their own ethical conceptions about the lives and futures *they* believed themselves to deserve. These ideas and critiques usually did not appear in the form of open expressions of protest. More often they appeared in subtle ways, such as the posing of seemingly innocent questions, the telling of equivocal jokes, the performance of overcompliance, or the lingering of moods. Sometimes these ethical contestations appeared through something as inoffensive as a song.

While the pedagogues enforced a strict policy of German language use in the home for young offenders, the young Eritrean men kept communicating with one another in Tigrinya through songs. Throughout their workdays, they hummed songs, usually popular tunes from exiled Eritrean musicians they followed on the internet. One afternoon, not long after the Post-it incident, the powerful critique hidden underneath these songs was brought home to me. As Abel, Kibrum, and Aaron were going about their work in the metal workshop, Aaron started to hum a tune. Picking up on his rhythm, the other two joined in, leading to a beautiful musical conversation. Every time one of the boys had finished a sentence, the next would chime in, as if they were responding to one another. They finished on a recurring refrain, the sound of Aaron's hammer creating the beats. When the song was over, Kibrum gave me an expectant look, asking me whether I had heard them sing. "It was beautiful," I confirmed. "You know what we were singing about?" Kibrum asked. I said that I did not know as the lyrics were in Tigrinya. Kibrum explained that the song was by Lulom Abreha, a man who had left behind his family to go to Europe.[1] The song talked about the terrible things he had witnessed as a migrant, the violence inflicted on him by human traffickers, and the desperation he encountered in the Libyan desert, the unspeakable horrors of seeing other migrants around him die. Kibrum said that he often wondered why the musician had chosen to leave his home. "This is no life," he said, alluding to his own life in Switzerland and the impossible existential balancing acts it confronted him with.

As Kibrum talked about the violent inequality the song conveyed, alternative readings of Europe's moral placement in the world became palpable. While not directly comprehensible to the pedagogues or work instructors, the simple act of humming a song contained a deep-seated questioning of Europe's self-understanding as a bastion of equality and human rights. Instead, the humming hinted at the darky underbelly of Europe's liberal facade, at the deserts and oceans forming the outer limits of its violently guarded wealth and sense of superiority. Kibrum's utterance "this is no life" also hinted at the fact that these borders do not end once refugees and migrants reach European soil. They make way for more opaque frontiers that do not mark out geographical territories but inner, affectively charged terrains of belonging. It was of all these layers of thought that the simple act of singing a song spoke. Like Abel's Post-it note, the everyday, subtle expressions of critique I am aiming at require some effort on the side of the anthropologist to become legible. They often only make themselves felt to bystanders in the form of hauntings—the ways human acts of ruination and disaster refuse to go away, stubbornly sticking around at the margins of the everyday, always carrying the potential of turning into a more profound, transformative critique.

In the pages that follow, I try to make visible the social ethics lurking underneath some of the hauntings I was confronted with in my work with the young Eritreans living in the home for young offenders. While the previous chapters have shown the variations of abandonment and ruination interior frontiers can foster, I want to end the book on the young people's everyday strivings for autonomy. The social afterlife of Abel's Post-it note uncovers the ambiguous balancing acts these strivings invoke. It shows how, in conditions of (politically produced) stasis, the playing with ideas of suicide, death, and the end of life can be deployed as powerful articulations of social and political critique. Thus, they hold the potential of producing an inner sense of forward movement, which thereby allows the young men to act upon the environments they find themselves cast into.

THE POST-IT NOTE'S SOCIAL AFTERLIFE

In the weeks and months following the Post-it incident, the questions about being and nothingness Abel had raised continued to reverberate through the young men's engagements with the social and educational reality they had been thrown into. Ideas of death and dying became crucial narrative vehicles through which they voiced some of their critical examinations.[2] They first appeared in postings on Facebook, in the form of YouTube videos, in images, or in comments in which the young men played with the idea of death, suicide, and being on the edge. In September 2015 Kibrum posted a photo of himself on his new bike, sadly looking back into the distance. "Fuck this world," the caption underneath it read. "I don't love this world, fuck it." A few weeks later he posted a selfie of Aaron, Abel, and himself in front of the restrooms at a shopping mall. "We are not happy because this life is shit," he commented on it. "We always worry and don't have time to laugh or play anymore." Abel posted an image of himself sitting in the train, staring into the distance. "I miss myself," he titled it. Another time he posted an image of a young girl standing dangerously close to an abyss. She was looking down, as if pondering whether or not to jump. Above the image hovered a saying from Psalm 56:3, written both in English and Tigrinya: "When I am afraid, I will trust in you." Kibrum responded by posting the link to a YouTube video of a song composed by a German girl whose entire social media channel dealt with the depression she was suffering from and the suicidal imaginings she was entertaining. The song was entitled "This Is My Goodbye-Song in Case I Am Leaving Early." It showed an image of her stretched-out arm bleeding from the cuts she had inflicted on herself, some of them dangerously close to the artery. Kibrum quoted the lyrics, saying, "Please tell me what I am living for, otherwise I will give up."

While the idea of suicide reverberated through the stories and images the young men shared on Facebook, they did not verbalize it explicitly in face-to-face conversations. Rather than imagining the act of suicide per se, they played with the idea of being dead, of escaping the pressures they were confronted with in their lives on earth. The following conversation snippet illustrates one moment when the young men brought up such ideas in an everyday situation. It occurred during German class. That afternoon, Lisa, the assistant teacher, was explaining the Swiss political landscape to the young men. Lisa suggested that she could organize an excursion for them to see a polling station in the nearby town hall before the parliamentary elections on October 18, 2015. This suggestion found little enthusiasm among the boys. Not only did they not feel inclined to give up the little free time they had by surrendering their weekend, but the fact that they had just learned that as refugees on humanitarian permits they were likely to be barred from political life in Switzerland for at least another decade made the expectation that they engage with the elections absurd. When Lisa asked if the boys were interested in going there on the weekend, there was an awkward silence in the room. Finally, Kibrum responded. He said that he did not know if they could go because perhaps they would not be in the home anymore. The teacher asked where they were going to be, if they had other plans for the weekend. Repeating some of the thoughts of Abel's Post-it note, Kibrum shrugged, noting that "perhaps we will be in heaven, maybe we will not be living on this earth anymore."

Lisa ignored Kibrum's statement, probably interpreting it as a joke. She went on to explain the various political parties in Switzerland and their election promises. When she came to the right-wing SVP party, she told the young men that the party had a tough stance on refugees, that it promoted the idea that Switzerland should only be for the Swiss and that no more refugees should be allowed in. Having taken in this information, Kibrum laughed with embitterment, saying that if it were up to him, he would like to leave Switzerland as soon as possible but that he could not, that he was not able to move about in the world as he wished. "Everything is a problem here," he said. "It would be better not to be on this earth." "Yes," Abel agreed, "we want to live somewhere else than on this earth." This sparked a discussion between the young men in which they played through imaginary scenarios of what life would look like if they did not have to live it on this earth. Life on earth, they agreed, was not good; it held nothing but trouble for them. While it had forced them to take radical steps, it never actually moved them into a better position.

These discussions about the end of life occurred regularly. Like the critique inherent in the Eritrean songs, they did not usually surface in explicit ways. Instead, they occurred as short intermezzos, brief moments in the midst of everyday interactions or conversations. Another way Abel's question of "Do I still live on this earth?" continued to arise was through the imagining of what being dead felt like. The young men endlessly fantasized about the feeling of being a corpse buried in the ground. While some of them believed that their souls would travel to another place, which, as Haileb put it, would be "like staying in a nightclub forever," others found the idea of there being nothing but cold earth and quietness comforting. They imagined how worms would slowly eat up their bodies and how, in the end, there would be nothing left of them but earth and a heap of bones.

The presence of these hauntings did not leave the staff working with the eight young men untouched. Especially in the first weeks of the project, the social pedagogues were deeply troubled by such moments. Yet they struggled with what to do with them, how to integrate them into a coherent narrative about the young Eritreans and their own roles in their lives. Abel's Post-it note and the morbid conversations it instigated at once troubled the social pedagogues and made them reach out for explanatory models that would allow them to dissolve this sense of unsettledness. The pedagogues soon came to interpret the presence of these narratives of death and dying in terms of the effect of the traumatic journeys the refugee youth had been through and the emotional instability caused by the separation from their parents. With the help of stories about refugee children's symptoms of trauma they had read about in the newspapers or professional guidelines, they were able to chase away the hauntings by reframing them as common behavioral patterns of unaccompanied refugee youth. Rather than seeing them as expressions of the dead end the young men found the education project and their presence in Switzerland to be, they used psychological models to make sense of these narratives. I can sympathize with the pedagogues' sense of unsettledness and with their attempts to explain the young men's confronting expressions through the professional angles they were accustomed to. Given the hegemonic power of the framework of trauma as an explanatory model for the emotional life of refugees, it requires critical intellectual work not to get pulled into its orbit. Didier Fassin and Richard Rechtman (2009) argue that since the mid-nineteenth century trauma has gradually evolved into such a powerful concept that it has led to the establishment of an "empire of trauma." They note that contemporary society now accepts without question the idea that "tragic and painful events, whether individually or collectively experienced, leave marks in the mind" and that these psychic wounds can only be healed with the help of psychologists or psychiatrists (4). How difficult it has become to engage with refugees' struggles beyond the prism of trauma also shows in academic discourse. The literature on unaccompanied refugee youth is rife with studies that focus on their psychic distress, and even in social science texts that do not explicitly follow a psychological angle, the topic of trauma appears again and again as a way of explaining refugee youths' experiences.

I do not intend to question the validity of these psychological perspectives or of the social pedagogues' inclination to scan the young men's behavior for signs of trauma. When the pedagogues sent some of the young men (including Abel and Kibrum) to speak to the institution's psychologist, they undoubtedly acted in the belief that they were taking the right measures to protect them. Yet the boys' refusal to speak to the therapist and their repeated insistence that their problems were not of psychological nature forced me to take their words and actions seriously and look for other means of understanding the appearance of the Post-it note and its social afterlife. As I spent more time with the young men and got to know some of their stories and experiences, I came to believe that there was much more to these everyday hauntings than could be captured in individualistically oriented psychological models. I came to believe that, more than anything, these imaginaries about the end of life and dying need to be understood in the context of the deeply felt existential misbalance the experience of enforced stasis provoked.

EXISTENTIAL BOREDOM

The experience of stasis, of thwarted hopes of movement through education spoke through the young men's discussions about boredom that often followed the imaginary toying with ideas about the end of life. While many of the young men were still struggling to speak in German, they incessantly used the German word for boredom, *Langeweile*. Whether to describe the lack of spice in the food they were eating, the work they had to perform in the workshops, or a quarrel with a friend, all these descriptions ended with the remark that "it's boring" (*es ist langweilig*). The kind of boredom they expressed was driven by more than a lack of meaningful activity or oversupply of time. It was a radical form of boredom with everything, including life itself. As I was sitting in on German class one October afternoon, this existential boredom became apparent. Mr. Liebig, the head teacher, started the lesson by addressing each of the young men in the room individually, asking them how they were doing. When it was Haileb's turn, he replied that he was healthy but that he was feeling very bored. The teacher asked him to explain why he was so bored. Haileb responded that he did not know, that life was just boring. Mr. Liebig suggested that this was normal, that everybody had a boring day every now and then. "But my life is always boring," Haileb answered. "No matter what I do, I always feel bored here. Life is just boring. I have to get used to a boring life."

In conversations with Mr. Liebig, this profound sense of boredom became a recurring theme. The teacher formed an important attachment figure for many of the young men, and his lessons provided a space of respite within the rigidly structured routine of the institution. Mr. Liebig was a serious but friendly man in his forties who had been teaching in the home for young offenders for over a decade. He took his educational mandate seriously and regularly stood up for his principles vis-à-vis the management of the institution. Unlike the social pedagogues, he did not frame his core educational task in terms of integration. Rather than seeing himself as a broker for Swiss society, Mr. Liebig understood his role as a social facilitator whose task it was to help his students acquire the skills they needed to become self-fulfilled and critically minded persons. In conversations during the coffee breaks, the teacher often confided in me, arguing that the pedagogical concept of the integration pilot was flawed, as it marginalized the role of the young men's academic development. He was critical of the project's strong focus on manual work skills, and he supported the boys' pleas for more schooling. Even though he did not have much success, he repeatedly tried to argue for more academic training with Mr. Brugger. Importantly, Mr. Liebig was receptive to the young men's difficult existential balancing acts. Convinced that it was crucial for the boys' social and educational advancement that they be able to discuss and express their experiences, he disregarded the home's rule not to ask the young men about their personal histories. The teacher often used German conversation lessons to instigate discussions about difficult questions. This included carefully guided conversations about their migratory journeys, the lives they had led in Eritrea, and the struggles they were facing in Switzerland. Unlike most of the other teachers I met throughout my fieldwork in Bern and Zürich, he encouraged the refugee youth to articulate their opinions about the discrimination they faced in their daily lives.

German classes with Mr. Liebig formed important breathing spells, small pockets of care in the unresponsive social environment the young men found themselves thrown into. They allowed for some of the troubling questions they had on their minds to be brought into the open, discussed, and analyzed. The sense of existential boredom and numbness they were struggling with was one such theme. In a discussion with Mr. Liebig one afternoon, Kibrum suggested that he was often thinking about life and where it was leading him. "What's there to think about in life?" Haileb asked provocatively. "I already know what it will look like, and it's boring: I am learning a trade here, I will start to work, get married, have kids, raise them, and die."

The boredom surfacing in these discussions with Mr. Liebig is close to the profound, existential kind of boredom Heidegger (1995, 81–155) describes in his work. He distinguishes between three forms of boredom: becoming bored by something, being bored with something, and profound boredom. While we instinctively react to the first two forms of boredom by preoccupying ourselves with activities and in doing so turn away from the nothingness of existence they confront us with, profound boredom does the opposite. It radically throws us back upon ourselves, into a being-here we cannot turn away from, thereby allowing bare existence to present itself (Gilliam 2013, 252). In the context of her work with Warlpiri men and women in Northern Australia, Yasmine Musharbash (2007, 309) describes existential boredom as an "all-encompassing boredom where the individual is bored independently of or detached from the world around them." She distinguishes between a situative kind of boredom that people are reflexive and reactive about and an existential boredom that (paraphrasing Heidegger) is characterized by a "silent fog of indifference." This fog of indifference is evident in Haileb's suggestion that there was nothing he could do about the boredom he was experiencing because it was life itself that was boring. From his perspective the vital stages characteristically thought to form a person's life trajectory—from birth to marriage to death—were inherently boring. With little room to change the monotonous flow of life, all there was left to do, he suggested, was to get used to it. The indifference about the world and life itself caused by the profound boredom the young men experienced was so far-reaching that it even stretched into their discussions about death and dying: When Haileb talked during German class about the monotony of his life in Switzerland, the teacher and other boys suggested activities that could help him feel less bored. While Fikur proposed a hobby like soccer or volleyball, Kibrum said he should go outside every evening and watch the sunset. When Haileb liked none of these suggestions, Kibrum teased him: "Perhaps the best thing for you is to go to heaven: there you'll never be bored." Haileb rejected this idea. "No," he responded. "Being dead is boring, too."

These discussions about boredom give glimpses into the damage interior frontiers can inflict on people. They show the numbness the experience of being made to feel out of place can cause in them, making them dissociate themselves from the world. In their research with unaccompanied refugee youth in Sweden, Kristina Gustafsson, Ingrid Fioretos, and Eva Norström (2012, 66) use the concept of "dislocation" to describe the lasting effects of the ambiguous exclusionary processes they were confronted with. Like the Eritrean youth, the young people they worked with often expressed feelings of estrangement—both from their surroundings and from themselves (75). The authors stress that to better understand the lifeworlds of unaccompanied minors, scholars need to develop a much more succinct understanding of the existential quandaries involved in their strivings for emplacement (76). The young Eritreans' repeated expressions of a profound, all-encompassing boredom bespeak this need for a more thorough scholarly engagement with refugee youths' existential balancing acts. Crucially, the discussions about boredom and the abyss of being stand for more than individual suffering. They have important stories to tell about contemporary global political processes and the uneven distribution of existential mobility they harbor. They prove that for many people across the world globalization is not characterized by excitement and accelerated speed but by downward social mobility and the sensation of "pattering in place" (Jansen 2014, 79). In combination with the young men's narratives about death and dying, their discussions about existential boredom show what happens when people's strivings for autonomy and existential mobility are cut short. The desire for death echoing through these conversations is a haunting reminder of what happens to young people who are dumped in zones of educational abandonment, in places that pretend to invest in their futures while cutting them off from the rest of the world.

While the young men's discussions about boredom reveal the ruinous potential of interior frontiers, I believe that they should not be interpreted solely as testaments of destruction. Precisely *because* of their ability to bring into the open some of these ruinous effects, they also form powerful vehicles of contestation, a way through which the youth could speak up against the structural violence inflicted on them. While the nothingness revealed in profound boredom is deeply unsettling, it should not be too easily discarded as a dead end, as a state of being devoid of motion or the possibility for agency. Boredom is often depicted as a painful state that is accompanied by feelings of emptiness, withdrawal, and meaninglessness. In these readings, boredom turns into a mood that is at odds with the openness of the world. Christian Gilliam (2013, 250) suggests that this is a misrepresentation of boredom, leading to the clichéd suggestion that the rediscovery of personal meaning is needed to cure this existential misattunement. He argues that it is "precisely the meaninglessness delivered through boredom" that is of critical existential importance. Similarly, Heidegger (1995, 164) insists that profound boredom represents the opposite of "being-away." In confronting us with the inescapability of our being-here (*Dasein*), it facilitates a state of existential understanding. In enduring this condition, he notes, in not fighting against the deep sense of uncanniness that accompanies the experience of profound boredom but in making room for it, in letting it "approach us and tell us what it wants," we open ourselves up to new possibilities (155).

The everyday discussions about death and profound boredom among the young men in the educational institution were not just expressions of a state of existential paralysis. The playing with nihilistic ideas enabled them to simultaneously think through radical new possibilities for selfhood and formulate critical assessments of their continued social and educational separation. The narratives of boredom and life coming to a halt thus paradoxically also became an important vehicle for the young men to regain a sense of agency, of acting upon the environment they found themselves cast into.

THE SOCIAL GRAMMARS OF EDGEWORK

Besides the debates about boredom and the end of life, the young men sometimes also explicitly talked about suicide. The busy road between the building complexes accommodating the refugee youth and young offenders turned into the main focus of these narratives. When I was helping the boys with their Friday-afternoon cleaning duties, I caught Abel standing by the kitchen window motionless, the cleaning cloth in his hand. As he observed the large trucks passing by from above, Abel started to laugh. "I would love to jump down," he said. He imagined people's reactions if he were to suddenly open the window and jump onto the road from the second floor of the building. This idea made Kibrum chuckle. "But you'd only be able to do it once," he suggested dryly. The idea of committing suicide on the road appeared again and again in everyday conversations. When crossing the road to get to the workshops, the boys repeatedly played with the idea of stopping short midway, causing the next big truck to hit them. Sometimes they tried to unnerve me or the pedagogues by intentionally slowing down, speeding up only at the last second in front of an approaching car. If one of the young men was late after the lunch break, they often joked that he had probably taken an "early exit" at the road.

Like the other hauntings I have detailed so far, the narratives of suicide did not surface in explicit, easily decipherable ways. They usually took the form of jokey conversations or of half-finished stories, the endings of which could only be sensed. Just as they did the social pedagogues, these small incidents unsettled me. Sometimes they shook me to the point that I struggled to verbalize them in my fieldnotes—as if the mere act of writing down these suicidal thoughts made me complicit, as if my decision not to intervene and call on the expertise of a psychologist was questionable. Yet my conversations with the young men made me see that their suicidal imaginaries should not be reduced to interventionist frameworks. The young men's fervent refusal to talk to the psychologist convinced me that it was important to find other means of approaching, understanding, and, indeed, valuing, their struggles. Elizabeth Cullen Dunn (2017, 54) aptly points out that frameworks of trauma tend to reduce refugees' existential struggles to individual battles devoid of links to the structural violence marking the here and now. She notes that anthropologists need to acknowledge that displacement creates "an existential injury to a community, not a psychic injury to an individual" (54). The boys' insistence that their problems were not of a psychological nature thus needs to be taken seriously. Even though they did not verbalize it explicitly, the hauntings they produced hinted at the *social* nature of their struggles. In their imperfect, unfinished, and sporadic appearance, the hauntings also revealed the intersubjective ways inclusive exclusion is made sense of in the everyday. When looked at from an existential rather than biomedical perspective, the language of self-destruction deployed by the young men has much to say about the agency at play in seemingly hopeless imaginaries of self-nullification.

As the most decisive of all acts, suicide throws up core questions about existence, agency, and voice. Ludek Broz and Daniel Münster (2015, 9) argue that rather than attempting to explain away suicide through powerful clinical discourses, anthropologists should study "suicide fields," which they define as "the wider domains of practices and of sense making, out of which realized, imaginary, or disputed suicides emerge." Similarly, Julie Livingston (2009, 659) argues that because of its defining role in modern social life, we need to understand the narrative quality of suicide, how it enters stories and discourses and comes to "serve as a cautionary vehicle through which people contemplate and comment on what they see as the fundamental existential questions of their time." Rather than interpreting the young men's imaginary suicides in medical terms, we can look at them as important narrative vehicles through which they could regain a sense of agency, as a means of overcoming the social and existential stalemate they found themselves locked into. Besides alluding to their struggles, they enabled them to imagine different scenarios of selfhood and being, and in doing so to critique their prolonged social and educational isolation.

In Western thought, the idea of children committing or contemplating suicide is horrifying. This horror is inextricably linked to modern ideas of childhood as a time of innocence that ought to be free of the burdens that motivate adults to end their lives. If young people commit suicide, it is therefore usually interpreted as a nonreflective repetition of adult behavior rather than as a conscious act. Tom Widger (2015) points out the flaws in this line of thought, arguing that it silences young people's critical and political potential. In his research in Sri Lanka, he found that the practice of suicide play was very common among children and teenagers. Building on the work of Allison James, he argues that like other forms of play, suicide play needs to be regarded as "a serious medium through which children conduct their social affairs" (James 1998, 104, quoted in Widger 2015, 178). The joking about and playing with ideas of suicide forms an important tool for young people to formulate societal critiques. By imitating and imagining suicidal practices, young people make "explicit statements about their lives, their relationship with others, and their perceived ability or inability to control or shape the future" (Widger 2015, 170). Similarly to the young Eritreans' suicidal imaginaries, Widger (2015, 171) found that it was often difficult to draw the line between joke, play, and real suicidal practices. He argues that it is precisely this ambiguity in suicide play that creates important spaces for young people to test out their identities (172).

The jokes about death and suicide that Abel's message initiated resemble the dynamics Widger describes. By imagining the end of their lives and toying with the idea of suicide, the young men were able to express and test out critical thoughts about their lives in Switzerland. While some of these debates took place among the youth themselves, they often included the social pedagogues and teachers. The telling of suicidal jokes did not occur coincidentally. They had a specific direction, tone, and function. In her research with adolescent men in a secure care unit in Denmark, Tea Bengtsson (2012, 527) observed the strategies they deployed to break with institutional constraints, the kind of boredom that "sits in the walls" (526). They often did so through small, risky actions that allowed them to achieve a momentary feeling of power and freedom. Bengtsson (2012, 531) uses Lyng's (2005) notion of "edgework" to describe the liminal and edgy ways youth seek to create meaning and gain control in situations over which they have little say. In a similar vein, the young Eritreans' narratives about suicide, existential boredom, and death also had a decidedly social function. In playing with these extreme imaginaries, they shocked the social workers, provoking them to leave their professional role for a moment and forcing them into a direct conversation. By engaging in this form of edgework, the young men were able to break through the monotony of life in the institution, thereby creating brief moments of excitement and empowerment when they felt that they were in control of the situation.

As short-lived and banal as these moments might appear to be, I believe that anthropologists need to take them seriously and include them in their theoretical engagements with educational institutions. In the context of the educational pilot project in the home for young offenders, these brief moments enabled the young men to voice a critique against the social and existential immobility the institution and Swiss asylum policy at large had forced them into. The playing with ideas of the most extreme form of stasis thus paradoxically allowed them to create a sense of forward movement, the feeling that they were confronting the seemingly insurmountable field of forces weighing down on them. What is more, through these discussions the idea of death itself lost its character as a terminal point. Instead, it came to stand for an ultimate sense of forward movement, one that nobody else could control.

The various hauntings presented throughout the chapter—the discussions about death, the desire to escape earthly life, the expressions of boredom, the suicidal imaginaries—show that Abel's Post-it note was not a coincidence, an extraordinary one-off incident. The thoughts he verbalized link into a wider vernacular framework of reference through which the young people attempted to assess, analyze, and critique their continued exclusion. As unsettling as the moments of edgework might be, they should not be misinterpreted as signs of trauma or capitulation. They need to be read as creative expressions of the social vocabulary the young men developed to make sense of the world they had been thrown into. This world, the book has shown, was interspersed with physical borders, educational hurdles, and affective roadblocks. While the hauntings are testament to a fundamental human striving to co-own and *be* co-owned by the world, they also bear witness to the fact that it is precisely this striving that interior frontiers take aim at.

The educational institutions I have zoomed in on have made visible the modus operandi of interior frontiers, the myriad ways they make refugee youth feel insufficient, different, or locked out. Schools are particularly interesting places from which such processes of boundary drawing can be observed. Just like the haunting responses they evoked in the young men, boundary work does not take place through loud, openly aggressive actions. It does so in silent, hidden ways, through social grammars that I have tried to capture through the metaphor of inclusive exclusion. These grammars include a language of care for the young people—a care, however, that is not driven by emancipative efforts but by the aim of preparing refugee youth for a future at the margins of society. They include the seemingly benevolent aim to promote the youths' *right* to integration while jealously policing *demands* for assimilation. They include a mantra of positivity, which upon closer inspection turns out to be a carefully guarded way of shushing critical questions about refugees' dehumanizing treatment. They include the promise of creating societal participation for marginalized youth groups while silently leading them to the lowest end of the social ladder. And they include a commitment to the accommodation of diversity while simultaneously sending

out messages of unwelcome. Summarized, the logic of inclusive exclusion oper-
ates on the basis of deception: the deception of permitting refugee youth entrance
into the shared affective space of Swissness while keeping them locked out of this
interiority by constantly moving the goalposts of belonging. The outcome of all
these processes is the creation of zones of educational abandonment—spaces
where refugee youth are cornered into social and educational dead ends. The
cruelty of these processes of abandonment has become apparent in the "inclusive"
education projects where my research took place. Rather than strengthening
refugee students' sense of self-worth, these so-called integration projects worked
as a means of warehousing youth labeled as problem cases, keeping them from
"contaminating" the educational standard of other, more deserving students.
The integration pilot in the home for young offenders is an example of how so-
phisticated these practices of abandonment are, and of how deeply they have set
their roots in contemporary education systems. While the book has focused on
the effects such practices have on unaccompanied refugee youth, they also affect
other youth figures labeled troubled, unruly, or dysfunctional. They correspond
with wider societal dynamics that force such youth to participate in make-believe
shows of inclusive education, while fostering the creation of new educational
underclasses.

Abel's Post-it note and its social afterlife demonstrate the ways these mechanisms of inclusive exclusion are enmeshed in the everyday, how they do not just
keep youth from becoming valued members of society, blocking them in their
drive for social mobility, but drastically restrain youths' ability to move forward
in the realms of their own lifeworlds. These vital blockages allude to the fact
that interior frontiers are so powerful exactly because they manage to permeate the most intimate domains of social life. Interior frontiers and the histories
of racism they are based on can therefore never be fully understood if we only
regard them as discursive social constructions. They need to be approached as
lived and material conditions of social life, as actively experienced realities that
are defined by their own social grammars. These grammars often only become
legible if we turn our attention to the edgework people perform at the interstices
of the private and the public. They usually do not appear in the form of clearly
demarcated statements or narratives but need to be looked for in the fragmentary
and unfinished ways people engage with the world. In the context of my research,
the social grammars of interior frontiers became graspable through the minutest
details, such as Thierno's utterance of "I cannot," Abel's statement "I am not alive,"
or the young men's suicidal imaginaries. These social grammars also became
decipherable through the small acts of boundary drawing the pedagogues were
engaged in: the focus on deficits, the acts of aspiration cooling, the emphasis on
cultural otherness. Paying ethnographic attention to the minor moments forming

the syntax of social grammars allows grasping both the cruelties interior frontiers foster and the ways people attempt to knit together their lives again. It is exactly these attempts of knitting together one's life again—the small moments of edgework the youth created to feel in control—that allow us to move beyond the realms of subjective experience and "sense the political" (Jansen 2014, 81). Rather than searching for the political solely in the structures, norms, and institutions of society, we need to regard the everyday as a crucial arena where the political takes shape (Das 2006). As I am coming to the end of this book, I make one last ethnographic leap. Besides making visible the existential balancing acts the young people had to perform, it brings up important conceptual questions about the interplay between the political and experiential.

BY WAY OF CONCLUSION: POLITICS OF VIABILITY

The moment I want to end this book with occurred during German class, about four months after the Post-it incident. I was sitting next to Kibrum. He was a brilliant student who always looked forward to the two hours a day when he could leave behind the workshop to go to the internal school. That afternoon, however, he was struggling to focus. He was moving back and forth in his chair, teasing the other boys with little jokes, kicking them under the table. No matter how often Mr. Liebig told him off, it was impossible for Kibrum to sit still. At some point his restlessness became so overpowering that the teacher suggested the boys take a ten-minute break to walk around and let off some steam. During the break I asked Kibrum why he was so restless. "I have this fever inside my body," he explained. At first, I thought that he was suggesting that the cold he had come down with the week before might have returned. I put my hand on his forehead to check whether he had a temperature, but it was cool. I told Kibrum that he did not seem to have a fever. "But I have this fever inside me, it's boiling," he responded. When the young men returned to the classroom, Mr. Liebig warned them that they needed to be more focused in the second half of the lesson. He said that Kibrum in particular needed to calm down, that he seemed to be very nervous that day. "Yes, I am boiling inside," Kibrum repeated. Pointing at his stomach, he added, "Everything inside me wants to move. It doesn't like to sit still." Later on, after the class had finished and as I was accompanying some of the boys to the carpentry workshop, I asked Kibrum where he believed the "fever" that was raging in his body stemmed from. "I don't know, maybe it's because I am unhappy," he said. I asked why he was so unhappy. "How can I say this?" he replied. "Where can I start?" He paused for a moment. "Why am I here?" "Would you like to be somewhere else instead?" I asked. "Yes," Kibrum responded. "But what can I do? I have to be here now."

This brief moment with Kibrum has much to say about the ambiguous potential of education as a motive and decelerating force in the lives of young refugees. It shows the consequences of a politics of stasis that pushes some people to the margins of social life, where they are exposed to boredom, lack of control, and lack of future prospects. The book has shown what happens when young people's hopes for education as a means of forward movement are systematically drained, thereby producing institutionalized forms of stasis, boredom, and hopelessness. In Kibrum's case the prolonged state of enforced educational immobility and, perhaps most importantly, the lack of anywhere else to turn to make his going-ness better caused him to "boil inside," to feel as if he did not have his body's motion under control. It made him feel unhappy, as he explained, for although everything inside him wanted to move, the educational institution where he was living prevented him from doing so.

Compared to the tens of thousands of people currently stuck en route to Europe, in such countries as Libya, Morocco, or Sudan, the young men I focused on in this book were among the lucky few who made it to Switzerland, which is one of the richest and safest countries in the world and which has a strong public education system. As this book has shown, the youth attached huge importance to the idea of gaining access to this education system as a means of moving forward in their lives. The idea of movement through education had propelled them on their dangerous journeys through the Libyan desert and across the Mediterranean. Yet Kibrum's statement reveals what happens when a place that is believed to form a perfect launching pad for social and existential mobility turns out to be everything but a springboard to a better future, instead producing a deep and utter sense of entrapment. Such experiences of existential stasis should not be reduced to the figure of the refugee or written into a domain of exceptionality. While they are clearly racialized, Georgina Ramsay (2020, 401) rightly stresses that such experiences have to be read against the backdrop of contemporary global capitalist modes of dispossession that push an increasing number of people—refugees and nonrefugees alike—into "zones of political containment in which time is slowed, unmeasured, unproductive." These processes of precaritization do not just hinder access to material and social resources but encroach on people's innermost sense of forward movement (401).

Kibrum's inner fever and the dramatic discussions about death and the nothingness of being provoked by Abel's Post-it message depict what happens when the kinetic energy of migratory journeys—here embodied in the metaphor of movement through education—slowly gets sucked out of people's bodies and minds by a bureaucratic system that weighs down on them, making every step forward feel heavy and lacking direction. Yet these experiences of stasis should not be misinterpreted as a lack of agency. Kibrum's statement that his entire being resisted the enforced stasis the educational institution produced, that "everything inside me wants to move," is telling. It shows the contradictory ways interior frontiers take hold of people's daily lives—how enforced social isolation can actually enter bodies and minds as an irresistible urge to move about and resist the forces holding one back. These dynamics also showed in Abel's message. Because we have zoomed in on the Post-it note and its social afterlife, it has become apparent how, in conditions of (politically produced) stasis, the playing with ideas of suicide, death, and the end of life could actually produce an inner sense of forward movement, thereby allowing the young men to act on their environment.

The epistemological shift from treating interior frontiers primarily as social constructs to looking at them as foundational to a distinct social grammar provokes profound questions—not just about exclusionary processes per se but also about the links between the political and experiential. Cullen Dunn (2017, 6) suggests that anthropologists of displacement need to be careful to distinguish between the "politics of life" and a "politics of living." While the former allows the capturing of the biopolitical techniques used by powerful actors and institutions to govern refugees as a population, the latter allows light to be shed on the existential balancing acts of people living in the shadows of refugee and humanitarian regimes. The provocative questions Abel posed in his Post-it note and the edgework it invoked confirm how important it is not to caricature refugees as powerless victims of an all-encompassing system, as mere bodies governed by abstract political regimes. Viewed through an existential epistemological lens, however, these two domains of life (the existential and the political) cannot always be so clearly separated. The young Eritrean men's experiences reveal that their intimate struggles for forward movement in the realms of their own lives cannot be divorced from the politics of life marking their treatment as problem cases in need of intervention. Ethnographically capturing how powerful ideas and discourses manage to trickle down into people's lived experiences does not equal reducing them to puppets of an all-encompassing system. The narratives, imaginaries, and actions the young Eritrean men deployed in response to the institutional and societal forces holding them back demonstrate that people are never solely determined by external factors, that human life can (and should) never be reduced to bare life. Fassin (2010, 82–83) has noted that the "seductive dualistic framework" haunting many anthropological engagements with marginalized groups tends to assume that there is a clear distinction between physical and existential life. He is critical of this distinction, arguing that even though individuals or groups might be subject to powerful forces of domination, they often manage to develop subtle tactics that enable them to "transform their physical life into a political instrument or a moral resource or an affective expression" (94).

The stories, experiences, and hauntings focused on in this book underscore Fassin's point. They show that just as there is no such thing as bare life, there is no such thing as absolute existential stasis. The sensation of life on hold provoked the young men to imagine nihilistic scripts that allowed them to combat the powerful forces holding them back. Abel's Post-it note and Kibrum's insistence that everything inside him was aching to move show the profound existential struggles for being involved in these processes. Pushing the forcefulness of these experiences into the spotlight helps us to see the dialectical ways interior frontiers permeate the lives of people—how refugees and migrants currently attempting to find their way in increasingly hostile social landscapes are propelled forward and onward by intimate hopes of self-fulfillment and transformation while simultaneously being pushed into zones of social abandonment. In the last decades scholars of education have often made use of a biopolitical angle to capture the power dynamics through which students are governed and controlled. While these studies have produced important insights into the mechanisms of control underwriting the schooling of marginalized youth groups, I agree with Hage's (2019) suggestion that the prism of biopolitics fails to capture the perfidious social grammars at play in contemporary societies. These grammars no longer consist of disciplinary mechanisms or open acts of containment. They are based on the production of "bearable life" rather than bare life. Such a bearable life is "the product of a search for the absolutely minimally-viable life, the just-bearable life" (Hage 2019, 82).

The bearable life Hage hints at is not based on the "in-your-face" kind of violence that could lead to deaths. It is a kind of life that constantly hovers "between the viable and non-viable, between the life that is worth living and the life that is not" (82). The politics of viability Hage points at perfectly captures the inner workings of inclusive exclusion and the forms of edgework it forces refugee youth to perform: while it does not permit the young people to become full members of society, it also does not allow them to renounce their membership. It is precisely these dynamics I am aiming to capture when describing educational projects such as the integration pilot as forms of social and educational abandonment. While instilling in students a feeling of their reasonable and benevolent nature, they continuously confront them with the presence of a social abyss.

Throughout the book I have tried to show the experiential quality of interior frontiers and the dramatic existential balancing acts they evoke. The politics of viability so poignantly captured by Hage bespeaks the importance of not romanticizing these balancing acts and misinterpreting them as demonstrations of simplistic, self-contained expressions of agency. While an existential, Heideggerian perspective allows us to capture the means the young men deployed to actively navigate the field of forces they were thrown into, the stories presented in the book simultaneously show the important role ethnography can play in moving existential theory beyond its tendency to produce removed, totalizing, and romanticizing depictions of social life. By shedding light on the details of life as lived and experienced by particular individuals and groups at particular moments in time, ethnographically driven research is able to show the limitations of an overly enthusiastic emphasis on the potentially emancipatory role of existential balancing acts. Although the discussions of death and existential boredom allowed the young men to gain a sense of forward movement and empowerment, it is important to keep in mind the field of forces these everyday moves were occurring in, where these acts were again and again thrown up against a wall of indifference.

At a time when migratory pathways are violently blocked, fenced off, or shut down, forcing people into desperate countermoves, it becomes almost impossible to distinguish desired from enforced forms of mobility or to disentangle the forces that push people forward from those holding them back. Yet, by taking the existential struggles involved in these balancing acts seriously, we can begin to grasp the complex and at times contradictory ways in which people's innermost quests for forward movement correspond with the fields of forces they find themselves thrown into. Rather than reducing these struggles to a language of biopolitics or intervention, a focus on refugees' existential balancing acts allows their meaning-making practices in response to and against these fields of forces to be captured. By recentering the epistemological focus to the realms of the everyday, we can begin to gain glimpses of the directionality and magnitude of life as it unfolds, while embedding this unfolding in a global political condition of thrownness (Lems and Tošić 2019).

In August 2018 I returned to the home for young offenders to attend the graduation ceremony. In many ways, the event was just as Sebastian had imagined it to be when he daydreamed about it in terms of a film script three years earlier. Except for Aaron, who had dropped out of the program after a year, all the young Eritreans had completed the integration pilot. From the seven remaining boys, six had not just successfully completed their two-year EBA apprenticeships but also been able to find a job and secure an apartment. During the graduation ceremony, however, it was not, as Sebastian had imagined, the young men who shed tears of thankfulness. It was he himself who was deeply moved by the moment. When Sebastian gave a speech, he could hardly contain his emotions, struggling to finish his talk. Despite the bitterness and suspicion he had so often shown toward the young men, in hindsight he regarded the time he had spent with them to be the most meaningful one in his career as a social pedagogue.

While the seven Eritreans were proud that they had successfully completed the project, their eyes remained dry that afternoon. The lowly qualified and badly paid work sectors they had been pushed into help explain why they were less inclined to look back on their time in the home for young offenders as a success story. Abel had completed an apprenticeship as a cook and was now working as a kitchen aid in a restaurant; Kidane, Yonas, and Fikur had completed a two-year training as metalworkers and were now employed as assistants in locksmith shops or at construction sites; Robel had finished a carpentry apprenticeship and had found work with a construction carpenter; Haileb had failed his final exams in the tire repair shop close to where he had been in training (the only youth whose training was outsourced), but he was hopeful that he would complete his education soon and continue to work in the tire shop as an assistant. The youths' relegation to the lowest ranks of the societal ladder once again proves the power interior frontiers hold over people's lives and their futures. But talking to Kibrum, I was reminded of the unintended forms of subversion interior frontiers can also bring about. He told me that, like Robel, he had completed an apprenticeship as a carpenter and was now living in an apartment in a village on the outskirts of Zürich, which he shared with Abel. When I asked Kibrum if he had also been able to find a job, he smiled. "Yes, and you will never guess as what," he said. Not awaiting my response, he told me that he was now working for a funeral parlor. He explained that he was not just responsible for building the coffins but was also working as a mortician. The irony that he had ended up in this profession was not lost on Kibrum. He said that he knew that many people despised this kind of work but that he was not afraid of working with dead people, that he actually enjoyed it. He said that he liked that it was so multifaceted and that he even found the strange atmosphere of graveyards appealing. "You know what I find the funniest?" Kibrum asked, laughing. "All the efforts the Swiss people put into keeping migrants out, and then they are carried to their graves by a little Black man."

NOTES

1. The song can be watched on YouTube (access date January 10, 2020): https://www.youtube.com/watch?v=qDa9Gi9V1IE).

2. Some of the ideas presented in this chapter were first published in an article for *Suomen: Journal of the Finnish Anthropological Society* (Lems 2019).

REFERENCES

Abu El-Haj, Thea Renda. 2010. "'The Beauty of America': Nationalism, Education, and the War on Terror." *Harvard Educational Review* 80 (2): 242–75.

———. 2015. *Unsettled Belonging: Educating Palestinian American Youth after 9/11.* Chicago: University of Chicago Press.

Achermann, Bruno. 2017. "Wo steht die Schweiz hinsichtlich Inklusion?" *VPOD Bildungspolitik* 201 (April 2017): 7–9.

Adams, Mary. 2009. "Stories of Fracture and Claim for Belonging: Young Migrants' Narratives of Arrival in Britain." *Children's Geographies* 7 (2): 159–71.

Affolter, Laura, Jonathan Miaz, and Ephraim Poertner. 2019. "Taking the 'Just' Decision: Caseworkers and Their Communities of Interpretation in the Swiss Asylum Office." In *Asylum Determination in Europe: Ethnographic Perspectives,* edited by Nick Gill and Anthony Good, 263–84. Cham: Springer International.

Ahmed, Sara. 2007. "A Phenomenology of Whiteness." *Feminist Theory* 8 (2): 149–68.

———. 2015. "Not in the Mood." *New Formations* 82:13–28.

Alcoff, Linda. 2006. *Visible Identities: Race, Gender, and the Self.* Oxford: Oxford University Press.

Ali, Mehrunnisa, Jagjeet Kaur Gill, and Svitlana Taraban. 2003. *Unaccompanied/ Separated Children Seeking Refugee Status in Ontario: A Review of Documented Policies and Practices.* Toronto: CERIS.

Allerton, Catherine. 2018. "Impossible Children: Illegality and Excluded Belonging among Children of Migrants in Sabah, East Malaysia." *Journal of Ethnic and Migration Studies* 44 (7): 1081–97.

Allsopp, Jennifer, and Elaine Chase. 2019. "Best Interests, Durable Solutions and Belonging: Policy Discourses Shaping the Futures of Unaccompanied Migrant and Refugee Minors Coming of Age in Europe." *Journal of Ethnic and Migration Studies* 45 (2): 293–311.

Allsopp, Jennifer, Elaine Chase, and Mary Mitchell. 2015. "The Tactics of Time and Status: Young People's Experiences of Building Futures While Subject to Immigration Control in Britain." *Journal of Refugee Studies* 28 (2): 163–82.

Amnesty International. 2017. *Flüchtlinge aus Guinea in der Schweiz.* Bern: Amnesty International.

———. 2018. *Guinea: Death Toll Rises as Repression of Opposition Protests Worsens.* London: Amnesty International.

Anagnostopoulos, Dorothea. 2006. "'Real Students' and 'True Demotes': Ending Social Promotion and the Moral Ordering of Urban High Schools." *American Educational Research Journal* 43 (1): 5–42.

Anderson, Bridget. 2015. *Us and Them? The Dangerous Politics of Immigration Control.* Oxford: Oxford University Press.

———. 2017. "The Politics of Pests: Immigration and the Invasive Other." *Social Research: An International Quarterly* 84 (1): 7–28.

Andersson, Ruben. 2019. *No Go World: How Fear Is Redrawing Our Maps and Infecting Our Politics.* Oakland, CA: University of California Press.

Anthias, Floya. 2013. "Moving beyond the Janus Face of Integration and Diversity Discourses: Towards an Intersectional Framing." *Sociological Review* 61 (2): 323–43.

Applebaum, Barbara. 2010. *Being White, Being Good: White Complicity, White Moral Responsibility, and Social Justice Pedagogy.* Lanham, MD: Lexington Books.

Arendt, Hannah. 1944. "The Jew as Pariah: A Hidden Tradition." *Jewish Social Studies* 6 (2): 99–122.

———. (1958) 1998. *The Human Condition.* Chicago: University of Chicago Press.

———. (1963) 2006. *Eichmann in Jerusalem: A Report on the Banality of Evil.* London: Penguin.

Arens, Markus. 2007. "Bildung und soziale Herkunft—die Vererbung der institutionellen Ungleichheit." In *Perspektiven der Bildung: Kinder und Jugendliche in formellen, nicht-formellen und informellen Bildungsprozessen,* edited by Marius Harring, Carsten Rohlfs, and Christian Palentien, 137–54. Wiesbaden: VS Verlag für Sozialwissenschaften.

Aries, Philippe. 1962. *Centuries of Childhood: A Social History of Family Life.* New York: Vintage Books.

Auyero, Javier. 2012. *Patients of the State: The Politics of Waiting in Argentina.* Durham, NC: Duke University Press.

Bachelet, Sebastien. 2019. "'Looking for One's Life': Trapped Mobilities and Adventure in Morocco." *Migration and Society* 2 (1): 40–54.

Balibar, Etienne. 1991. "Is There a Neo-racism?" In *Race, Nation, Class: Ambiguous Identities,* edited by Etienne Balibar and Immanuel Wallerstein, 17–28. London: Verso.

———. 1994. "Fichte and the Internal Border: On Addresses to the German Nation." In *Masses, Classes, Ideas: Studies on Politics and Philosophy before and after Marx,* edited by Etienne Balibar, 61–84. New York: Routledge.

BASS. 2016. *Bestandsaufnahme zur Bildungsbeteiligung von spät eingereisten Jugendlichen und jungen Erwachsenen.* Bern: Büro für Arbeits- und sozialpolitische Studien (BASS).

Baumann, Gerd. 2004. "Introduction: Nation-State, Schools and Civil Enculturation." In *Civil Enculturation*, edited by Werner Schiffauer, Gerd Baumann, Riva Kastoryano, and Steven Vertovec, 1–18. New York: Berghahn.

Bean, Tammy, Elisabeth Eurelings-Bontekoe, and Philip Spinhoven. 2007. "Course and Predictors of Mental Health of Unaccompanied Refugee Minors in the Netherlands: One Year Follow-Up." *Social Science & Medicine* 64 (6): 1204–15.

Becker, Rolf. 2009. "Entstehung und Reproduktion dauerhafter Bildungsungleichheiten." In *Lehrbuch der Bildungssoziologie*, edited by Rolf Becker, 85–129. Wiesbaden: VS Verlag für Sozialwissenschaften.

Becker, Rolf, and Wolfgang Lauterbach. 2004. "Dauerhafte Bildungsungleichheiten—Ursachen, Mechanismen, Prozesse und Wirkungen." In *Bildung als Privileg? Erklärungen und Befunde zu den Ursachen der Bildungsungleichheit*, edited by Rolf Becker and Wolfgang Lauterbach, 9–40. Wiesbaden: VS Verlag für Sozialwissenschaften.

Belloni, Milena. 2016. "'My Uncle Cannot Say "No" If I Reach Libya': Unpacking the Social Dynamics of Border-Crossing among Eritreans Heading to Europe." *Human Geography* 9 (2): 47–56.

———. 2019. *The Big Gamble: The Migration of Eritreans to Europe*. Berkeley: California University Press.

———. 2020. "Family Project or Individual Choice? Exploring Agency in Young Eritreans' Migration." *Journal of Ethnic and Migration Studies* 46 (2): 336–53.

Bengtsson, Tea Torbenfeldt. 2012. "Boredom and Action—Experiences from Youth Confinement." *Journal of Contemporary Ethnography* 41 (5): 526–53.

Bernstein, Robin. 2011. *Racial Innocence: Performing American Childhood from Slavery to Civil Rights*. New York: New York University Press.

Besteman, Catherine. 2014. "On Ethnographic Unknowability." *Savage Minds* (blog). November 10, 2014. https://savageminds.org/2014/11/10/on-ethnographic-knowability/.

Bhabha, Jacqueline. 2007. *Seeking Asylum Alone—a Comparative Study: Unaccompanied and Separated Children and Refugee Protection in Australia, the UK and the US*. Sydney: Themis.

Biehl, João. 2005. *Vita: Life in a Zone of Social Abandonment*. Berkeley: University of California Press.

———. 2012. "Care and Disregard." In *A Companion to Moral Anthropology*, edited by Didier Fassin, 242–63. Oxford: Wiley-Blackwell.

Bildungsdirektion Kanton Zürich. 2017. "Bildung und Integration." Überarbeitete Empfehlungen. Zürich: Kanton Zürich Bildungsdirektion.

Bonilla-Silva, Eduardo. 2006. *Racism without Racists: Color-Blind Racism and the Persistence of Racial Inequality in the United States*. 2nd ed. New York: Rowman & Littlefield.

Bourdieu, Pierre. 2000. *Pascalian Meditations*. Stanford, CA: Stanford University Press.

Bozzini, David M. 2011. "Low-Tech Surveillance and the Despotic State in Eritrea." *Surveillance & Society* 9 (1): 93–113.

———. 2015. "The Fines and the Spies: Fears of State Surveillance in Eritrea and in the Diaspora." *Social Analysis* 59 (4): 32–49.

Bredeloup, Sylvie. 2013. "The Figure of the Adventurer as an African Migrant." *Journal of African Cultural Studies* 25 (2): 170–82.

Broz, Ludek, and Daniel Münster, eds. 2015. *Suicide and Agency: Anthropological Perspectives on Self-Destruction, Personhood and Power.* Farnham: Ashgate.

Bryan, Catherine, and Myriam Denov. 2011. "Separated Refugee Children in Canada: The Construction of Risk Identity." *Journal of Immigrant & Refugee Studies* 9 (3): 242–66.

Bryant, Rebecca. 2016. "On Critical Times: Return, Repetition, and the Uncanny Present." *History and Anthropology* 27 (1): 19–31.

Bucholtz, Mary. 2002. "Youth and Cultural Practice." *Annual Review of Anthropology* 31 (1): 525–52.

Butler, Judith. 2009. *Frames of War: When Is Life Grievable?* London: Verso.

Cabot, Heath. 2014. *On the Doorstep of Europe: Asylum and Citizenship in Greece.* Philadelphia: University of Pennsylvania Press.

———. 2019. "The Business of Anthropology and the European Refugee Regime." *American Ethnologist* 46 (3): 261–75.

Carastathis, Anna, Nathalie Kouri-Towe, Gada Mahrouse, and Leila Whitley. 2018. "Introduction: Intersectional Feminist Interventions in the 'Refugee Crisis.'" *Refuge* 34 (1): 3–15.

Castagno, Angelina. 2008. "'I Don't Want to Hear That!': Legitimating Whiteness through Silence in Schools." *Anthropology & Education Quarterly* 39 (3): 314–33.

Catalano, Theresa. 2017. "When Children Are Water: Representation of Central American Migrant Children in Public Discourse and Implications for Educators." *Journal of Latinos and Education* 16 (2): 124–42.

Çelikaksoy, Eskil, and Aycan Wadensjö. 2015. "Unaccompanied Minors and Separated Refugee Children in Sweden: An Outlook on Demography, Education and Employment." In *IZA Discussion Paper No. 8963.* Bonn: Forschungsinstitut zur Zukunft der Arbeit.

Chalhi, Sabah, Martijn Koster, and Jeroen Vermeulen. 2018. "Assembling the Irreconcilable: Youth Workers, Development Policies and 'High Risk' Boys in the Netherlands." *Ethnos* 83 (5): 850–67.

Chase, Elaine. 2010. "Agency and Silence: Young People Seeking Asylum Alone in the UK." *British Journal of Social Work* 40 (7): 2050–68.

Chimni, B. S. 1998. "The Geopolitics of Refugee Studies: A View from the South." *Journal of Refugee Studies* 11 (4): 350–74.

Christiansen, Catrine, Mats Utas, and Henrik Vigh, eds. 2006. *Navigating Youth, Generating Adulthood: Social Becoming in an African Context.* Uppsala: Nordiska Afrikainstitutet.

Cohen, Stanley. 1972. *Folk Devils and Moral Panics: The Creation of the Mods and Rockers.* London: MacGibbon and Kee.

Coleman-Fountain, Edmund. 2016. "Youthful Stories of Normality and Difference." *Sociology* 51 (4): 766–82.

Comaroff, Jean, and John Comaroff. 2005. "Reflections on Youth, from the Past to the Postcolony." In *Makers and Breakers: Children and Youth in Postcolonial Africa*, edited by A. Howana and F. De Boeck, 267–81. Oxford: Currey.

Council of Europe. 2014. *Unaccompanied and Separated Asylum-Seeking and Refugee Children Turning Eighteen: What to Celebrate?* Strasbourg: Council of Europe.

Council of the European Union. 2011. "Directive 2011/95/EU of the European Parliament and of the Council of 13 December 2011 on Standards for the Qualification of Third-Country Nationals or Stateless Persons as Beneficiaries of International Protection, for a Uniform Status for Refugees or for Persons Eligible for Subsidiary Protection, and for the Content of the Protection Granted (Recast)." *Official Journal* L 337, 9–26. http://www.refworld.org/docid/4f197df02.html.

Crawley, Heaven. 2007. *When Is a Child Not a Child? Asylum, Age Disputes and the Process of Age Assessment*. London: Immigration Law Practitioners' Association (ILPA).

Crawley, Heaven, and Dimitris Skleparis. 2018. "Refugees, Migrants, Neither, Both: Categorical Fetishism and the Politics of Bounding in Europe's 'Migration Crisis.'" *Journal of Ethnic and Migration Studies* 44 (1): 48–64.

Crea, Thomas M., Robert G. Hasson III, Kerri Evans, Jodi Berger Cardoso, and Dawnya Underwood. 2018. "Moving Forward: Educational Outcomes for Unaccompanied Refugee Minors (URM) Exiting Foster Care in the United States." *Journal of Refugee Studies* 31 (2): 240–56.

Cullen Dunn, Elizabeth. 2017. *No Path Home: Humanitarian Camps and the Grief of Displacement*. New York: Cornell University Press.

Dahinden, Janine, Kerstin Duemmler, and Joëlle Moret. 2014. "Disentangling Religious, Ethnic and Gendered Contents in Boundary Work: How Young Adults Create the Figure of 'The Oppressed Muslim Woman.'" *Journal of Intercultural Studies* 35 (4): 329–48.

D'Amato, Gianni. 2010. "Switzerland: A Multicultural Country without Multicultural Policies?" In *The Multiculturalism Backlash: European Discourses, Policies and Practices*, edited by Steven Vertovec and Susanne Wessendorf, 130–51. London: Routledge.

———. 2012. "Jenseits der Integrationspolitik als politisches Ritual?" In *Alltag und Ritual: Staatsübergänge und Ritualisierungen in sozialen und politischen Feldern. Festschrift zu Ehren von Hans-Rudolf Wicker*, edited by Judith Hangartner, Ueli Hostettler, Anja Sieber Egger, and Angelica Wehrli, 87–105. Zürich: Seismo.

Darby, Derrick, and John L. Rury. 2018. *The Color of Mind: Why the Origins of the Achievement Gap Matter for Justice*. Chicago: University of Chicago Press.

Das, Veena. 1995. *Critical Events: An Anthropological Perspective on Contemporary India*. Delhi: Oxford University Press.

———. 2006. *Life and Words: Violence and the Descent into the Ordinary*. Berkeley: University of California Press.

———. 2012. "Ordinary Ethics." In *A Companion to Moral Anthropology*, edited by Didier Fassin, 133–49. Malden, MA: Wiley-Blackwell.

D-EDK. 2016. *Lehrplan 21: Grundlagen*. Luzern: Deutschschweizer Erziehungsdirektoren-Konferenz.

De Genova, Nicholas. 2013. "Spectacles of Migrant 'Illegality': The Scene of Exclusion, the Obscene of Inclusion." *Ethnic and Racial Studies* 36 (7): 1180–98.

———, ed. 2017. *The Borders of "Europe": Autonomy of Migration, Tactics of Bordering*. Durham, NC: Duke University Press.

———. 2018. "The 'Migrant Crisis' as Racial Crisis: Do Black Lives Matter in Europe?" *Ethnic and Racial Studies* 41 (10): 1765–82.

De Genova, Nicholas, Glenda Garelli, and Martina Tazzioli. 2018. "Autonomy of Asylum? The Autonomy of Migration Undoing the Refugee Crisis Script." *South Atlantic Quarterly* 117 (2): 239–65.

De Graeve, Katrien. 2017. "Classed Landscapes of Care and Belonging: Guardianships of Unaccompanied Minors." *Journal of Refugee Studies* 30 (1): 71–88.

Del Percio, Alfonso, and Alexandre Duchêne. 2014. "Sprache und sozialer Ausschluss: Eine Genealogie des schulischen Berufsintegrationsprozesses jugendlicher MigrantInnen in der Schweiz." In *Mehrsprachigkeit und (Un-)Gesagtes*, edited by Anna Schnitzer and Rebecca Mörgen, 194–216. Basel: Beltz.

Dhaliwal, Sukhwant, and Kirsten Forkert. 2016. "Deserving and Undeserving Migrants." *Soundings: A Journal of Politics and Culture* 61 (1): 49–61.

Ditton, Hartmut. 2007. "Der Beitrag von Schule und Lehrern zur Reproduktion von Bildungsungleichheit." In *Bildung als Privileg: Erklärungen und Befunde zu den Ursachen der Bildungsungleichheit*, edited by Rolf Becker and Wolfgang Lauterbach, 243–71. Wiesbaden: VS Verlag für Sozialwissenschaften.

Douglas, Mary. 1966. *Purity and Danger: An Analysis of Concepts of Pollution and Taboo*. London: Routledge.

Dovemark, Marianne, and Dennis Beach. 2016. "From Learning to Labour to Learning for Precarity." *Ethnography and Education* 11 (2): 174–88.

Dupire, Marguerite. 1962. *Peuls nomades: Etude descriptive des Wodaabe du Sahel Nigerien*. Paris: Institut d'Ethnologie.

Eidgenössisches Department des Inneren (EDI). 1999. *Interpellation 98.3656 Antwort des Bundesrates vom 31. Mai 1999: "Getrennte Klassen? Ein Dossier zu den politischen Forderungen nach Segregation fremdsprachiger Kinder in der Schule."* Bern: Schweizer Nationalrat.

Eigenmann, Philipp. 2017. *Migration macht Schule. Bildung und Berufsqualifikation seitens Italienerinnen und Italiener in Zürich, 1960–1980*. Zürich: Chronos.

Engeler, Michelle. 2016. "Being Young in the Guinée Forestière: Members of Youth Associations as Political Entrepreneurs." *Stichproben. Wiener Zeitschrift für kritische Afrikastudien* 30 (2016): 63–86.

———. 2019. *Youth and the State in Guinea: Meandering Lives*. Bielefeld: Transcript.

European Migration Network (EMN). 2010. *Policies on Reception, Return and Integration Arrangements for, and Numbers of, Unaccompanied Minors: An EU Comparative Study.* Brussels: European Commission.

Eurostat. n.d. "Asylum Applicants Considered to Be Unaccompanied Minors by Citizenship, Age and Sex—Annual Data (Rounded)." Accessed June 5, 2018. http://appsso.eurostat.ec.europa.eu/nui/show.do?dataset=migr_asyunaa&lang=en.

Fanon, Frantz. 1986. *Black Skin, White Masks.* London: Pluto.

Fassin, Didier. 2005. "Compassion and Repression: The Moral Economy of Immigration Policies in France." *Cultural Anthropology* 20 (3): 362–87.

———. 2010. "Ethics of Survival: A Democratic Approach to the Politics of Life." *Humanity: An International Journal of Human Rights* 1 (1): 81–95.

———. 2011a. *Humanitarian Reason: A Moral History of the Present.* Berkeley: University of California Press.

———. 2011b. "The Trace: Violence, Truth, and the Politics of the Body." *Social Research* 78 (2): 281–98.

Fassin, Didier, and Carolina Kobelinsky. 2012. "How Asylum Claims Are Adjudicated: The Institution as a Moral Agent." *Revue Française de Sociologie* 53 (4): 657–88.

Fassin, Didier, and Richard Rechtman. 2009. *The Empire of Trauma: An Inquiry into the Condition of Victimhood.* Princeton, NJ: Princeton University Press.

Ferguson, James G. 1999. *Expectations of Modernity: Myths and Meanings of Urban Life on the Zambian Copperbelt.* Berkeley: University of California Press.

———. 2002. "Of Mimicry and Membership: Africans and the 'New World Society.'" *Cultural Anthropology* 17 (4): 551–69.

Fichte, Johann Gottlieb. 1845. "Reden an die deutsche Nation." In *Johann Gottlieb Fichtes sämmtliche Werke,* edited by Johann Gottlieb Fichte, 259–459. Berlin: Veit und Com.

Fioratta, Susanna. 2015. "Beyond Remittance: Evading Uselessness and Seeking Personhood in Fouta Djallon, Guinea." *American Ethnologist* 42 (2): 295–308.

Fisher, William F. 1997. "Doing Good? The Politics and Antipolitics of NGO Practices." *Annual Review of Anthropology* 26 (1): 439–64.

Fischer-Tiné, Harald, and Patricia Purtschert, eds. 2015. *Colonial Switzerland: Rethinking Colonialism from the Margins.* Basingstoke: Palgrave.

Foucault, Michel. 1977. *Discipline and Punish: The Birth of the Prison.* New York: Random House.

———. 1997. "Technologies of the Self." In *Ethics: Subjectivity and Truth (Essential Works of Foucault 1954–1984),* edited by Paul Rabinow, 223–54. London: Penguin.

Gaibazzi, Paolo. 2015. "The Quest for Luck: Fate, Fortune, Work and the Unexpected among Gambian Soninke Hustlers." *Critical African Studies* 7 (3): 227–42.

———. 2019. "Moving-with-Others: Restoring Viable Relations in Emigrant Gambia." *Migration & Society* 2 (1): 26–39.

Gaibazzi, Paolo, Alice Bellagamba, and Stephan Dünnwald, eds. 2017. *EurAfrican Borders and Migration Management: Political Cultures, Contested Spaces, and Ordinary Lives.* Basingstoke: Palgrave.

Gillborn, David. 2005. "Education Policy as an Act of White Supremacy: Whiteness, Critical Race Theory and Education Reform." *Journal of Education Policy* 20 (4): 485–505.

Gilliam, Christian. 2013. "Existential Boredom Re-examined: Boredom as Authenticity and Life-Affirmation." *Existential Analysis* 24 (2): 250–61.

Gilliam, Laura, and Eva Gullov. 2016. *Children of the Welfare State: Civilising Practices in Schools, Childcare and Families.* London: Pluto.

Gingrich, Andre. 2004. "Concepts of Race Vanishing, Movements of Racism Rising? Global Issues and Austrian Ethnography." *Ethnos* 69 (2): 156–76.

Global Detention Project. 2018. *Immigration Detention in Libya.* Geneva: Global Detention Project.

Gold, Marina. 2019. "The Swiss Paradox." *Social Analysis* 63 (1): 22–43.

Gomolla, Mechthild, and Frank-Olaf Radtke. 2007. *Institutionelle Diskriminierung: Die Herstellung ethnischer Differenz in der Schule.* Wiesbaden: VS Verlag.

Gonon, Philipp, Kathrin Kraus, Jürgen Oelkers, and Stefanie Stolz, eds. 2006. *Work, Education and Employability.* Bern: Peter Lang.

Gullestad, Marianne. 2002. "Invisible Fences: Egalitarianism, Nationalism and Racism." *Journal of the Royal Anthropological Institute* 8 (1): 45–63.

Gustafsson, Kristina, Ingrid Fioretos, and Eva Norström. 2012. "Between Empowerment and Powerlessness: Separated Minors in Sweden." *New Directions for Child and Adolescent Development* 2012 (136): 65–77.

Haas, Bridget M. 2017. "Citizens-in-Waiting, Deportees-in-Waiting: Power, Temporality, and Suffering in the U.S. Asylum System." *Ethos* 45 (1): 75–97.

Haeberlin, Urs, Christian Imdorf, and Winfried Kronig. 2004. *Von der Schule in die Berufslehre: Untersuchungen zur Benachteiligung von ausländischen und von weiblichen Jugendlichen bei der Lehrstellensuche.* Bern: Haupt.

———. 2005. "Verzerrte Chancen auf dem Lehrstellenmarkt: Untersuchungen zu Benachteiligungen von ausländischen und von weiblichen Jugendlichen bei der Suche nach beruflichen Ausbildungsplätzen in der Schweiz." *Zeitschrift für Pädagogik* 51 (1): 116–34.

Hage, Ghassan. 2003. *Against Paranoid Nationalism: Searching for Hope in a Shrinking Society.* Annandale: Pluto.

———. 2009. "Waiting Out the Crisis: On Stuckedness and Governmentality." In *Waiting,* edited by Ghassan Hage, 97–106. Melbourne: Melbourne University Press.

———. 2017. *Is Racism an Environmental Threat?* Cambridge: Polity.

———. 2019. "Afterword: Bearable Life." *Suomen Anthropologi: Journal of the Finnish Anthropological Society* 44 (2): 81–83.

Halvorsen, Kate. 2002. "Separated Children Seeking Asylum: The Most Vulnerable of All." *Forced Migration Review* 12 (January): 34–36.

Haney, Lynne Allison. 2003. *Inventing the Needy: Gender and the Politics of Welfare in Hungary.* Berkeley: University of California Press.

Heidbrink, Lauren. 2014. *Migrant Youth, Transnational Families, and the State: Care and Contested Interests.* Philadelphia: University of Pennsylvania Press.

Heidegger, Martin. 1995. *The Fundamental Concepts of Metaphysics: World, Finitude, Solitude*. Bloomington: Indiana University Press.

———. 2001. *Being and Time*. Oxford: Blackwell.

Hess, Julia Meredith, and Dianna Shandy. 2008. "Kids at the Crossroads: Global Childhood and the State." *Anthropological Quarterly* 81 (4): 765–76.

Hilt, Line Torbjørnsen. 2016. "'They Don't Know What It Means to Be a Student': Inclusion and Exclusion in the Nexus between 'Global' and 'Local.'" *Policy Futures in Education* 14 (6): 666–86.

———. 2017. "Education without a Shared Language: Dynamics of Inclusion and Exclusion in Norwegian Introductory Classes for Newly Arrived Minority Language Students." *International Journal of Inclusive Education* 21 (6): 585–601.

Hirt, Nicole, and Abdulkader Saleh Mohammad. 2013. "'Dreams Don't Come True in Eritrea': Anomie and Family Disintegration Due to the Structural Militarisation of Society." *Journal of Modern African Studies* 51 (1): 139–68.

Hochschild, Arlie Russell. 1979. "Emotion Work, Feeling Rules, and Social Structure." *American Journal of Sociology* 85 (3): 551–75.

Hofstetter, Daniel. 2017. *Die schulische Selektion als soziale Praxis: Aushandlungen von Bildungsentscheidungen beim Übergang von der Primarschule in die Sekundarstufe I*. Basel: Beltz.

Honwana, Alcida. 2012. *The Time of Youth: Work, Social Change, and Politics in Africa*. Sterling: Kumarian.

Horton, Sarah. 2008. "Consuming Childhood: 'Lost' and 'Ideal' Childhoods as a Motivation for Migration." *Anthropological Quarterly* 81 (4): 925–43.

Human Rights Watch. 2019a. *Guinea: Events of 2018*. New York: Human Rights Watch.

———. 2019b. *No Escape from Hell: EU Policies Contribute to Abuse of Migrants in Libya*. New York: Human Rights Watch.

Imdorf, Christian. 2005. *Schulqualifikation und Berufsfindung: Wie Ecolect und nationale Herkunft den Übergang in die Berufsbildung strukturieren*. Wiesbaden: VS Verlag für Sozialwissenschaften.

———. 2010. "Wie Ausbildungsbetriebe soziale Ungleichheit reproduzieren: Der Ausschluss von Migrantenjugendlichen bei der Lehrlingsselektion." In *Bildungsungleichheit revisited: Bildung und soziale Ungleichheit vom Kindergarten bis zur Hochschule*, edited by Heinz-Hermann Krüger, Ursula Rabe-Kleberg, Rolf-Torsten Kramer, and Jürgen Budde, 259–74. Wiesbaden: VS Verlag für Sozialwissenschaften.

Inderbitzin, Ivan. 2003. "The Foreignisation Process in Switzerland: The Swiss and Their Ausländer." Doctoral thesis, Monash University.

International Organization for Migration (IOM). 2019. *Migrate to Succeed: Understanding Youth Migration Trajectories in Eritrea*. Dakar: International Organization for Migration.

Iyob, Ruth. 1995. *The Eritrean Struggle for Independence: Domination, Resistance, Nationalism, 1941–1993*. Cambridge: Cambridge University Press.

Jackson, Michael. 1998. *Minima Ethnographica: Intersubjectivity and the Anthropological Project*. Chicago: University of Chicago Press.

———. 2002. *The Politics of Storytelling: Violence, Transgression, and Intersubjectivity*. Copenhagen: Museum Tusculanum Press.

———. 2013. *The Wherewithal of Life: Ethics, Migration, and the Question of Well-Being*. Berkeley: University of California Press.

Jackson, Michael, and Albert Piette, eds. 2015. *What Is Existential Anthropology?* New York: Berghahn.

Jaffe-Walter, Reva. 2016. *Coercive Concern: Nationalism, Liberalism, and the Schooling of Muslim Youth*. Stanford, CA: Stanford University Press.

James, Allison. 1998. "Play in Childhood: An Anthropological Perspective." *Child Psychology and Psychiatry Review* 3 (3): 104–9.

James, Allison, and Alan Prout. 1990. *Constructing and Reconstructing Childhood: New Directions in the Sociological Study of Childhood*. London: Falmer.

Jansen, Stef. 2014. "On Not Moving Well Enough: Temporal Reasoning in Sarajevo Yearnings for 'Normal Lives.'" *Current Anthropology* 55 (S9): S74–S84.

Jefferies, Julián. 2014. "Fear of Deportation in High School: Implications for Breaking the Circle of Silence Surrounding Migration Status." *Journal of Latinos and Education* 13 (4): 278–95.

Joppke, Christian. 2007. "Beyond National Models: Civic Integration Policies for Immigrants in Western Europe." *West European Politics* 30 (1): 1–22.

Jørgensen, Martin Bak, and Trine Lund Thomsen. 2016. "Deservingness in the Danish Context: Welfare Chauvinism in Times of Crisis." *Critical Social Policy* 36 (3): 330–51.

Jubany, Olga. 2011. "Constructing Truths in a Culture of Disbelief: Understanding Asylum Screening from Within." *International Sociology* 26 (1): 74–94.

Jupp, James C., and Timothy J. Lensmire. 2016. "Second-Wave White Teacher Identity Studies: Toward Complexity and Reflexivity in the Racial Conscientization of White Teachers." *International Journal of Qualitative Studies in Education* 29 (8): 985–88.

Kalb, Don, and Gabor Halmai, eds. 2011. *Headlines of Nation, Subtexts of Class: Working-Class Populism and the Return of the Repressed in Neoliberal Europe*. New York: Berghahn.

Kamm, Martina, Denise Efionayi-Mäder, Anna Neubauer, Phillippe Wanner, and Fabienne Zannol. 2003. *Aufgenommen—aber ausgeschlossen? Die vorläufige Aufnahme in der Schweiz*. Bern: Schweizerisches Forum für Migrations- und Bevölkerungsstudien (SFM) & Eidgenössische Kommission gegen Rassismus (EKR).

Kantonspolizei Zürich. 2014. *Polzeiliche Kriminalstatistik Kanton Zürich*. Zürich: Kantonspolizei Zürich.

———. 2017. *Polizeiliche Kriminalstistik 2017*. Zürich: Kantonspolizei Zürich.

Karakayali, Serhat. 2009. "Paranoic Integrationism: Die Integrationsformel als unmöglicher (Klassen) Kompromiss." In *No Integration?! Kulturwissenschaftliche*

Beiträge zur Integrationsdebatte in Europa, edited by Sabine Hess, Jana Binder, and Johannes Moser, 95–103. Bielefeld: Transcript.

Kaufmann, Eric. 2011. "Reflections on the Swiss Sonderfall." *Nations and Nationalism* 17 (4): 815–20.

Keetharuth, Sheila. 2014. *Report of the Special Rapporteur on the Situation of Human Rights in Eritrea*. Geneva: United Nations General Assembly.

Khosravi, Shahram. 2020. "Afterword: Experiences and Stories along the Way." *Geoforum* 116:292–95.

Kleinman, Arthur. 1997. "'Everything That Really Matters': Social Suffering, Subjectivity, and the Remaking of Human Experience in a Disordering World." *Harvard Theological Review* 90 (3): 315–35.

———. 2006. *What Really Matters: Living a Moral Life amidst Uncertainty and Danger*. Oxford: Oxford University Press.

Kleist, Nauja, and Stef Jansen. 2016. "Introduction: Hope over Time—Crisis, Immobility and Future-Making." *History and Anthropology* 27 (4): 373–92.

Knierzinger, Johannes, Michelle Engeler, and Carole Ammann. 2016. "Guinea: Spearhead of Change or Eternal Maverick?" *Stichproben. Wiener Zeitschrift für kritische Afrikastudien* 30 (2016): 1–8.

Kohli, Ravi. 2006. "The Comfort of Strangers: Social Work Practice with Unaccompanied Asylum-Seeking Children and Young People in the UK." *Child & Family Social Work* 11 (1): 1–10.

Konferenz der kantonalen Sozialdirektorinnen und Sozialdirektoren (SODK). 2016. *Empfehlungen der Konferenz der kantonalen Sozialdirektorinnen und Sozialdirektoren (SODK) zu unbegleiteten minderjährigen Kindern und Jugendlichen aus dem Asylbereich (MNA-Empfehlungen)*. Bern: SODK Generalsekretariat.

Kronauer, Martin. 2010a. *Exklusion: Die Gefährdung des Sozialen im hoch entwickelten Kapitalismus*. Frankfurt: Campus.

———. 2010b. "Inklusion—Exklusion. Eine historische und begriffliche Annäherung an die soziale Frage der Gegenwart." In *Inklusion und Weiterbildung: Reflexionen zur gesellschaftlichen Teilhabe in der Gegenwart*, edited by Martin Kronauer, 24–58. Bielefeld: Bertelsmann.

Kronig, Winfried, Urs Haeberlin, and Michael Eckhart. 2000. *Immigrantenkinder und schulische Selektion: Pädagogische Visionen, theoretische Erklärungen und empirische Untersuchungen zur Wirkung integrierender und separierender Schulformen in den Grundschuljahren*. Bern: Haupt.

Kury, Patrick. 2003. *Über Fremde reden: Überfremdungsdiskurs und Ausgrenzung in der Schweiz, 1900–1945*. Zürich: Chronos.

Kvittingen, Anna. 2010. Negotiating Childhood: Age Assessment in the UK Asylum System. In *Refugee Studies Centre Working Papers Series*. Oxford: Refugee Studies Centre.

Lamont, Michele, and Virag Molnar. 2002. "The Study of Boundaries in the Social Sciences." *Annual Review of Sociology* 28: 167–95.

Lavanchy, Anne. 2015. "Glimpses into the Hearts of Whiteness." In *Colonial Switzerland: Rethinking Colonialism from the Margins*, edited by Patricia Purtschert and Harald Fischer-Tiné, 278–95. London: Palgrave.

Lee, Stacey. 2006. *Up against Whiteness: Race, School and Immigrant Youth.* New York: Teachers College Press.

Lems, Annika. 2016. "Placing Displacement: Place-Making in a World of Movement." *Ethnos* 81 (2): 315–37.

———. 2018. *Being-Here: Placemaking in a World of Movement.* New York: Berghahn.

———. 2019. "Existential Kinetics of Movement and Stasis: Young Eritrean Refugees' Thwarted Hopes of Movement-through-Education." *Soumen Anthropologi: Journal of the Finnish Anthropological Society* 44 (2): 59–80.

———. 2020. "Being Inside Out: The Slippery Slope between Inclusion and Exclusion in a Swiss Educational Project for Unaccompanied Refugee Youth." *Journal of Ethnic and Migration Studies* 46 (2): 405–22.

Lems, Annika, Kathrin Oester, and Sabine Strasser. 2020. "Children of the Crisis: Ethnographic Perspectives on Unaccompanied Refugee Youth in and En Route to Europe." *Journal of Ethnic and Migration Studies* 46 (2): 315–35.

Lems, Annika, and Jelena Tošić. 2019. "Preface: Stuck in Motion? Capturing the Dialectics of Movement and Stasis in an Era of Containment." *Soumen Anthropologi: Journal of the Finnish Anthropological Society* 44 (2): 3–19.

Lenz, Christoph. 2016. "Warum sind so viele Flüchtlinge 18 Jahre alt?" *Blick*, May 12, 2016. https://www.blick.ch/news/schweiz/datenrecherche-zeigt-der-bund-laesst -kinder-fluechtlinge-im-stich-id5021987.html.

Lewis, Tyson E. 2010. "Understanding the Logic of Educational Encampment: From Illich to Agamben." *International Journal of Illich Studies* 1 (1): 28–36.

Leyvraz, Anne-Cécile. 2017. "Ein Verfahren mit zahlreichen Hürden für unbegleitete Minderjährige." *Fakten statt Mythen*, September 14, 2017. https://www .sachdokumentation.ch/bestand/ds/868.

Livingston, Julie. 2009. "Suicide, Risk, and Investment in the Heart of the African Miracle." *Cultural Anthropology* 24 (4): 652–80.

Lucht, Hans. 2012. *Darkness before Daybreak: African Migrants Living on the Margins in Southern Italy Today.* Berkeley: University of California Press.

Ludi, Regula. 2014. "More and Less Deserving Refugees: Shifting Priorities in Swiss Asylum Policy from the Interwar Era to the Hungarian Refugee Crisis of 1956." *Journal of Contemporary History* 49 (3): 577–98.

Lyng, Stephen. 2005. "Edgework and the Risk-Taking Experience." In *Edgework*, edited by Stephen Lyng, 17–50. New York: Routledge.

Mains, Daniel. 2007. "Neoliberal Times: Progress, Boredom, and Shame among Young Men in Urban Ethiopia." *American Ethnologist* 34 (4): 659–73.

———. 2011. *Hope Is Cut: Youth, Unemployment, and the Future in Urban Ethiopia.* Philadelphia: Temple University Press.

Malkki, Liisa. 1995. "Refugees and Exile: From 'Refugee Studies' to the National Order of Things." *Annual Review of Anthropology* 24 (1): 495–523.

———. 1996. "Speechless Emissaries: Refugees, Humanitarianism, and Dehistoricization." *Cultural Anthropology* 11 (3): 377–404.

———. 2010. "Children, Humanity, and the Infantilization of Peace." In *In the Name of Humanity*, edited by Ilana Feldman and Miriam Ticktin, 58–85. Durham, NC: Duke University Press.

Manela, Tony. 2015. "Gratitude." In *Stanford Encyclopedia of Philosophy*, edited by Edward N. Zalta. https://plato.stanford.edu/archives/fall2019/entries/gratitude.

Markom, Christa. 2014. *Rassismus aus der Mitte: Die soziale Konstruktion der "Anderen" in Österreich.* Bielefeld: Transcript.

Matias, Cheryl. 2016. *Feeling White: Whiteness, Emotionality, and Education.* Rotterdam: Sense.

McGovern, Mike. 2012. *Unmasking the State: Making Guinea Modern.* Chicago: Chicago University Press.

Mead, Margaret. 1928. *Coming of Age in Samoa.* New York: William Morrow.

Meanwell, Emily, and Julie Swando. 2013. "Who Deserves Good Schools? Cultural Categories of Worth and School Finance Reform." *Sociological Perspectives* 56 (4): 495–522.

Michel, Noémi. 2015. "Sheepology: The Postcolonial Politics of Raceless Racism in Switzerland." *Postcolonial Studies* 18 (4): 410–26.

Mitchell, David. 2014. "Gay Pasts and Disability Future(s) Tense: Heteronormative Trauma and Parasitism in *Midnight Cowboy*." *Journal of Literary & Cultural Disability Studies* 8 (1): 1–16.

Monsutti, Alessandro. 2018. "Mobility as a Political Act." *Ethnic and Racial Studies* 41 (3): 448–55.

Müller, Tanja R. 2008. "Bare Life and the Developmental State: Implications of the Militarisation of Higher Education in Eritrea." *Journal of Modern African Studies* 46 (1): 111–31.

Musharbash, Yasmine. 2007. "Boredom, Time, and Modernity: An Example from Aboriginal Australia." *American Anthropologist* 109 (2): 307–17.

Nardone, Mariana, and Ignacio Correa-Velez. 2016. "Unpredictability, Invisibility and Vulnerability: Unaccompanied Asylum-Seeking Minors' Journeys to Australia." *Journal of Refugee Studies* 29 (3): 295–314.

Netzwerk Kinderrechte Schweiz. 2002. *Swiss NGO Report: Kommentar zum Bericht der schweizerischen Regierung an den UNO Kinderrechtsausschuss.* Bern: Netzwerk Kinderrechte.

Niederberger, Josef Martin. 2004. *Ausgrenzen, assimilieren, integrieren: die Entwicklung einer schweizerischen Integrationspolitik.* Zürich: Seismo.

Ní Raghallaigh, Muireann. 2013. "The Causes of Mistrust amongst Asylum Seekers and Refugees: Insights from Research with Unaccompanied Asylum-Seeking Minors Living in the Republic of Ireland." *Journal of Refugee Studies* 27 (1): 82–100.

Oertli, Johannes Balthasar. 2019. "Forensic Age Estimation in Swiss Asylum Procedures: Race in the Production of Age." *Refuge* 35 (1): 8–17.

Oester, Kathrin, and Bernadette Brunner. 2015. *Von Kings und Losern: Eine Performance-Ethnografie mit Schülerinnen und Schülern im transnationalisierten Stadtteil Bern West.* Wiesbaden: Springer VS.

Oester, Kathrin, Ursula Fiechter, and Elke-Nicole Kappus. 2008. *Schulen in transnationalen Lebenswelten: Integrations- und Segregationsprozesse am Beispiel von Bern West.* Zürich: Seismo.

Oester, Kathrin, and Annika Lems. 2017. "Zwischen Inklusion und Exklusion: Zur Bildungssituation unbegleiteter jugendlicher Asylsuchender." *VPOD Bildungspolitik* 203:6–8.

———. 2019. "Recht auf Bildung? Unbegleitete Minderjährige zwischen Inklusion und Exklusion." In *Kindheit(en) in formalen, nonformalen und informellen Bildungskontexten: Ethnografische Beiträge aus der Schweiz,* edited by Anja Sieber Egger, Gisela Unterweger, Marianna Jäger, Melanie Kuhn, and Judith Hangartner, 239–58. Wiesbaden: Springer Fachmedien Wiesbaden.

Office of the High Commissioner for Human Rights (OHCR). 2018. *Desperate and Dangerous: Report on the Human Rights Situation of Migrants and Refugees in Libya.* Geneva: Office of the High Commissioner for Human Rights.

Oorschot, Wim van. 2000. "Who Should Get What, and Why? On Deservingness Criteria and the Conditionality of Solidarity among the Public." *Policy & Politics* 28 (1): 33–48.

———. 2006. "Making the Difference in Social Europe: Deservingness Perceptions among Citizens of European Welfare States." *Journal of European Social Policy* 16 (1): 23–42.

Pankhurst, Alula. 2003. "Introduction: Dimensions and Conceptions of Marginalisation." In *Peripheral People: The Excluded People of Ethiopia,* edited by Dana Freeman and Alula Pankhurst, 1–26. Lawrenceville, NJ: Red Sea.

Papadopoulos, Dimitris, and Vassilis S. Tsianos. 2013. "After Citizenship: Autonomy of Migration, Organisational Ontology and Mobile Commons." *Citizenship Studies* 17 (2): 178–96.

Piette, Albert. 2015. *Existence in the Details: Theory and Methodology in Existential Anthropology.* Berlin: Duncker & Humblot.

Piñeiro, Esteban. 2015. *Integration und Abwehr: Genealogie der schweizerischen Ausländerintegration.* Zürich: Seismo.

Piñeiro, Esteban, Isabelle Bopp, and Georg Kreis. 2009. "Einleitung: Fördern und Fordern revised: Seismografien zum gegenwärtigen Integrationsdiskurs." In *Fördern und Fordern im Fokus,* edited by Esteban Piñeiro, Isabelle Bopp, and Georg Kreis, 9–20. Zürich: Seismo.

Pupavac, Vanessa. 2001. "Misanthropy without Borders: The International Children's Rights Regime." *Disasters* 25 (2): 95–112.

Purtschert, Patricia. 2015. "The Return of the Native: Racialised Space, Colonial Debris and the Human Zoo." *Identities* 22 (4): 508–23.

Purtschert, Patricia, Barbara Lüthi, and Francesca Falk, eds. 2014. *Postkoloniale Schweiz: Formen und Folgen eines Kolonialismus ohne Kolonien.* Bielefeld: Transcript.

Quenzel, Gudrun, and Klaus Hurrelmann, eds. 2010. *Bildungsverlierer: Neue Ungleichheiten*. Wiesbaden: VS Verlag für Sozialwissenschaften.

Ramsay, Georgina. 2017. *Impossible Refuge: The Control and Constraint of Refugee Futures*. London: Routledge.

———. 2020. "Time and the Other in Crisis: How Anthropology Makes Its Displaced Object." *Anthropological Theory* 20 (4): 385–413.

Rau, Simone, and Barnaby Skinner. 2016. "Das sind die härtesten Asylrichter der Schweiz." *Tagesanzeiger* (blog). October 8, 2016. https://blog.tagesanzeiger.ch /datenblog/index.php/12556/je-nach-richter-dreimal-hoehere-erfolgschancen.

Reeves, Madeleine. 2019. "The Queue: Distributed Legality, Bureaucratic Time and Waiting-Work in Migrant Moscow." *Soumen Anthropologi: Journal of the Finnish Anthropological Society* 44 (2): 20–39.

Rey, Pascal. 2016. "Une gouvernance locale à l'épreuve du temps. Politiques nationales, pouvoirs locaux et stratégies des miniers en Guinée." *Stichproben: Wiener Zeitschrift für kritische Afrikastudien* 16 (30): 87–110.

Riggan, Jennifer. 2013. "Imagining Emigration: Debating National Duty in Eritrean Classrooms." *Africa Today* 60 (2): 84–106.

Rouch, Jean. 1956. *Migrations au Ghana, Gold Coast, enquêtes 1953–1955*. Paris: Société des Africanistes.

Rytter, Mikkel. 2019. "Writing against Integration: Danish Imaginaries of Culture, Race and Belonging." *Ethnos* 84 (4): 678–97.

Sacks, Harvey. 1984. "On Doing 'Being Ordinary.'" In *Structures of Social Action: Studies in Conversational Analysis*, edited by Maxwell Atkinson and John Heritage, 413–29. Cambridge: Cambridge University Press.

Salis Gross, Corina. 2004. "Struggling with Imaginaries of Trauma and Trust: The Refugee Experience in Switzerland." *Culture, Medicine and Psychiatry* 28 (2): 151–67.

Sartre, Jean Paul. (1943) 2003. *Being and Nothingness: An Essay on Phenomenological Ontology*. London: Routledge.

———. 1956. "Existentialism Is a Humanism." In *Existentialism from Dostoyevsky to Sarte*, edited by Walter Kaufman, 287–311. New York: Meridian.

Schader, Basil, and Andrea Haenni Hoti. 2006. *Albanischsprachige Kinder und Jugendliche in der Schweiz: Hintergründe, schul- und sprachbezogene Untersuchungen*. Zürich: Pestalozzianum.

Scheper-Hughes, Nancy, and Carolyn Sargent, eds. 1998. *Small Wars: The Cultural Politics of Childhood*. Berkeley: University of California Press.

Schroven, Anita. 2019. *Playing the Marginality Game: Identity Politics in West Africa*. London: Berghahn.

Schweizerische Stiftung des Internationalen Sozialdienstes (SSI). 2016. Handbuch zur Betreuung unbegleiteter Minderjähriger in der Schweiz: Praxisorientierter Leitfaden. Geneva: Schweizerische Stiftung des internationalen Sozialdienstes.

Schwiter, Karin. 2013. "Neoliberal Subjectivity: Difference, Free Choice and Individualised Responsibility in the Life Plans of Young Adults in Switzerland." *Geographica Helvetica* 68 (3): 153–59.

Scott, James. 1985. *Weapons of the Weak: Everyday Forms of Peasant Resistance.* New Haven, CT: Yale University Press.

Seawright, Gardner. 2018. "Questioning the White Body: On Applying a Phenomenological Mode of Inquiry to Whiteness Studies in Education." *International Studies of Qualitative Studies in Education* 31 (10): 911–34.

Sheller, Mimi, and John Urry. 2006. "The New Mobilities Paradigm." *Environment and Planning A* 38 (2): 207–26.

Shukla, Nikesh, ed. 2016. *The Good Immigrant.* London: Unbound.

Siegl, Veronika. 2018. "Aligning the Affective Body: Commercial Surrogacy in Moscow and the Emotional Labour of Nastraivatsya." *Tsantsa* 23:63–72.

Silverman, Stephanie. 2016. "'Imposter-Children' in the UK Refugee Status Determination Process." *Refuge* 32 (3): 30–39.

Skenderovic, Damir, and Gianni D'Amato. 2008. *Mit dem Fremden politisieren: rechtspopulistische Parteien und Migrationspolitik in der Schweiz seit den 1960er Jahren.* Zürich: Chronos.

Slaby, Jan. 2010. "The Other Side of Existence: Heidegger on Boredom." In *Habitus in Habitat II: Other Sides of Cognition*, edited by Sabine Flach, Daniel Margulies, and Jan Söffner, 101–20. Bern: Peter Lang.

Slater, Jenny. 2015. *Youth and Disability: A Challenge to Mr Reasonable.* Farnham: Ashgate.

Slee, Roger. 2011. *The Irregular School: Exclusion, Schooling, and Inclusive Education.* London: Routledge.

Söhn, Janina. 2011. *Rechtsstatus und Bildungschancen: Die staatliche Ungleichbehandlung von Migrantengruppen und ihre Konsequenzen.* Wiesbaden: VS Verlag für Sozialwissenschaften.

Sossi, Federica. 2006. *Migrare: Spazi di Confinamento e Strategie di Esistenza.* Milan: Il Saggiatore.

Staatssekretariat für Migration (SEM). 2016. "Unbegleitete Minderjährige Asylsuchende in der Schweiz: Statistiken/ Vergleichstabelle." January 23, 2016. https://www.sem.admin.ch/dam/data/sem/publiservice/statistik/asylstatistik /statistiken_uma/uma-2016-d.pdf.

———. 2017a. "Asylstatistik 2016." January 23, 2017. https://www.sem.admin.ch/dam /data/sem/publiservice/statistik/asylstatistik/2016/stat-jahr-2016-kommentar-d .pdf.

———. 2017b. "Unbegleitete Minderjährige Asylsuchende in der Schweiz: Statistiken/ Vergleichstabelle." https://www.sem.admin.ch/dam/data/sem /publiservice/statistik/asylstatistik/statistiken_uma/uma-2017-d.pdf.

Stack, Carol. 1974. *All Our Kin: Strategies for Survival in a Black Community.* New York: Harper and Row.

Stenning, Derrick. 1959. *Savannah Nomads: A Study of the Wodaabe Pastoral Fulani of Western Bornu Province, Northern Region, Nigeria.* Oxford: Oxford University Press.

Stephens, Sharon. 1995. "Children and the Politics of Culture in 'Late Capitalism.'" In *Children and the Politics of Culture*, edited by Sharon Stephens, 3–48. Princeton, NJ: Princeton University Press.

Stoler, Ann Laura. 2017. "'Interior Frontiers' as Political Concept, Diagnostic, and Dispositif." *Cultural Anthropology* (blog). January 18, 2017. https://culanth.org /fieldsights/interior-frontiers-as-political-concept-diagnostic-and-dispositif.

———. 2018. "Interior Frontiers." In *Political Concepts: A Critical Lexicon*, edited by J. M. Bernstein, Adi Ophir, and Ann Laura Stoler. New York: Fordham University Press. Online book. https://www.politicalconcepts.org/interior-frontiers-ann -laura-stoler/.

Straker, James. 1990. *Youth, Nationalism, and the Guinean Revolution*. Bloomington: Indiana University Press.

Strasser, Sabine, and Elif Eda Tibet. 2020. "The Border Event in the Everyday: Hope and Constraints in the Lives of Young Unaccompanied Asylum Seekers in Turkey." *Journal of Ethnic and Migration Studies* 46 (2): 354–71.

Streckeisen, Ursula, Denis Hänzi, and Andrea Hungerbühler. 2007. *Fördern und Auslesen: Deutungsmuster von Lehrpersonen zu einem beruflichen Dilemma*. Wiesbaden: VS Verlag für Sozialwissenschaften.

Svaton, Carla Jana. 2017. "Die Integrierten: Eine Ethnografie über Übersetzungs- und Inskriptionsprozesse einer 'integrativen Volksschule.'" Doctoral diss., University of Bern.

Tekle, Fisseha. 2018. "A Cruel Graduation: In Eritrea, School Remains a One-Way Ticket to the Army." *East African*, August 1, 2018. https://www.theeastafrican.co.ke/oped /comment/Eritrea-forced-national-service/434750-4691740-jydtmc/index.html.

Terre des Hommes (TDH). 2009. *Disappearing, Departing, Running Away. A Surfeit of Children in Europe?* Lausanne: Terre des Hommes.

Terrio, Susan. 2008. "New Barbarians at the Gates of Paris? Prosecuting Undocumented Minors in the Juvenile Court—the Problem of the 'Petits Roumains.'" *Anthropological Quarterly* 81 (4): 873–901.

Thommen, Anna. 2013. *Neuland*. Zürich: Filmcoopi AG.

Ticktin, Miriam. 2016. "Thinking Beyond Humanitarian Borders." *Social Research* 83 (2): 255–71.

———. 2017. "A World without Innocence." *American Ethnologist* 44 (4): 577–90.

Treiber, Magnus. 2018. "From Revolutionary Education to Futures Elsewhere: Children and Young Refugees Fleeing from Eritrea." In *Research Handbook on Child Migration*, edited by Jacqueline Bhabha, Jyothi Kanics, and D. Senovilla Hernandez, 49–65. Northampton: Edward Elgar.

UNESCO. 1994. *The Salamanca Statement and Framework for Action on Special Needs Education*. Salamanca: United Nations & Ministry of Education and Science Spain.

United Nations Committee on the Rights of the Child. 2015. *Concluding Observations on the Combined Second to Fourth Periodic Reports of Switzerland*. Geneva: United Nations Committee on the Rights of the Child.

United Nations General Assembly (UNCRC). 1989. *Convention on the Rights of the Child*. Geneva: High Commissioner for Human Rights.

United Nations High Commissioner for Refugees (UNHCR). 2018. *Global Trends: Forced Displacement in 2017*. Geneva: United Nations High Commissioner for Refugees.

United Nations Human Rights Council. 2016. *Detailed Findings of the Commission of Inquiry on Human Rights in Eritrea*. Geneva: Human Rights Council.

Vonarburg, Fabio. 2018. "Wer sich nicht an den Integrationsvertrag hält, wird ab nächstem Jahr bestraft." *Watson* (blog). August 18, 2018. https://www.watson.ch /schweiz/gesellschaft%20&%20politik/259061391-wer-sich-nicht-an-den-integrations -vertrag-haelt-wird-ab-naechstem-jahr-bestraft.

Watters, Charles. 2007. "Refugees at Europe's Borders: The Moral Economy of Care." *Transcultural Psychiatry* 44 (3): 394–417.

Wellgraf, Stefan. 2012. *Hauptschüler: zur gesellschaftlichen Produktion von Verachtung*. Bielefeld: Transcript.

Wernesjö, Ulrika. 2012. "Unaccompanied Asylum-Seeking Children: Whose Perspective?" *Childhood* 19 (4): 495–507.

Wicker, Hans-Rudolf. 2003. "Einleitung: Migration, Migrationspolitik und Migrationsforschung." In *Migration und die Schweiz*, edited by Hans-Rudolf Wicker, Rosita Fibbi, and Werner Haug, 12–62. Zürich: Seismo.

———. 2009. "Die neue schweizerische Integrationspolitik." In *Fördern und Fordern im Fokus: Leerstellen des schweizerischen Integrationsdiskurses*, edited by Esteban Piñeiro, Isabelle Bopp, and Georg Kreis, 23–47. Zürich: Seismo.

Widger, Tom. 2015. "Learning Suicide and the Limits of Agency: Children's 'Suicide Play' in Sri Lanka." In *Suicide and Agency*, edited by Ludek Broz and Daniel Münster, 166–81. Farnham: Ashgate.

Willen, Sarah S. 2012. "How Is Health-Related 'Deservingness' Reckoned? Perspectives from Unauthorized Im/migrants in Tel Aviv." *Social Science & Medicine* 74 (6): 812–21.

———. 2015. "Lightning Rods in the Local Moral Economy: Debating Unauthorized Migrants' Deservingness in Israel." *International Migration* 53 (3): 70–86.

Willis, Paul E. 1977. *Learning to Labour: How Working Class Kids Get Working Class Jobs*. Aldershot: Gower.

Wimmer, Andreas. 2011. "A Swiss Anomaly? A Relational Account of National Boundary-Making." *Nations and Nationalism* 17 (4): 718–37.

Yuval-Davis, Nira. 2006. "Belonging and the Politics of Belonging." *Patterns of Prejudice* 40 (3): 197–214.

INDEX

Aargauer Zeitung (newspaper), 40
Aaron (Eritrean refugee): dropping out of
  program, 202; hopes and story of, 1–2,
  148–49, 160–61; mood swings of, 168, 170;
  Post-it incident and, 3, 28; Tigrinya songs
  and, 185–86
abandonment. *See* educational abandonment;
  social abandonment
Abdi (Somali refugee from Ethiopia), 81–82,
  113, 114–15, 147
Abel (Eritrean refugee): asylum procedure
  and, 2; hopes and story of, 1–3, 148–49,
  160–61, 162; life after integration pilot,
  203; mental health of, 161; mood swings of,
  168; Post-it incident and, 3, 26, 27–28, 167,
  182–85, 196, 197; selection for integration
  pilot and, 154; sense of abandonment and,
  177–79; suicidal thoughts and, 193; Tigrinya
  songs and, 185–86
Abreha, Lulom, 185–86
Abu El-Haj, Thea, 76
affect aliens, 170–76, 184–85
Afghanistan, 7
Afwerki, Isaias, 16–17, 62–63
agency, 44–45, 83, 133–34, 139, 192–93, 201–2
Ahmed, Sara, 128–29, 168, 170–71
alienation, 55–57
"American Oxygen" (song), 47
anchor babies, 11
Anderson, Bridget, 13, 173
anticipation, 126

apprenticeships: asylum procedure and, 98;
  integration classes (Bern) and, 65, 66–67,
  77–79, 96–97, 107–9, 111, 113–14, 143–44;
  integration pilot (Zürich) and, 1, 148, 168,
  202. *See also* four-year apprenticeships
  (*Eidgenössisches Fähigkeitszeugnis*, EFZ);
  Schnupperlehren (trial apprenticeships);
  short-term apprenticeships
  (*Eidgenössisches Berufsattest*, EBA)
Arendt, Hannah, 52–53, 78, 138
aspiration cooling (*Aspirationsabkühlung*),
  109
asylum procedure (European Union), 9–11, 94
asylum procedure (Switzerland): impact on
  psychological wellbeing of, 124–26; luck
  and, 113–20, 124–25; overview of, 9–12;
  selection for integration pilot (Zürich) and,
  153–54; uncertainty and, 82, 95–98; un/
  deservingness and, 10–12, 81–83, 97–98,
  113–16, 126–28, 131–32, 137–45; West African
  asylum seekers and, 117
attunement (*Befindlichkeit*), 176
Austria, 10–11
autonomy, 93–95, 149, 186
autonomy of migration, 94

Bachelet, Sebastien, 119
Balibar, Etienne, 5–6
Baumann, Gerd, 172
Beach, Dennis, 109–10
Befindlichkeit (attunement), 176

ANNIKA LEMS is head of the independent research group Alpine Histories of Global Change: Time, Self, and the Other in the German-Speaking Alpine Region at the Max Planck Institute for Social Anthropology. She is author of *Being-Here: Placemaking in a World of Movement*.

www.ingramcontent.com/pod-product-compliance
Lightning Source LLC
Chambersburg PA
CBHW030408270326
41926CB00009B/1321